CALL to CELEBRATE
RECONCILIATION & EUCHARIST

Author

Maureen A. Kelly, MA

Program Consultants

Nylda Aldarando

Mary Birmingham

Rita Ferrone

Gael Gensler, OSF

Mary Ann Getty-Sullivan

Rev. Joe Kempf

Tom Kendzia

Rev. Paul Turner

Reviewers

Rosie Papion-Brown

David Haas

Rev. Robert J. Hater, Ph.D.

Contributing Artist

Michael O'Neill McGrath, OSFS

Our Sunday Visitor

Curriculum Division

www.osvcurriculum.com

The Ad Hoc Committee to Oversee the Use of the Catechism, United States Conference of Catholic Bishops, has found the doctrinal content of this teacher manual, copyright ©2007, to be in conformity with the *Catechism of the Catholic Church.*

Author
Maureen A. Kelly, M.A.

Nihil Obstat
Msgr. Louis R. Piermarini

Imprimatur
✠ Most Rev. Robert J. McManus, S.T.D.
Bishop of Worcester
June 12, 2006

The Imprimatur is an official declaration that a book or pamphlet is free of doctrinal or moral error. No implication is contained therein that anyone who granted the Imprimatur agrees with the contents, opinions, or statements expressed.

> Write:
> **Our Sunday Visitor Curriculum Division**
> **Our Sunday Visitor, Inc.**
> 200 Noll Plaza, Huntington, Indiana 46750

Call to Celebrate is a registered trademark of Our Sunday Visitor Curriculum Division, Our Sunday Visitor, 200 Noll Plaza, Huntington, Indiana 46750.

For permission to reprint copyrighted material, grateful acknowledgment is made to the following sources:

Division of Christian Education of the National Council of the Churches of Christ in the U.S.A.: Scripture quotations from the *New Revised Standard Version Bible: Catholic Edition.* Text copyright © 1993 and 1989 by the Division of Christian Education of the National Council of the Churches of Christ in the U.S.A

GIA Publications, Inc., 7404 S. Mason Ave., Chicago, IL 60638 www.giamusic.com, 800-442-1358. Lyrics from "We Are Called" by David Haas. Lyrics © 1988 by GIA Publications, Inc.

International Commission on English in the Liturgy: Excerpts from the English translation of *Rite of Baptism for Children* © 1969, International Commission on English in the Liturgy Corporation (ICEL); excerpts from the English translation of *Directory for Masses with Children* © 1973, ICEL; excerpts from the English translation of *Rite of Penance* © 1974, ICEL; excerpts from the English translation of *Rite of Confirmation (Second Edition)* © 1975, ICEL; excerpt from the English translation of *A Book of Prayers* © 1982, ICEL; excerpts from the English translation of *Book of Blessings* © 1988, ICEL; excerpts from the English translation of *The Roman Missal* © 2010, ICEL. All rights reserved.

United States Conference of Catholic Bishops, Inc., Washington, D.C.: From the English translation of the *Catechism of the Catholic Church* for the United States of America. Translation copyright © 1994 by United States Catholic Conference, Inc. – Libreria Editrice Vaticana. From the English translation of the *Catechism of the Catholic Church: Modifications from the Editio Typica.* Translation copyright © 1997 by United States Catholic Conference, Inc. – Libreria Editrice Vaticana.

John Burland: Lyrics from *And With Your Spirit: Songs for Deepening Children's Understanding of the Mass.* Our Sunday Visitor Curriculum Division, printed in partnership with Ovation Music Service. © 2011 John Burland.

Photo Credits
36 Bettmann/Corbis; 66 Leif Skoogfors/CORBIS; 116 Bettman/CORBIS

Illustration Credits
Dan Brown/Artworks 122–123; Shane Marsh/Linden Artists, Ltd. 62–63, 92–93, 142–143; Roger Payne/Linden Artists, Ltd. 42–43, 52–53, 112–113; Francis Phillips/Linden Artists, Ltd. 22–23, 32–33, 162–163; Tracy Somers 36, 56; Clive Spong/Linden Artists, Ltd. 12–13, 102–103, 132–133, 152–153.

Call to Celebrate Reconciliation and Eucharist Catechist Edition
ISBN: 978-1-59-276974-2
Item Number: CU5051

5 6 7 8 9 10 015016 22 21 20 19 18
Webcrafters, Inc., Madison, WI, USA; August 2018 Job# 138333

Contents

Philosophy and Process v

Reconciliation Scope and Sequence .... vi–vii

Eucharist Scope and Sequence .... viii–ix

Components and Web Site x

Catechetical Communities xi

Young People and the Sacrament of
 Reconciliation xii

Restored Order xiii

Sacraments and Liturgical Catechesis.......... xiv–xv

The Role of Music..................... xvi

Respecting Cultures..................... xvii–xviii

Reconciliation xix

Welcome..................... xx–xxi

Reconciliation Young People's Lessons

Chapter 1 We Are Called 8A–17

Ritual Focus: Signing with the Cross
 God Gives Everyone Life (Acts 17:16–34)

Faith Focus: God calls us to a life of happiness with him
 and gives us grace through the sacraments.

Liturgical Focus: The Sacraments of Initiation

Chapter 2 We Are Welcomed 18A–27

Ritual Focus: Renewal of Baptismal Promises
 Zacchaeus (Luke 19:1–10)

Faith Focus: The Sacrament of Reconciliation forgives
 sins committed after Baptism.

Liturgical Focus: Reception of the Penitent

Chapter 3 We Reflect 28A–37

Ritual Focus: Reverencing the Word
 The Great Commandment (Luke 10:25–28)

Faith Focus: Scriptures show us how God wants us
 to live.

Liturgical Focus: The Examination of Conscience

Chapter 4 We Are Sorry.............................. 38A–47

Ritual Focus: Examination of Conscience and
 Act of Contrition
 A Woman Who Was Sorry (Luke 7:36–38,
 44–48, 50)

Faith Focus: Sorrow for sin is the most important part
 of the Sacrament of Reconciliation.

Liturgical Focus: The Confession of Sin and Penance

Chapter 5 We Are Forgiven 48A–57

Ritual Focus: Prayer over the Candidates
 The Forgiving Father (Luke 15:11–24)

Faith Focus: The Sacrament of Reconciliation forgives
 sins and reconciles us with God and
 one another.

Liturgical Focus: Prayer of Absolution

Chapter 6 We Go Forth 58A–67

Ritual Focus: Sprinkling with Water and
 the Sign of Peace
 Jesus Appears to the Disciples
 (John 20:19–23)

Faith Focus: We are sent forth to bring forgiveness
 and peace to others.

Liturgical Focus: Proclamation of Praise and Dismissal

Catholic Source Book

Words of Faith 68–73

Celebrating Reconciliation......................... 74–75

Sources of Morality......................... 76–77

Catholic Prayers......................... 78–81

Program Resources and Activity Masters

We Are Called CE1

We Are Welcomed CE2

We Reflect CE3

We Are Sorry CE4

We Are Forgiven CE5

We Go Forth CE6

Eucharist
Young People's Lessons

Eucharist 82–83

Welcome 84–85

Faith Journey 86–87

Chapter 7 We Belong 88A–97

Ritual Focus: Renewal of Baptismal Promises
                     The Vine and the Branches (John 15:1–17)

Faith Focus: The Sacraments of Initiation, Baptism,
                     Confirmation, and Eucharist make us
                     members of the Church.

Liturgical Focus: Sacraments of Initiation

                     For Restored Order implementation, use these
                     two sessions after Chapter 7:

                     Restored Order (Confirmation):
                     Gifts of the Spirit CE15–25

                     Restored Order (Confirmation):
                     We Are Holy CE26–36

Chapter 8 We Gather 98A–107

Ritual Focus: Procession and Gloria
                     The Early Christians (Acts 2:42–47)

Faith Focus: We gather as a united community.

Liturgical Focus: Introductory Rites, Gloria

Chapter 9 We Are Forgiven 108A–117

Ritual Focus: Penitential Act
                     The Call of Matthew (Matthew 9:9–13)

Faith Focus: Eucharist is a Sacrament of unity
                     and forgiveness.

Liturgical Focus: Penitential Act

Chapter 10 We Listen 118A–127

Ritual Focus: Signing
                     The Sower (Matthew 13:1–23)

Faith Focus: God is present in Scripture.

Liturgical Focus: The Liturgy of the Word

Chapter 11 We Prepare 128A–137

Ritual Focus: Honoring the Cross
                     The Washing of the Feet (John 13:1–16)

Faith Focus: The Mass is a sacrifice.

Liturgical Focus: Preparation of the Gifts

Chapter 12 We Remember and
               Give Thanks 138A–147

Ritual Focus: Mystery of Faith
                     The Last Supper (Matthew 26:26–28,
                     Luke 22:14–20)

Faith Focus: We remember the many ways God has
                     saved us.

Liturgical Focus: Eucharistic Prayer, Consecration,
                  Mystery of Faith, Great Amen

Chapter 13 We Share a Meal 148A–157

Ritual Focus: Sharing a Meal
                     The Bread of Life (John 6:30–58)

Faith Focus: We receive the Body and Blood of Jesus,
                     the Bread of Life.

Liturgical Focus: Communion Rite

Chapter 14 We Go Forth .... 158A–16?

Ritual Focus: Blessing for Mission
                     Pentecost (Acts 2:1–41)

Faith Focus: The Holy Spirit helps us do Jesus' work.

Liturgical Focus: Dismissal

Catholic Source Book

Words of Faith .... 168–17?

Order of Mass .... 174–18?

Receiving Communion .... 186–18?

Catholic Prayers .... 188–19?

Index .... 19?

Program Resources and Activity Masters

We Belong .... CE?

    Restored Order (Confirmation):
    Gifts of the Spirit .... CE15–2?

    Restored Order (Confirmation):
    We Are Holy .... CE26–3?

We Gather .... CE?

We Are Forgiven .... CE?

We Listen .... CE1?

We Prepare .... CE1?

We Remember and Give Thanks .... CE1?

We Share a Meal .... CE1?

We Go Forth .... CE1?

Philosophy and Process

Philosophy

Call to Celebrate: Reconciliation and Eucharist flows from the traditional Church teachings that:

- Liturgy, the public worship of the Church, is the central activity of the People of God.

- The continual call to conversion is an essential part of the proclamation of the kingdom and is a response to God's love and mercy.

- In the celebration of these sacraments, the People of God are transformed by their immersion in symbols, rituals, prayers, and participation in the celebration.

- Participation in the sacraments brings people to a newness of life.

Call to Celebrate: Reconciliation and Eucharist upholds the principle that preparing young people for participation in the sacraments is a two-part process. First, it is a process that is best done in the midst of family, peers, and the whole community. Second, it is a process of liturgical catechesis that respects how individuals—both young people and adults—come to know the mysteries of the sacraments through participation in symbol and ritual.

Catechetical Process

At its heart, *Call to Celebrate: Reconciliation and Eucharist* follows a liturgical-catechetical method in three steps:

CELEBRATE

Every session begins with a celebration that includes a ritual focus. These celebrations involve young people, families, or whole communities in a gradual unfolding of the rites, symbols, and prayers of the sacraments. The celebration is immediately followed by a reflection on what was experienced.

REMEMBER

In every session a Scripture passage which pertains to the meaning of the rite is proclaimed and broken open. The doctrines which form the body of teaching about the sacraments are presented, and a specific part of the Rite of each sacrament is explained.

LIVE

Every session includes an activity that helps young people integrate the theme into daily living.

Activity Strand Every session is developed around an activity strand:

- Reflect
- Share
- Respond

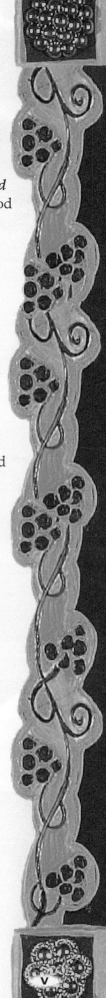

Our Catholic Teachings...

...today's Church needs to become more aware of the need to show in all her work the mercy of God and to follow the example of Jesus himself.

See John Paul II, *On the Mercy of God*, 12

The goal of liturgical catechesis is to prepare people for and initiate them into the mystery of Jesus Christ and in the full, conscious, and active participation in the Liturgy. It is through catechesis that we understand the nature, rites, and symbols of our faith.

See *Constitution on the Sacred Liturgy*, 10; *National Directory for Catechesis*, 33; John Paul II, *Catechesi Tradendae*, 23; and *Catechism of the Catholic Church*, 1075.

Scope and Sequence

	Chapter **1** **WE ARE CALLED**	Chapter **2** **WE ARE WELCOMED**	Chapter **3** **WE REFLECT**
Ritual Focus	Signing with the Cross	Renewal of Baptismal Promises	Reverencing the Word
Scripture	God Gives Everyone Life (Acts 17:16–34)	Zacchaeus (Luke 19:1–10)	The Great Commandment (Luke 10:25–28)
Faith Focus	• In Baptism, God calls us to a life of happiness with him. • A sacrament is a holy sign that comes from Jesus and gives us grace. • Jesus is the greatest sign of God the Father's love.	• At Baptism we are called to walk in the light. • Sin is a choice. • The Sacrament of Reconciliation forgives sins committed after Baptism.	• We prepare for the Sacrament of Reconciliation with an examination of conscience, using the word of God. • The Holy Spirit guides us in examining our conscience. • Conscience is the capacity to know right from wrong.
Catechism of the Catholic Church	1420–1421, 1425-1429	1441–1445	1454
Liturgical Focus	Sacraments of Initiation	Reception of the Penitent	The Examination of Conscience
Signs of Faith	baptismal name Baptism Holy Trinity	holy water candles Reconciliation room	bowing Bible Precepts of the Church

Chapter 4	Chapter 5	Chapter 6
WE ARE SORRY	**WE ARE FORGIVEN**	**WE GO FORTH**
Examination of Conscience and Act of Contrition	Prayer over the Candidates	Sprinkling Rite and Sign of Peace
A Woman Who Was Sorry (Luke 7:36–38, 45–48, 50)	The Forgiving Father (Luke 15:11–24)	Jesus Appears to the Disciples (John 20:19–23)
• The Holy Spirit helps us to be sorry for our sins. Sorrow for sin is the most important part of the Sacrament of Reconciliation. • A penance is a prayer or action that shows we are truly sorry for our sins.	• God is always ready to forgive us. • God wants us to be one with him. *Reconciliation* means "bringing together again, or reuniting." • Through the power of the Holy Spirit and the ministry of the priest, we are reconciled with God and one another.	• The Sacrament of Reconciliation is a sacrament of conversion. • The mission of reconciliation is to bring forgiveness and peace to others. • The Holy Spirit remains with us to help us grow and become more like Jesus.
450–1453	1455–1460	1468–1470
Confession of Sins and Penance	Prayer of Absolution	Proclamation of Praise and Dismissal
kneeling contrition penitent	laying on of hands Heaven: together forever purple stole	sprinkling with holy water Sign of Peace bishops and priests

Scope and Sequence

	Chapter 7 WE BELONG	Restored Order: Use these sessions if also preparing for Confirmation.		Chapter 8 WE GATHER	Chapter 9 WE ARE FORGIVEN
		GIFTS OF THE SPIRIT	WE ARE HOLY		
Ritual Focus	Renewal of Baptismal Promises	Blessing	Blessing	Procession and Gloria	Penitential Act
Scripture	The Vine and the Branches John 15:1–17	Jesus Promises the Holy Spirit John 14:15–26	Jesus Teaches about Holiness Luke 4:16–30	The Early Christians Acts 2:42–47	The Call of Matthew Matthew 9:9–13
Faith Focus	• A sacrament is a holy sign that comes from Jesus and gives us grace. • Baptism, Confirmation, and Eucharist are Sacraments of Initiation. • The Sacraments of Initiation make us full members of the Church.	• The Holy Spirit is the third Person of the Holy Trinity. • The Holy Spirit is our Advocate, our helper. • We receive the seven gifts of the Holy Spirit at Confirmation.	• The gifts of the Holy Spirit help us do God's work. • The Holy Spirit makes us holy. • Being *holy* means "being close to God and choosing what God wants."	• The Church is the People of God and Body of Christ. • The Eucharist, or Mass, is the Church's most important action of praise and thanks. • The Introductory Rites gather us as a community of faith.	• The Eucharist is a sacrament of unity and forgiveness. • Sin keeps us from being one People of God. • At Mass we ask God's forgiveness during the Penitential Act.
Catechism of the Catholic Church	1212, 1275–1277, 1285, 1316–1317, 1321–1327	1830–1831	1302–1305	1153, 1156–1158	1393–1395
Liturgical Focus	Sacraments of Initiation	Bishop's Imposition of Hands, Prayer for the Gifts of the Holy Spirit	Anointing, Final Blessing	Introductory Rites, Gloria	Penitential Act
Signs of Faith	water Paschal candle Holy Trinity	imposition of hands chrism bishop	fire miter and crozier saint	assembly procession prayer and singing	*Kyrie, eleison* (Lord Have Mercy) silence sprinkling with holy water

Chapter 10 WE LISTEN	Chapter 11 WE PREPARE	Chapter 12 WE REMEMBER & GIVE THANKS	Chapter 13 WE SHARE A MEAL	Chapter 14 WE GO FORTH
Signing	Honoring the Cross	Mystery of Faith	Sharing a Meal	Blessing for Mission
The Sower Matthew 13:1–23	The Washing of the Feet John 13:1–16	The Last Supper Matthew 26:26–28; Luke 22:14–20	I Am the Bread of Life John 6:30–58	Pentecost Acts 2:1–41
• The Bible is God's word written in human words. • We listen to the word of God during the Liturgy of the Word. • When we listen to God's word, we want to share it with others.	• Jesus sacrificed his life for us when he died on the cross. • The Mass is a sacrifice. • At Mass through the power of the Holy Spirit and the words and actions of the priest, Jesus offers again the gift of himself to his Father.	• The Eucharistic Prayer is a prayer of thanksgiving, remembering, and consecration. • Through the power of the Holy Spirit and the words and actions of the priest, the bread and wine become the Body and Blood of Jesus. • At the Great Amen, the assembly says "yes" to all of God's saving actions and promises.	• The Mass is a meal of thanksgiving. • Jesus is the Bread of Life. • In Holy Communion, we are united to Jesus and the Church. We share in the promise of life forever with God.	• The Eucharist changes us. • The Holy Spirit helps us to live out our mission. • At Mass we are sent forth in peace to share the good news.
101–104, 136, 141, 1154, 1190, 1349, 1408	1333–1336	1362–1366	1382–1398	1391–1397
Liturgy of the Word	Preparation of the Gifts	Eucharistic Prayer, Consecration, Mystery of Faith, Great Amen	Communion Rite	Dismissal
Sign of the Cross	cross	kneeling	Sign of Peace	blessing
Bible	altar	priest	paten, ciborium, and chalice	witness
readings	bread and wine	Blessed Sacrament	Agnus Dei (Lamb of God)	deacon

Components and Website

Candidate's Book helps young people reflect on the mystery of Eucharist, Confirmation, and Reconciliation and forgiveness through celebrations, colorful and appealing visuals, and interactive pages with activities and prayers. Faith at Home features and pages help families support young people in their preparation.

 Catechist Edition provides everything the catechist needs to be successful—easy-to-use planners, theological, spiritual, and historical background, an easy-to-use three-step lesson process, a wealth of resources and activities, plus activity masters and Scripture pantomimes, dramas, and narrations.

Family Guide features reflections for all adult family members who are preparing young people and also offers step-by-step outlines for families preparing young people in the home.

 Songs of Celebration CD offers the songs used in the celebrations for *Call to Celebrate: Reconciliation and Eucharist*. It may be used in the catechetical sessions and by families at home.

My Mass Book and **My Reconciliation Book** are delightfully illustrated guidebooks for young people that present and guide them through both sacraments, respectively.

 Sacraments Source Book provides a wealth of information and practical resources, including professional development articles, catechist and parent orientation and training sessions, family centered sessions, and parish assembly sessions.

GO online **www.osvcurriculum.com**

These sites provide more background and activities for young people, parents, and catechists.

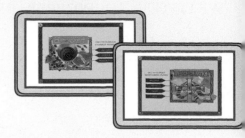

- Print Planner with Links
- Music Sample
- Illustrated Glossary
- Timeline of Jesus' Life
- Catechist Edition Activity Masters
- Catechist Edition Gospels
- FAQs
- Extended Saint Stories
- Symbol Chart

Catechist's Companion series includes helpful guides for catechists on how to successfully instruct young people on the sacraments, and a guide to help catechists more fully understand and apply the revised Roman Missal changes.

Catholic Parent Know-How series will help parents more fully participate in their child's Eucharist and Reconciliation journeys.

And With Your Spirit: Songs for Deepening Children's Understanding of the Mass by acclaimed Catholic songwriter and performer John Burland and Dr. Jo Ann Paradise includes 14 songs with lyrics based on the revised Roman Missal to enrich your lessons with the young people.

Catechetical Communities

Family

The primary place where catechesis occurs is in the family. It is within the family that young people first learn about God. The family is where they continue to develop values, practice their faith, and observe and witness to a faithful life lived in common everyday experiences.

In *Call to Celebrate: Reconciliation and Eucharist,* "family" encompasses all those people who make up the basic unit of a young person's primary community: parents, siblings, and extended family members. Both programs involve the family through:

- Faith at Home activities and pages in the *Candidate's Book*
- A *Family Guide* for Eucharist and one for Reconciliation
- Parent sessions in the *Sacraments Source Book*

Catechist

Your role as a catechist for sacrament preparation for young people is significant. As a person of faith, your witness and sharing of faith is vital. You create the environment for celebrating and learning. Through you, young people will come to know the mystery of God's forgiveness in the Sacrament of Reconciliation and of God's love in the Eucharist in a unique way. In your role as catechist for *Call to Celebrate: Reconciliation and Eucharist,* you are called upon to preside, proclaim the word, listen, reflect, and teach. Your ministry is a gift to each young person because through your efforts they will come to a deeper appreciation of the sacraments and the signs, symbols, and rituals associated with them. They will also be led to a fuller experience of Jesus and the Church.

Assembly

The participation of the worshipping community is important to young people's initiation. The vitality and faith life of the assembly shapes and forms the faith of its young people. The *Sacraments Source Book* provides blessings, Prayer of the Faithful, and bulletin notices to alert the assembly to remember and pray for the young people as they prepare to celebrate the Sacraments of Eucharist, Confirmation, and Reconciliation for the first time. It also provides assembly gatherings in which members of the assembly and families can engage together to reflect on the rites and their meaning. This program encourages the *full, active,* and *conscious* participation of the whole community. Remind young people and their families of the importance of participating with the assembly every week at Mass.

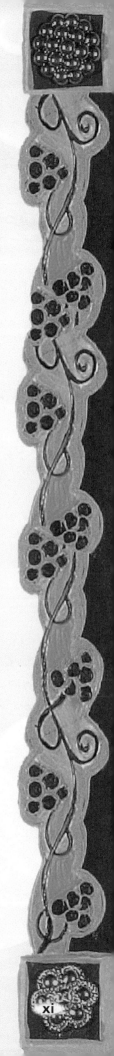

Young people and the Sacrament of Reconciliation

As you prepare young people to celebrate the Sacrament of Reconciliation, keep in mind that their sense of sin and forgiveness depends on a variety of things. While many of them may have very good self images, some of them will not. Their images of God may vary from a God who is unconditional in loving and forgiving them to a God who is judgmental and withholding of love and forgiveness. Some of them will be at a level of moral development where they do know the difference between right and wrong. Others will still think that mistakes and accidents are sinful and will not understand that sin has to do with choices and relationships. Some of them will come from family situations where forgiveness and reconciliation are granted easily and generously and others from environments where they are withheld or granted sparingly.

This program is designed to help the young person navigate these differences in ways that respect his or her circumstances. At the same time, through participation in rituals and activities, the program calls him or her to grow and develop so as to be able to enter fully into the celebration of the Sacrament of Reconciliation at the end of this preparation.

The overall goal in preparing young people to celebrate the Sacrament of Reconciliation is to help them understand that:

- through Baptism they are graced children of God.
- God is merciful and forgiving and calls us to friendship with him.
- sometimes we choose to do things that either break or weaken our friendship with God.
- the Holy Spirit helps us recognize sin and gives us the strength to avoid it.
- God always welcomes us back when we are sorry.
- in the Sacrament of Reconciliation we always experience the forgiveness of God and the Church.

Young people show readiness to celebrate the Sacrament of Reconciliation when:

- *They know the difference between right and wrong.*
- *They know the difference between sin and accidents or mistakes.*
- *They are capable of saying "I am sorry" on their own.*
- *They are capable of reflecting on their actions when asked about them.*
- *They understand that God will always forgive them.*
- *They show a sincere desire to right wrongs.*

Restored Order

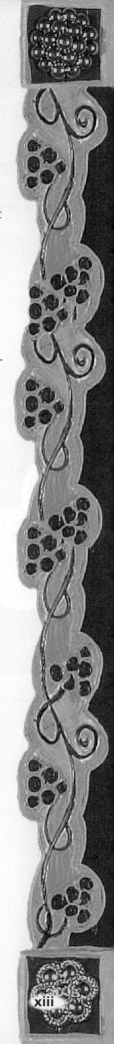

In the early Church, Christian Initiation was one event. Adults or young people were baptized, anointed, or had hands laid upon them, and then participated in the Eucharist, all at the same celebration. For a variety of reasons this practice gradually became separated into three different events. In 1910, Pius X recommended in his encyclical *Quam Singulari* that the First Communion of young people should not be deferred too long after they had reached the age of reason. Previous to his urging, young people who had been baptized as infants usually celebrated First Communion in the early teen years, and Confirmation usually was celebrated at an earlier age. However, once young people began to participate fully in the Eucharist at an earlier age, the age for Confirmation was varied and not necessarily tied to reception of First Communion.

As a result of Rites issued by the Church after the Second Vatican Council, many dioceses and parishes throughout the United States have adopted the practice of celebrating Confirmation prior to First Communion. This is often referred to as *restored order*.

Some of these dioceses celebrate the Sacrament of Confirmation at the same Eucharistic celebration in which young people celebrate their First Communion. Other dioceses celebrate at a different time, but before First Communion.

Other dioceses choose to celebrate Confirmation sometime after First Communion. All of these practices are approved by the United States Bishops Conference, which has given approval to the celebration of Confirmation for young people baptized as infants anytime between the ages of seven and sixteen.

Call to Celebrate: Reconciliation and Eucharist includes two sessions for those parishes that are practicing restored order. These sessions are found on pages CE15–36 of this *Catechist Edition*. If you are preparing young people for both sacraments, you would use these sessions after session one.

Our Catholic Teachings...

There is a great deal of variation from diocese to diocese for the age of confirmation in the United States. The Sacrament of Confirmation can be celebrated at any time between the age of discretion and sixteen years. It has been determined that a single catechesis cannot be assigned for this sacrament.

See *National Directory for Catechesis*, 36 A, 2.

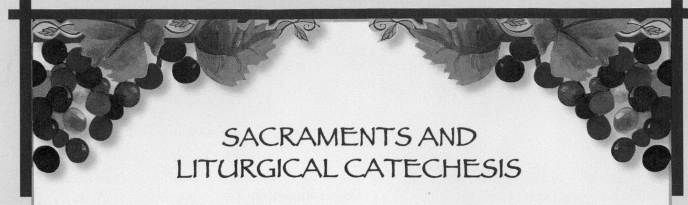

SACRAMENTS AND LITURGICAL CATECHESIS

Liturgical Catechesis

There is an ancient Latin phrase which is still used today that reinforces the importance of liturgical experience for an authentic appropriation of Christian faith. It is *lex orandi legem credendidi statuit,* which means, "the rule of prayer establishes the rule of faith." Liturgical catechesis is the activity of bringing communal faith to consciousness through participation in and celebration of the rites of the community. It has a solid historical tradition in our Church since liturgy has long been regarded as the Church's "school of faith," an expression which recognizes the formative value of ritual celebration on participants. The story of Emmaus shows that it is precisely in the ritual "breaking of the bread" that the disciples come to know and understand the mystery of Jesus (*Luke 24:13–35*).

Candidates

Liturgical catechesis meets a young person's readiness to learn. Research shows that young people are impressed most deeply in the context of rituals and symbols. They are capable of entering into them and able to express profound insight into the meanings expressed in religious symbol and ritual. Participation in religious ritual and symbol landscapes their imaginations and provides formative experiences that go beyond the written or spoken word. In *Call to Celebrate: Reconciliation and Eucharist,* young people are gradually led through celebration with symbol, ritual, and gesture to understand the mystery of the sacraments in an age appropriate way. Every session begins with a celebration that is an essential part of the lesson. These celebrations help young people better understand and enter into the liturgical life of the Church. Taking their cue from the *Directory for Masses with Children,* "…the liturgy itself always exerts its own inherent power to instruct" (12); the celebrations are meant to be the cornerstone on which each session is built.

Prayer Space

Therefore, it is very important for you to take care to prepare the prayer space ahead of time and to lead the celebration in a way that will call young people to prayer, participation in the ritual action, and reflection after the celebration.

The prayer space needs to be a place where the movement of processions and rituals are easily and reverently participated in. Prepare it ahead of time. You may choose to set aside a space in your meeting place, or you may find the church or another room to be more suitable. When you have chosen a space, arrange it in such a way that

young people can move easily and can see and hear everything that is happening. Decorate the space with plants or flowers. Always have available a large clear bowl with holy water, a Bible and stand, and a candle. Check your planning page each week to be sure you have everything you need for the celebration.

The Celebration

Each of the celebrations is built around a song, a Scripture reading, and a ritual action. With the exception of Chapter 9, all of the celebrations also include a procession. Take time to conduct the procession reverently and slowly. Involve young people in song, either by leading it yourself, using the *Songs of Celebration* or *And With Your Spirit* CD, or inviting a song leader into your group. You may choose to proclaim the Scripture from the adapted version in the *Candidate's Book* or from the Bible. Be sure to familiarize yourself with the ritual action ahead of time so that you are able to be fully engaged with the young people during the celebration. The celebration is in the *Candidate's Book*; if you find that having them use the books during the celebration is distracting, you may wish to do the celebration without the books and guide their responses.

Leader of Prayer

During the celebration you are the leader of prayer. The way you preside is important. Here are some tips:

- Learn the script ahead of time. Be familiar with it, so that you are able to lead and be present with the young people without being distracted or fumbling for "what comes next."

- Use your body to communicate. Stand tall. Use broad and expansive gestures. Be aware of your facial expressions and tone of voice.

- Watch your timing. Let there be silence between parts of the prayer. Take time with each young person during the ritual actions. Do not be afraid of pauses or silence. They often lead them to deeper prayer and reflection.

Reflection

Liturgical catechesis does not end with the celebration. It is important to allow young people the opportunity to reflect on the celebration and to articulate what they have experienced. During this segment of the session, it is more important that you listen to the candidate's responses and take your lead from them than for you to tell them what it means.

THE ROLE OF MUSIC

It is difficult to imagine anyone who would reject the life-giving power of music for young people and adults. Music taps into feelings and imagination and at times provides a sense of the transcendent. Songs can tell a story and they can be a textbook. Music and song that touch our lives and are related to significant experiences often come back over the years.

These same things can be said of the music used in liturgy in general and in the celebrations of *Call to Celebrate: Reconciliation and Eucharist* in particular. It is an important catechetical element, since music forms, shapes, and gives voice to what we believe, truly "echoing" God's word and action in our lives.

The program includes a *Songs of Celebration* Music CD to use in the celebrations. Alternative suggestions are also given in each session, including selections from *And With Your Spirit* by John Burland and Dr. Jo Ann Paradise, which features 14 songs that correlate to the revised Roman Missal. If you are not confident in your musical abilities, use the CD or engage a musician to help you and the candidate experience the fullness of the celebration and closing prayer. You can also use the music throughout the lesson as background while young people are working on activities.

Song Titles

And With Your Spirit

And With Your Spirit
Through My Fault
When We Praise You
We Glorify You
Glory to God
Incarnate One
Yes Lord I Believe
     (English/Spanish version)
It Is Right and Just
Holy Lord God of Hosts
We Proclaim Your Death, O Lord
Savior of the World
The Supper of the Lamb
Under My Roof
And With Your Spirit (acoustic version)

Songs of Celebration

Reconciliation
We Are Called, David Haas
     © GIA Publications
We Are Marching, South African Traditional
Del Señor viene la misericordia © Bob Hurd.
     Published by OCP
Remember Your Love © 1978 Damean Music,
     Distributed by GIA Publications
Children of God © Christopher Walker.
     Published by OCP
Coming Back Together ©2000 John Burland

Eucharist
Yes Lord, I Believe! © 2000 John Burland
Glory to God, Marty Haugen
     © GIA Publications

Create in Me © Tom Kendzia.
     Published by OCP
Open My Eyes © Jesse Manibusan.
     Published by OCP
We Praise You © 1978 Damean.
     Distributed by GIA Publications
Te alabaré, Señor/I Will Praise You,
     Lord/Tony Alonso © GIA Publications
We Come to the Table © 2005 John Burland
Lead Us to the Water © Tom Kendzia
     and Gary Daigle. Published by OCP

Confirmation
Send Us Your Spirit, David Haas © GIA
Publications
We Are Marching, South African Traditional

Our Catholic Teachings...

Religious music and singing give voice to the faithful as they celebrate devotions, sacred exercises, and liturgical services. Sacred music is an integral and priceless part of the Church's celebrations, solemn liturgies, and traditions, and should be fostered and encouraged among all members. Children are especially responsive to the joyful expression that music brings...

See *Directory for Masses with Children*, 30; *Musicam Sacram*, 16; and *Constitution on the Sacred Liturgy*, 118.

*A song that reflects the revised Roman Missal changes to the Gloria is also available at
www.osvcurriculum.com: Glory to God © 2007, 2009 Daniel L. Schutte. Published by OCP

RESPECTING CULTURES

The Catholic Church is, by her very name and nature, universal. The Eucharist is a primary celebration of the church's universality, but it is also a celebration that recognizes and draws forth the unique cultural contributions of people throughout the world. The *Catechism of the Catholic Church* states that "the mystery of Christ is so unfathomably rich that it cannot be exhausted by its expression in any single liturgical tradition" (1201) and "the celebration of the liturgy, therefore, should correspond to the genius and culture of the different peoples" (1204).

Universality of the Church

When we celebrate the sacraments we enter into a deeper relationship with the whole Body of Christ. One of the elements of preparing young people for the reception of sacraments is to give them a sense of the universal dimension of the church. This involves a two-fold responsibility for the catechist— to incorporate an understanding of the universality of the Church in sacramental preparation and to ensure that she or he is aware of the diversity of cultures that may be present among young people preparing for the sacrament.

Tips for Respecting Cultures

The richness of our faith invites diverse cultures to celebrate a life with Christ. This concept can be tangibly expressed to young people through the use of multicultural symbols and objects that celebrate the diversity of God's people. Use the following tips to help young people learn that people around the world profess their faith in a variety of ways, and we are all children of God and beloved by him. During the preparation time, use these ideas to encourage respect:

- Christ, the Light of the World, represents the fullness of life to all people. Give each young person a white paper plate to create a mandala, an ancient symbol of wholeness through all cultures. Discuss what symbols young people might use to show Jesus as the Light of the World.

- Listen to sacred music in another language.

- If a young person in the class speaks another language, invite him/her to say the "Our Father" in his/her language.

Our Catholic Teachings...

The multicultural and pluralistic society of the United States poses unique opportunities and challenges for the faith. Through the inculturation of the Gospel message, faith and life are linked, and the faithful can receive Jesus in every aspect of their lives.

See *National Directory for Catechesis*, 21C.

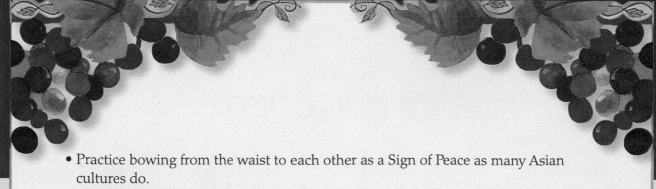

- Practice bowing from the waist to each other as a Sign of Peace as many Asian cultures do.

- Write a new lyric to the tune of "He's Got the Whole World in His Hands" using the names of countries throughout the world.

- To illustrate the baptismal call to make the world a better place have the young people create a chain of good deeds with construction paper and place the chain around a globe. Place the globe in a prominent place.

- Create a multicultural prayer table by placing a multicultural cloth or cloth map (available at fabric stores) and place items on the table that represent different cultures. Gather young people around the prayer table and ask them to close their eyes and think of what the world would be like if everyone lived in peace.

- Teach the young people to say "thank you" and "peace" in a variety of languages.

- Write a class poem titled "Called to Walk in the Light," in which each line has only two words. If students speak more than one language, write the poem using words from other languages also.

- The kanga is a rectangular piece of brightly printed cloth worn by women in the African countries of Kenya and Uganda. Give each young person a rectangular piece of light colored cloth (muslin or old sheets work well for this) approximately 18" x 12". Have each write "Love one another as I have loved you" in the center of the cloth with a marker. Provide a variety of sponge pieces or cut vegetables such as carrots, potatoes, and onions and have young people create colorful designs by dipping the vegetables or sponges into tempera paint and printing around the words on the kanga.

- Place a picture of the globe in the center of a bulletin board or on a sheet of poster board. Have young people trace one hand, cut it out, and write their name in the center. Place the finished hands around the globe like a wreath to show that we can circle the world with love and caring.

- Make a "Creation Tree." Place a dead tree branch into a container of sand. Give each young person one or more cardstock circles approximately 3" in diameter. Have young people cover either side of the circle with pictures of people and natural objects, or have them draw and color pictures illustrating the beauties of creation. Use a paper punch to make holes at the top of the circles and attach them to the tree with pieces of yarn. Talk about how the tree illustrates our connection with nature and others.

- Give each young person a piece of light-colored construction paper to make a peace flag using different words for peace and creating their own designs. Flags can be attached to a dowel stick with tape or displayed on a bulletin board.

CALL to CELEBRATE

RECONCILIATION

CALL to CELEBRATE
RECONCILIATION

Welcome

Dear Candidate,

This is a very special time for you. You are preparing to take another step in your journey of friendship with Jesus and the Church. Your journey began when you were baptized. This journey of faith never ends. You will keep growing in your friendship with Jesus and the Church for your whole life.

Sometimes on our journey with Jesus we act in ways that hurt our friendship with him. We are sorry and want to be forgiven. We want to change and grow even closer to him. The Church gives us the Sacrament of Reconciliation to help us know that God forgives us and brings us back to him.

vi

Pages vi and vii provide a welcome to the program and the process of preparation.

Dear Candidate

▶ Read aloud the first paragraph.

▶ Tell young people that everyone receives the Sacrament of Reconciliation before First Communion.

▶ Summarize the second paragraph.

▶ Discuss how the Sacrament of Reconciliation prepares our hearts and minds to receive the gift of Jesus Christ.

You are getting ready to celebrate the Sacrament of Reconciliation for the first time. In this Sacrament, Jesus forgives your sins through the actions and prayers of the priest.

In *Call to Celebrate: Reconciliation*, you will
• learn that God is a God of mercy and forgiveness
• pray with your classmates and family
• listen to the stories of Jesus and the Apostles
• learn how to celebrate the Sacrament of Reconciliation

What is one thing you would like to learn this year?

_____

_____

_____

vii

Read aloud the four bulleted points in the second paragraph.

? Invite young people to ask questions about the rite before answering the question in their books.

Rite of Penance

"Reconciliation between God and his people was brought about by Our Lord Jesus Christ in the mystery of his death and resurrection (*see Romans 5:10*). The Lord entrusted the ministry of reconciliation to the Church in the person of the apostles (see *2 Corinthians 5:18ff.*)."

Decree from the Sacred Congregation For Divine Worship

Catechism Connection

To deepen your own background and reflection on Penance and conversion, refer to the *Catechism of the Catholic Church, 1420–1421, 1425–1429.*

Catechist Resources

 Sacraments: Celebrations of God's Life *(45 min)*

Oblate Media and Communications

Explores how the Eucharist developed from the Last Supper to the present and explains the Mass

 From Age to Age: How Christians Have Celebrated the Eucharist

Edward Foley
Liturgy Training Publications, 1991

Tells how Christians through the ages have celebrated and understood the Eucharist

Young People's Resources

 Close Encounters with the Sacraments *(12 min)*

Oblate Media and Communications

Helps young people (ages 8–12) understand what Sacraments mean in everyday life

 Francis, Brother of the Universe

Roy Gasnick O.F.M.
Paulist Press

A comic-book format publication of the life of Saint Francis

Catechist Formation

"Now [God] commands
all people everywhere to repent."

Acts of the Apostles 17:30

Created for Harmony

The picture of the Garden of Eden, where all creation is in harmony with God, is a strong contrast to a picture of the world today. But this picture from Genesis reveals what God originally intended for the world: men and women who are joined perfectly with him and who reveal, by the way they live, the harmony between heaven and earth.

The first humans disrupted the harmony of the Garden of Eden in a powerful way, but not powerful enough to overcom God's own grace and mercy. God the Father showed the dept of this divine love by seeking to restore the order of creation by sending his Son, Jesus, to reconcile the world and restore harmony through his death on the cross.

Turning Away

Though humans enter the world with original sin, the Sacrament of Baptism cleanses us from sin and restores the union of life that is shared in Jesus Christ. Baptism also calls us to live in the pattern of Christ. Yet, because we are created in God's image with the gift of freedom, we do at times freely choose to turn away from God, others, and sometimes ourselves. We sin. Our actions disrupt the harmony of union with God.

It is through the Sacrament of Penance that we are able to respond again and again to our baptismal call, and renew and deepen our relationship with God. It gives us a fresh start. Because the mercy of God is unlimited, Christians need not despair over the power of sin and evil.

What does it mean for you to reject sin and live as God's child?

How has the Sacrament of Penance helped you to renew your life?

Catechist Prayer

God of creation, renew in me the life of the waters of Baptism Help me to die and rise with Christ daily in my words and in my deeds. Amen.

Lesson Planner

www.osvcurriculum.com
Visit our website for additional resources and information.

		OBJECTIVES	LESSON PROCESS	☀ ACTIVITIES	MATERIALS
CELEBRATE	15 minutes Pages 8–9	Ritual Focus *Signing with the Cross* To experience a celebration of the word, including signing and being called by name	Celebrate the opening prayer.		PROGRAM RESOURCES *Songs of Celebration* CD, track 1 OTHER MATERIALS Bible, prayer table, candle, large glass bowl filled with water
	Pages 10–11	To explore the meaning of the ritual actions To explain that at Baptism we become children of God	Complete the activity. ✝ Read about and discuss baptismal names. Share stories of Baptism. ✝ Read about and discuss Baptism.	☀ Reflect Young people reflect on the experience of the celebration.	
REMEMBER	30 minutes Pages 12–13	Faith Focus *How does God show his love for us?* To reinforce that God gave us life	Discuss how we know that God loves us. 📖 Proclaim the Scripture/Bible story. *Acts 17:22–34* Complete the activity.	☀ Share Young people make lists of words about God. ▰ Faith at Home Suggested activities for the home	PROGRAM RESOURCES Copies of Activity Master 1, p. CE1
	Pages 14–15	Faith Focus *What are the sacraments?* To explain that sacraments are signs of God's love	Identify original sin and the sacraments. ✝ Read about and discuss the Holy Trinity. Discuss the Sacraments of Initiation as a group and as individual sacraments.	▰ Faith at Home Suggested activities for the home	
LIVE	15 minutes Page 16	To lead young people in expressing praise in belonging to the Church	Introduce the activity. Pray the Closing Blessing. Read aloud the People of Faith story about Francis of Assisi.	☀ Respond Young people write about what it means to be a member of the Church.	PROGRAM RESOURCES *Songs of Celebration* CD, track 1
FAITH AT HOME	Page 17	▰ Faith at Home To introduce the different parts of the Faith at Home page	Review the Faith at Home page. Encourage young people to share this page at home.	☀ Act Suggested activities for the home	PROGRAM RESOURCES Reconciliaton Family Guide, pp.16–17

CELEBRATE

Objective

To experience a celebration of the word, including signing and being called by name

Preparation

Familiarize yourself with the movements of the ritual focus for signing and calling by name on page 8.

Prepare the prayer space ahead of time. You will need:

- a Bible
- a table covered with a white cloth
- a candle and a large glass bowl filled with water on the prayer table
- 🎼 Use the *Songs of Celebration* CD, track 1, to rehearse the suggested song, "We Are Called," or one of the optional music suggestions on page 9.

Select a young person to carry the Bible in procession.

We Gather

Invite young people to assemble with their books for a procession.

- Direct them to follow you and the young person carrying the Bible.
- 🎼 As you process, lead young people in singing using the *Songs of Celebration* CD, track 1.
- When all are assembled in the prayer space, light the prayer candle.
- Begin the prayer, and lead young people in the Sign of the Cross.

Follow the order of prayer on pages 8–9.

We Listen

For the proclamation of the Gospel, you may use a Bible or the adapted reading in the *Candidate's Book* on pages 12–13.

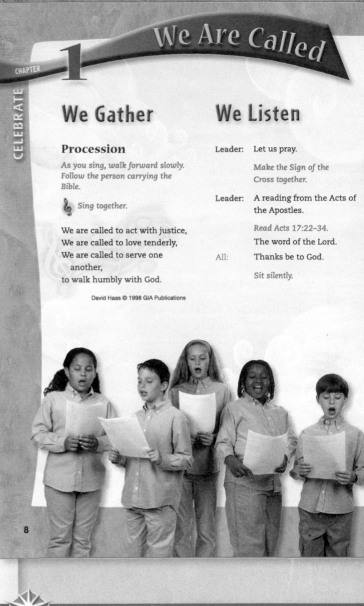

We Gather

Procession

As you sing, walk forward slowly. Follow the person carrying the Bible.

🎼 *Sing together.*

We are called to act with justice,
We are called to love tenderly,
We are called to serve one another,
to walk humbly with God.

David Haas © 1998 GIA Publications

We Listen

Leader: Let us pray.

Make the Sign of the Cross together.

Leader: A reading from the Acts of the Apostles.

*Read Acts 17:22–34.
The word of the Lord.*

All: Thanks be to God.

Sit silently.

8

✦ Ritual Background

Called by name   The practice of naming is traditionally associated with Baptism because Baptism is about identity. Who you are, and what you want to become are questions that Baptism celebrates.

In many scripture stories, when God decisively intervenes in a person's life, that person is given a new name. Abram became Abraham, and Sarai became Sarah. Jacob received the name Israel.

Jesus called Simon by a new name: Peter; and after his conversion, Saul of Tarsus was called Paul. Baptism is just such a decisive moment in the life of a Christian. A new life is beginning, and that person is called by name.

Ritual Focus: Signing with the Cross

Leader: Let us call to mind the goodness of God who gives us all good things. God gives us life and breath, and in him we live and move and have our being.

Come to the water to be marked with the Sign of the Cross.

[Name], God calls you by name to live in love with him always.

Candidate: Amen.

We Go Forth

Leader: Let us join in the prayer that Jesus taught us:

Pray the Lord's Prayer together.

Leader: Loving God, our source of life, bless us, protect us from all evil, and bring us to everlasting life.

All: Amen.

 Sing the opening song together.

9

Ritual Focus: Signing with the Cross

- Invite young people to stand and gather around the prayer table.
- Call each young person forward one by one.
- Make the Sign of the Cross on their foreheads with holy water.
- You may want to have young people refer to page 79 of their books for the words of the Lord's Prayer.
- When all of the young people have been signed, invite them to raise their hands in prayer and pray the Lord's Prayer together.

We Go Forth

- Lead the closing prayer.
- As the group processes back to their seats, have them sing *Songs of Celebration* CD, track 1, "We Are Called," or one of the optional music suggestions.

Optional Music Suggestions

"Donde hay amor y caridad,"
© Pedro Rublacava. Published by OCP

"Yes Lord, I Believe,"
© John Burland

"All People That on Earth Do Dwell,"
Traditional/Old 100th

✦ Liturgical Background

The Lord's Prayer When Jesus' disciples asked him to teach them to pray, he gave them the Lord's Prayer.

The Church has always treated this prayer with great reverence. In the early centuries, Christians customarily prayed it three times a day.

Liturgically, there was a solemn ceremony to "hand over" the Lord's Prayer to those preparing for Baptism. This rite is still practiced in the Church today with adults and older children who are preparing for Baptism at Easter.

The Lord's Prayer first appeared in the Mass during the fourth century. Because of its mention of bread and mutual forgiveness, it is well placed in the Communion Rite of the Eucharist.

CELEBRATE

Objective

To explore the meaning of the ritual actions of Signing with the Cross and being called by name

To explain that at Baptism we become children of God

Liturgical Catechesis

The purpose of this section is to help young people reflect on their experiences of the signs, rituals, prayers, and gestures of the celebration and to lead them to express their own meaning of the experiences. Allow young people to share their experiences without commenting on them.

God Calls

- On the board or on chart paper, write the following questions: What did you see? What did you hear? What did you do?

- Guide young people to reflect on the celebration by reviewing what happened in the prayer.

- Invite young people to share their responses to the questions.

Reflect

- Ask young people to write their responses in the book.

- Have volunteers share their responses.

Baptismal Name

- Ask young people to share how their name was chosen.

- Read aloud the text.

God Calls

Baptismal Name
We are each given a special name at **Baptism**. Usually it is the name or some form of the name of a saint or Mary, the Mother of Jesus. It may be the name of an Old Testament person. The name given at Baptism does not have to be a saint's name. Sometimes the word for a virtue, such as Faith, Hope, or Charity, is used as a name.

Reflect

Signing with the cross Think about the celebration, and in the space provided, write responses to two of the following questions.

1. What did the celebration tell you about God?

2. What did you think was the most important part of the celebration for you? Why?

3. What does it mean to be signed with the Sign of the Cross?

4. How did you feel when you heard the words, "God calls you by name"?

Question ____

_____

_____

_____

Question ____

_____

_____

_____

10

Additional Activity

Research a saint   The young people may enjoy learning more about saints and the significance of their names.

- Have books about saints and saint names available; if your classroom has Internet connections, find a few websites that give information about saints.

- Allow time for young people to research their first and/or middle name to find out about their patron saints.

- Young people whose names do not lend themselves to research can investigate any saint's name of their choosing.

- Have young people report their findings to the group.

God's Children

At our Baptism the priest or deacon calls us by name. The whole community welcomes us with great joy. We are baptized in the name of God the Father, God the Son, and God the Holy Spirit. The priest or deacon makes the Sign of the Cross on our forehead. The Sign of the Cross is a sign we belong to God. It marks us as a Christian, a follower or disciple of Jesus.

God calls us to a life of happiness with him. He promises us his grace. **Grace** is a sharing in God's own life. Imagine that! God wants us to share his life; he wants us to be his children. He chooses us to love him and each other.

SIGNS OF FAITH

Baptism

Baptism is the Sacrament that makes us children of God and members of the Body of Christ, the Church. Baptism takes away Original Sin and all personal **sin**. It unites us to Jesus and it makes us temples of the Holy Spirit. It promises us eternal life in Heaven. In Baptism we celebrate God's promise that he will live in friendship with us forever.

11

God's Children

- Invite young people to share any stories they know about their own Baptism.

- Ask if any of them have participated in a Baptism and have them share their experiences.

- Use the Teaching Tip below to familiarize or review the Sacrament of Baptism with the young people.

- Summarize the first paragraph.

- Have young people read the second paragraph silently and then ask them to respond to the phrase "Because God calls me to a life of happiness and chooses me to be his child, I…."

Baptism

- Organize young people into small groups or pairs. Have them read the text silently and as a group choose one of the effects of Baptism and talk about why it is important for them. Have pairs or groups share their responses with the whole group.

Teaching Tip

Seeing the sacraments   Young people will have a greater understanding of the Sacraments of Initiation if they have a chance to observe the rituals. Find out when your parish is celebrating a Baptism or Confirmation, and plan for your group to attend.

As an alternative, ask if any young people have home videos of their own or other family members' Baptism, First Communion, or Confirmation celebrations that they would be willing to show the group. You could also obtain any of several commercially produced videos on the sacraments, and play them in your session.

Objective

To reinforce that God gave us life

Faith Focus

How does God show his love for us?
List young people's responses on the board or on chart paper.

God Loves Us

Call attention to the illustration. Have young people speculate on the time and place as well as what is happening in the illustration. It is set in the ancient world in the time of the early Church. Paul is preaching.

- Confirm the speculation by having a young person read the first paragraph of text aloud.

 Scripture   ACTS 17:22–34

God Gives Everyone Life

- Gather the group in a story circle or in the prayer space. Remind them that they will be hearing the story from Acts again.

- Ask what they remember from hearing the story during the celebration.

- Select two strong readers to proclaim the story as Paul would have spoken.

- Ask for evidence from the story that the Greeks were convinced by Paul's teachings. Some of them were baptized.

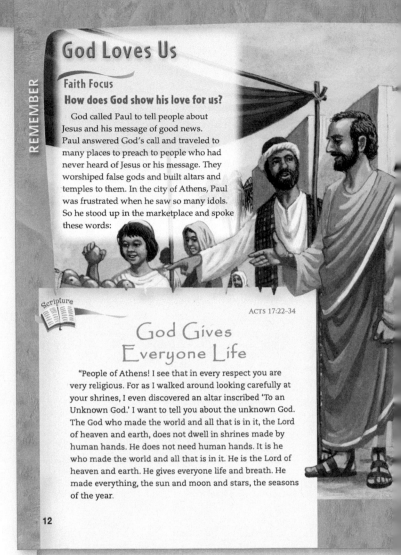

God Loves Us

REMEMBER

Faith Focus

How does God show his love for us?

God called Paul to tell people about Jesus and his message of good news. Paul answered God's call and traveled to many places to preach to people who had never heard of Jesus or his message. They worshiped false gods and built altars and temples to them. In the city of Athens, Paul was frustrated when he saw so many idols. So he stood up in the marketplace and spoke these words:

Scripture   ACTS 17:22–34

God Gives Everyone Life

"People of Athens! I see that in every respect you are very religious. For as I walked around looking carefully at your shrines, I even discovered an altar inscribed 'To an Unknown God.' I want to tell you about the unknown God. The God who made the world and all that is in it, the Lord of heaven and earth, does not dwell in shrines made by human hands. He does not need human hands. It is he who made the world and all that is in it. He is the Lord of heaven and earth. He gives everyone life and breath. He made everything, the sun and moon and stars, the seasons of the year.

12

📖📖 Scripture Background

Paul in Athens   The Book of Acts of the Apostles describes how the Gospel spread from its roots in Jerusalem all the way to Rome. In those days Rome represented "the ends of the earth" *(Acts 1:8)*. In the beginning of Acts, Peter and John are the main preachers of the Gospel. But Paul soon extends the message to the Gentiles, beginning in Philippi, Thessalonica, Athens, and eventually going all the way to Rome.

The Athenians were Gentiles, and Paul encouraged them to give up idolatry. They would have to forsake their false gods and embrace the one true and living God, made known through Jesus.

"He wants people to search for him because he is not far from any one of us. For, 'In him we live and move and have our being.' We are his offspring, his children. Since we are his offspring, we should not think of God as an image fashioned from gold or silver or stone by human art or imagination. Until now God overlooked your ignorance, but now he demands that all people everywhere repent and believe in him."

Some of the Greeks believed what Paul told them and became followers of Jesus.

BASED ON ACTS 17:22–34

 Faith at Home

Read the Scripture story with your family members. Discuss the different ways you and your family have come to know God. Examples could be through other people, events, and prayer. Make a list of those ways and use it by yourself or with family members as a litany of thanksgiving at mealtimes or other times when you are together. Read each item and respond, "We give you thanks, good and gracious God."

? What does Paul teach the people of Athens about God?

? How do you answer God's call to search for him?

Share

Make a list With a partner or in small groups, make a list of words that you can share with other young people that would tell them where they can search for God.

13

? Invite young people to work in pairs or small groups to summarize what Paul taught about God. Have them share their responses with the whole group. Possible responses: God is near us; God is our Father; God wants us to know him.

? Allow time for personal reflection as young people think about their answers to the second question. Encourage volunteers to share their reflections. Possible responses: by praying, by being kind to others, by sharing with others, by taking care of creation.

Share

- Keep young people in pairs or groups.
- Supply writing materials.
- Encourage young people to brainstorm responses for the activity.
- Have each group report two or three responses to the group.

Review

- God made everything and everyone.
- We are created to love God.

✴ Cultural Background

Looking for answers   In the first century people looked to magic, philosophy, and religion for answers to life's questions.

- Magic was considered a way to manipulate the deities who appeared to control the world according to principles and rules most people could not understand.

- Philosophy, a term that means "love of wisdom," appeared useful for a human understanding that the rational principles that lead to truth, beauty, and goodness would also lead to happiness, life, and prosperity.

- Religions also promised a way out of human misery through imitation and union with deities, who could be known through religious practices and the contemplation of sacred mysteries.

This was the environment Paul encountered in Athens as he proceeded to preach the message of Jesus.

REMEMBER

Objective
To explain that sacraments are signs of God's love

Faith Focus

What are the sacraments?
List young people's responses on the board or on chart paper.

Signs of God's Love

- Write *original sin* on the board; explain this term as you summarize the first paragraph.

- Invite young people to consider how they feel when someone rejects their friendship. Point out that God sent Jesus to us even after people turned away from God's love. This shows God's incredible love for us.

- Have students read the bulleted material silently and then restate it to demonstrate that they understand it.

The Holy Trinity

- Write the word *Trinity* on the board or on chart paper. Ask young people what the prefix *tri-* means. three

- Have young people speculate on what *Trinity* means. Confirm or correct their predictions as you work through the text.

- Ask young people to recall prayers that honor the Trinity. the Sign of the Cross, the Doxology (Glory Be to the Father), the Creed

Signs of God's Love

The Holy Trinity
God the Father, God the Son, and God the Holy Spirit are the three Persons in one God. We call them the **Holy Trinity**. Each of them can be called God. Belief in the Trinity is the most important part of our faith. When we make the Sign of the Cross, we are saying we believe in the Trinity.

Faith Focus

What are the Sacraments?

From the very beginning, God wanted people to be friends with him. He shared his life with humans. But the first humans turned away from God's friendship. They disobeyed him and sinned. We call this first sin **Original Sin**. Original Sin affects all people. Because of it, suffering came into the world and people tend to sin.

Even after the first humans turned away from him, God still wanted to live in friendship with people. So, God our Father sent his Son, Jesus, to show us how much he loves us. Jesus is the most important sign of God's love.

- Jesus showed us how to live in friendship with God.
- Jesus died on the cross to save us from sin.
- Jesus showed us that even when we turn from God's friendship, God will forgive us.

14

Additional Activity

Explore Original Sin Using the song and lyrics for "Incarnate One" (track 6) provided with the *And With Your Spirit* music CD, help your students explore the concept of Original Sin:

- Print each verse of "The Incarnate One" on a separate sheet of paper. Make the letters large enough that the young people can easily read the words from their desks.
- Tape verses across the board (or wall) in consecutive order.
- Provide paper and markers and have young people work in groups of two to illustrate one of these stories:
  - God makes the world
  - God makes Adam and Eve
  - Adam and Eve choose to eat from the tree
  - Mary and Baby Jesus
  - Jesus on the cross
- Attach pictures under the appropriate verses.
- Recount the story of salvation by reminding the young people that God made us to be with him forever. We chose sin. But God saved us from Original Sin by sending his Son (true God and true man) to save us.

14 CHAPTER 1

The Sacraments of Initiation

Jesus gave us the Sacraments, so we would know God's love, forgiveness, healing, and call to service. A **Sacrament** is an effective sign that comes from Jesus. The Seven Sacraments give us grace.

Baptism is the first of the three **Sacraments of Initiation**. In Baptism we are united to Jesus and receive new life. In **Confirmation** the Holy Spirit gives us strength to live as followers of Jesus. Baptism and Confirmation mark us with a special character, so we can only receive them once.

In the **Eucharist** we receive the Body and Blood of Jesus. We can participate in the Eucharist often. The Eucharist helps us be more like Jesus. It helps us live and move and have our being in God. We need to celebrate Reconciliation before First Eucharist.

These three Sacraments together make us full members of the Church. The Church is a sign of God's love. God calls us to live in community with other people who believe in him. The Church family helps us grow as God's children.

? What are some signs of God's love in your life?

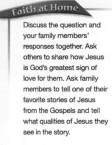

Faith at Home

Discuss the question and your family members' responses together. Ask others to share how Jesus is God's greatest sign of love for them. Ask family members to tell one of their favorite stories of Jesus from the Gospels and tell what qualities of Jesus they see in the story.

15

Liturgical Background

Revised Roman Missal On November 27, 2011, the First Sunday of Advent, we began to use a revised translation of the text of the Mass. Throughout the history of the Church, there have been only a few times when *official* changes in the text of the Mass prayers have occurred, and it is important to remember that the key elements of Catholic worship have remained constant since the time of the early Church. None of the changes, including the Third Edition of the *Roman Missal*, ever changes the original ritual and essence of Jesus' actions at the Last Supper. By the power of the Holy Spirit, the Church, from apostolic time to the present, preserves the fundamental structure of the Mass everywhere in the Church. The Mass is the center of the Church's life.

The Sacraments of Initiation

Write the terms *sacrament* and *Sacraments of Initiation* on the board or on chart paper. Challenge young people to name the seven sacraments.

- Work through the text with the young people paragraph by paragraph; invite volunteers to share why each of the sacraments is important.

- Write the name of each Sacrament of Initiation at the top of a segment of the board or on a sheet of chart paper. Have young people write informative phrases about each sacrament under its name.

- Have young people note which picture goes with each sacrament. Ask which part of each picture helped them recognize the sacrament.

- Recall the opening celebration. Which sacrament did the marking with water recall? Baptism

- Discuss why these sacraments are important as a group.

? Invite volunteers to answer the question. Possible responses: Jesus, the Sacraments, the Church, creation, family

Activity Master

You may wish to use Activity Master 1 on page CE1 to reinforce young people's knowledge of the Sacraments of Initiation.

▲ Activity Master 1

Review

- When people turned away from God, they brought suffering and sin into the world.

- Jesus gave us the sacraments as a sign of God's love for us.

LIVE

Objective

To lead young people in expressing praise in belonging to the Church

Being a Member

☀ Respond

- Explain the activity.
- Distribute writing materials and divide the group into pairs or small groups.
- Set a time limit.
- Invite volunteers to share the actions that they wrote in the building blocks.

Closing Blessing

- Gather the group in a prayer circle with their books.
- Begin with the Sign of the Cross.
- Read aloud the People of Faith story about Francis of Assisi.
- Pray the prayer.
- ♪ End with *Songs of Celebration* CD, track 1, "We Are Called," or one of the optional music suggestions on page 9.

Being a Member

☀ Respond

Build a church With a partner or small group, talk about what it means to be a member of the Church. Then, in each of the building blocks below, write one thing that members of the Church do to show they are active members. Choose one of the actions that you are able to do and do it this week.

Closing Blessing

Gather and begin with the Sign of the Cross.

Leader: God, our Father, you give us all the living creatures.

All: We praise and thank

Leader: Jesus, our Savior, yo give us life.

All: We praise and thank

Leader: Holy Spirit, our Help you make us holy.

All: We praise and thank

Leader: Let us go forth in pe and love.

All: Thanks be to God.

♪ *Sing together.*

We are called to act with justice,
We are called to love tenderly
We are called to serve one another,
to walk humbly with God.

David Haas © 1998 GIA Publication

16

☀ People of Faith: A Story

Francis of Assisi As a child and a young man, Francis did not like school very much. He loved to have a good time. He was funny. He loved to sing and get dressed up. He was handsome and courteous. People liked him. Francis came from a rich family. He wasted money sometimes. But he always took care of the poor.

When Francis was a young man, he heard God call him to help others. He left his family and his rich life. But he kept his happy ways, and he spent his life with other followers who spread God's love wherever they went.

Francis loved animals. He asked the emperor to make a special law that said people must provide for the birds and the beasts, as well as for the poor. His feast day is October 4th.

C. 1181–1226

Faith Focus

- In Baptism God calls us to a life of happiness with him.

- A Sacrament is an effective sign that comes from Jesus and gives us grace.

- Jesus is the greatest sign of God the Father's love.

Ritual Focus
Signing with the Cross

The celebration focused on being signed with holy water. You came to the water, were called by name, and signed with the Sign of the Cross. During the week, sign yourself with the Sign of the Cross when you wake up and remember that you belong to God.

Family Prayer

God, our Father, thank you for calling us to be your children. We know your love, and we want to share it with others. Send your Holy Spirit to help us love and care for everything you have created. We ask this in the name of your Son, Jesus. Amen.

Act

Share Together   Read Isaiah 43:1–4. Invite family members to share how the reading makes them feel. Then talk together about the phrase, "I have called you by name, you are mine." Invite family members to share why they have the names they do. Then ask individuals to share what they like about their names. Have everyone be still and imagine God saying each of their names and adding, "You are mine."

Do Together   God calls us to live in harmony with nature and to enjoy it. With your family, choose one of the following to do as a family this week:

- Go on a nature walk.
- Discuss how your family can be stewards of water.
- Find an environmental project to become involved in.
- Volunteer to help take care of an elderly neighbor's yard.

GO online **www.osvcurriculum.com**
Visit our website for weekly Scripture readings and questions, family resources, and more activities.

17

Faith at Home

Review the five parts of the Faith at Home page with young people.

Encourage them:

- to ask family members to review the **Faith Focus** statements with them

- to share the **Ritual Focus: Signing with the Cross** with family members

- to do at least one of the ✦ **Act** activities with family members

- to pray the **Family Prayer** with their family at times when the family is together

- to encourage their family members to go to **www.osvcurriculum.com** with them and do the activities for this chapter sometime during the week

Looking Ahead

For Chapter 2, you will need:

- a Bible

- a large glass bowl filled with water

- a small tree branch

- a candle

- a prayer table

 the *Songs of Celebration* CD

- copies of Activity Master 2 on p. CE2 for each young person

Rite of Penance

"By receiving repentant sinners and leading them to the light of the truth, the confessor fulfills a paternal function; he reveals the heart of the Father and reflects the image of Christ, the Good Shepherd" (no. 10c).

Catechism Connection

To deepen your own background and reflection on the Sacrament of Reconciliation, refer to the *Catechism of the Catholic Church, 1441–1445.*

Catechist Resources

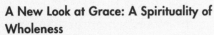

A New Look at Grace: A Spirituality of Wholeness

Bill Huebsch
Twenty-Third Publications

Helps the reader rediscover the power and beauty of God's grace

Blessings and Prayers Throughout the Year: A Resource for School and Parish

Elizabeth McMahon Jeep
Liturgy Training Publications

Provides prayers, blessings, rituals, and songs for occasions throughout the school year

Young People's Resources

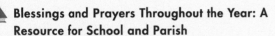

Jesus, I Feel Close to You

Denise Stuckey
Paulist Press

Children recount how their everyday lives parallel experiences Jesus had

Jesus Stories: Zacchaeus *(17 min)*

Vision Video

The "Jesus Heals" segment of this video recounts the story of Zacchaeus

Catechist Formation

"I must stay at your
house today."

Luke 19:5

We Belong to God

When we hurt someone, we are often afraid to approach the person to say we are sorry and to ask forgiveness. We may hesitate because we fear retaliation or a rebuff. When a break occurs in our relationship with God, however, we have no need for such fear. Jesus, in his life and ministry, showed us the face of a God, who always welcomes the sinner. Many times Jesus gathered with sinners, and each time he proclaimed the compassion and mercy of God the Father.

Christians die and rise with Christ in the Sacrament of Baptism. The Sacrament of Penance and Reconciliation provide sinners with an opportunity to renew their union with God. In this sacrament the priest represents the person of Christ in a loving and welcoming way.

We Are Welcome

The Rite of Penance conveys God's welcome through its opening greeting and through the proclamation of God's word that recalls his endless love for all people. The priests who celebrate this sacrament make every attempt to be people who reflect the care, acceptance, and mercy of Christ. In this way, those who participate in this sacrament hear Jesus speaking to them, and they encounter Christ as people of two thousand years ago encountered him. The light of Christ, seen in the baptismal candle, is once again rekindled in the lives of those who seek God's mercy.

Which people in your life have reflected God's love and mercy to you?
What scripture passages most help you understand God's great mercy?

Catechist Prayer

God of love, visit me this day with your tender mercy. Give me the confidence to live fully as your own child, created in your image. Amen.

Lesson Planner

		OBJECTIVES	LESSON PROCESS	☀ ACTIVITIES	MATERIALS
CELEBRATE	15 minutes Pages 18–19	Ritual Focus *Renewal of Baptismal Promises* To experience a celebration of the word, including the Renewal of Baptismal Promises	Celebrate the opening prayer.		PROGRAM RESOURCES *Songs of Celebration* CD, track 2 OTHER MATERIALS Bible, prayer table, candle, large glass bowl filled with water, small tree branch with leaves
	Pages 20–21	To explore the meaning of the ritual action	Complete the activity. ✝ Read about and discuss holy water. Present what sin is. ✝ Read about and discuss candles.	☀ Reflect Young people reflect on the experience of the celebration and the meaning of the Renewal of Baptismal Promises.	
REMEMBER	30 minutes Pages 22–23	Faith Focus *What happens when Jesus welcomes us?* To show that Jesus welcomes sinners	Discuss how Jesus brings us good news. 📖 Proclaim the Gospel story. *Luke 19:1–10* Complete the activity.	☀ Share Young people write a song about welcoming Jesus. ✎ Faith at Home Suggested activities for the home	PROGRAM RESOURCES *Songs of Celebration* CD, track 2 Copies of Activity Master 2, p. CE2
	Pages 24–25	Faith Focus *How are we welcomed in the Sacrament of Reconciliation?* To explain how we are welcomed in the Sacrament of Reconciliation	Identify Reconciliation as a second chance at living a good life. ✝ Discuss free will, mortal sin, venial sin, and communal and individual celebrations of Reconciliation. Read about the Reconciliation room.	✎ Faith at Home Suggested activities for the home	
LIVE	15 minutes Page 26	To reflect on preparing for Reconciliation	Introduce the activity. Pray the Closing Blessing. Read aloud the People of Faith story about Saint Monica.	☀ Respond Young people sketch ways of preparing for Reconciliation.	PROGRAM RESOURCES *Songs of Celebration* CD, track 2
FAITH AT HOME	Page 27	✎ Faith at Home To introduce the different parts of the Faith at Home page	Review the Faith at Home page. Encourage young people to share this page at home.	☀ Act Suggested activities for the home	PROGRAM RESOURCES Reconciliation Family Guide, pp. 18–19

CELEBRATE

Objective

To experience a celebration of the word, including the Renewal of Baptismal Promises

Preparation

Familiarize yourself with the movements of the ritual focus for the Renewal of Baptismal Promises on page 18.

Prepare the prayer space ahead of time. You will need:

- a Bible
- a table covered with a white cloth
- a candle and a large glass bowl filled with water on the prayer table
- a small tree branch
- Use the *Songs of Celebration* CD, track 2, to rehearse the suggested song, "We Are Marching/Siyahamba," or one of the optional music suggestions on page 19.

Select a young person to carry the Bible in procession.

We Gather

Invite young people to assemble with their books for a procession.

- Direct them to follow you and the young person carrying the Bible.
- As you process, lead young people in singing using the *Songs of Celebration* CD, track 2.
- When all are assembled in the prayer space, light the prayer candle.
- Begin the prayer, and lead young people in the Sign of the Cross.

Follow the order of prayer on pages 18–19.

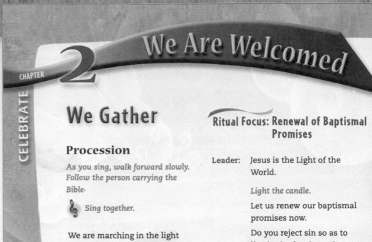

We Gather

Procession

As you sing, walk forward slowly. Follow the person carrying the Bible.

♪ *Sing together.*

We are marching in the light
  of God,
We are marching in the light
  of God,
We are marching, we are
  marching in the light of God.
We are marching, we are
  marching in the light of God.

South African Traditional

Leader: Let us pray.

Make the Sign of the Cross together.

Ritual Focus: Renewal of Baptismal Promises

Leader: Jesus is the Light of the World.

Light the candle.

Let us renew our baptismal promises now.

Do you reject sin so as to live in the freedom of God's children?

All: I do.

Leader: Do you reject Satan, and all his works, and all his empty promises?

All: I do.

18

Ritual Background

Bearing the Light of Christ   One of the beautiful "explanatory rites" following the water bath of Baptism is the giving of a candle lit from the Paschal candle. The gesture of taking the flame from the Paschal candle expresses that this lighted candle signifies a sharing in the light of Christ.

The words the priest says at this point also recall the parable of the wise and foolish maidens. The wise young women kept their lamps burning, and were ready to enter the marriage feast when the bridegroom came.

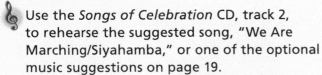

When the newly baptized receive their candles, the priest urges them to "keep the flame of faith alive in your hearts. When Christ comes, may you go out to meet him with all the saints in the heavenly kingdom."

Leader: Do you believe in God, the Father almighty; in Jesus Christ, his only Son, our Lord; in the Holy Spirit and the holy catholic Church?

All: I do.

BASED ON RITE OF BAPTISM FOR CHILDREN, 145–146

Sprinkle young people with water.

Make the Sign of the Cross as you are sprinkled with water.

We Listen

Leader: Good and gracious Father, send us the Holy Spirit to open our hearts to the good news of your Son, Jesus, the Light of the World. We ask this in his name.

All: Amen.

Leader: A reading from the holy Gospel according to Luke.

All: Glory to you, O Lord.

Leader: *Read Luke 19:1–10.*

The Gospel of the Lord.

All: Praise to you, Lord Jesus Christ.

Sit silently.

We Go Forth

Leader: Loving Father, thank you for the Light of Christ. Send us the Holy Spirit to help us live as children of the light.

All: Amen.

 Sing the opening song together.

19

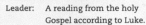 **Liturgical Background**

Renewal of Baptismal Promises   The practice of renewing Baptismal Promises is relatively new to the liturgy. It dates from 1951, when the Easter Vigil was reformed under Pope Pius XII.

The Renewal of Baptismal Promises was:

- an attempt to revitalize the faith of the congregation
- an attempt to strengthen the baptismal focus of Easter
- intended to help everyone understand the connection between the new life of Baptism and the Resurrection of Jesus celebrated at Easter

In the United States, all the faithful renew baptismal promises at the Masses of Easter day.

Ritual Focus: Renewal of Baptismal Promises

- Invite young people to gather around the prayer table.
- Lead the Renewal of Baptismal Promises.
- Dip the small branch in the water, and sprinkle young people with water.

We Listen

For the proclamation of the Gospel, you may use a Bible or the adapted reading in the *Candidate's Book* on pages 22–23.

We Go Forth

- Lead the closing prayer.

 As the group processes back to their seats, have them sing *Songs of Celebration* CD, track 2, "We Are Marching/Siyahamba," or one of the optional music suggestions.

Optional Music Suggestions

"Yes Lord I Believe,"
© John Burland,
Ovation Music Service

"Salmo 99: Nosotros somos su pueblo,"
© Jaime Cortez. Published by OCP

"All Are Welcome,"
Marty Haugen © GIA Publications

CELEBRATE

Objective
To explore the meaning of the ritual action of the Renewal of Baptismal Promises

Liturgical Catechesis
The purpose of this section is to help young people reflect on their experiences of the signs, rituals, prayers, and gestures of the celebration, and to lead them to express their own meaning of the experiences. Allow young people to share their experiences without commenting on them.

The Light of Christ
- On the board or chart paper, write the following questions: What did you see? What did you hear? What did you do?
- Guide young people to reflect on the celebration by reviewing what happened in the prayer.
- Invite young people to share their responses to the questions.

Reflect
- Have the young people complete the activity.
- Invite volunteers to share their responses.

Holy Water
- Invite a volunteer to read aloud the text.
- Explain where holy water fonts or baptismal pools are located in your parish church. Encourage young people to use the holy water from the font or pool to make the Sign of the Cross the next time they are in church.

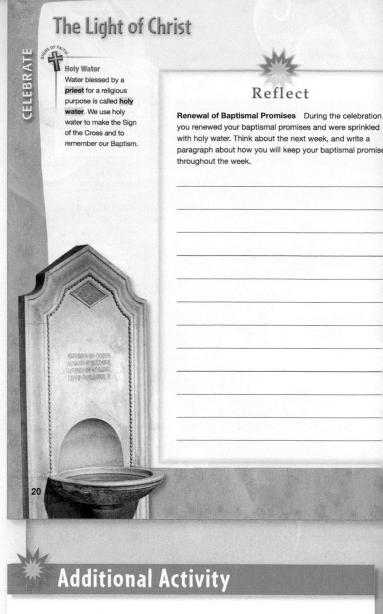

The Light of Christ

CELEBRATE

SIGNS OF FAITH

Holy Water
Water blessed by a **priest** for a religious purpose is called **holy water**. We use holy water to make the Sign of the Cross and to remember our Baptism.

Reflect

Renewal of Baptismal Promises During the celebration you renewed your baptismal promises and were sprinkled with holy water. Think about the next week, and write a paragraph about how you will keep your baptismal promise throughout the week.

20

Additional Activity

Paraphrase Baptismal Promises Obtain the full text of the Baptismal Promises from a ritual booklet.

- Make a handout listing the promises. Leave space after each promise.
- Invite young people to paraphrase the promises with words that are meaningful to them.
- Do one or two promises as a class to help young people understand the exercise.
- Have young people work in pairs or small groups to complete the sheet.
- When they have finished, have volunteers share their paraphrases.

Children of the Light

At Baptism we receive a candle. The priest prays that we will walk as children of the light. We are children of the light when we make choices to grow in our friendship with Jesus and the Church, and to love and care about other people.

Sometimes we do not act like children of the light. Even though we love our family or friends, we may choose to do things that are unloving. Even though we feel sorry for people who are poor or in need, we do not reach out to them. Sometimes we choose not to care about or share what we have with them. When we do that, we choose sin.

We know what it is like to choose to do something wrong. We know what it is like to feel sorry and want to make up. What if we never got a second chance?

SIGNS OF FAITH

Candles

Candles are signs of Christ, the Light of the World. Candles are used at the altar during Mass. The most important candle used in the Sacraments is the **Paschal candle**. This candle is blessed at the Easter Vigil and burned during the Masses of the Easter season. It is also burned at Baptisms and funerals throughout the year. Sometimes candles are placed before the altars of Mary and the saints. These candles are a sign of respect and prayer.

21

Children of the Light

- Invite young people to read the first paragraph silently.

- Organize the group into smaller groups and give them 2 minutes to make a list of choices young people can make to grow in their friendship with Jesus and the Church. Have them share the lists with the whole group.

- Summarize the second paragraph and spend some time talking about what sin is and is not.

- Use the teaching tip below to help you.

- Discuss young people's experiences of getting a second chance.

✚ Candles

- Invite volunteers to read the text aloud.

- Have young people recall where candles are located in the parish church.

💡 Teaching Tip

Clarifying concepts   Some young people may have difficulty distinguishing among mistakes, accidents, and sins.

- Provide the class with several age-appropriate examples of each.

- Discuss each example with young people, asking them to suggest why the action was or was not sinful.

- Remind them that sins are deliberate wrong and hurtful actions. Mistakes and accidents are not done on purpose and therefore are not sins.

REMEMBER

Objective
To show that Jesus welcomes sinners

Faith Focus

What happens when Jesus welcomes us?
List young people's responses on the board or on chart paper.

Jesus Brings Good News

- Ask young people how they can tell whether someone cares about them. Possible responses: The person spends time with them; the person tries to get to know them.

- As you summarize the paragraph, point out how Jesus showed that he cared about people.

 Scripture   LUKE 19:1–10

Zacchaeus

- Gather the group into a story circle or in the prayer space. Remind them that they will be hearing the Gospel story from Luke again.

- Ask what they remember from hearing the Gospel during the celebration.

- Call attention to the illustration. Ask young people to point out the main characters.

- Invite several young people to mime the actions of Jesus, Zacchaeus, and the crowd as other volunteers read the story aloud.

Jesus Brings Good News

Faith Focus

What happens when Jesus welcomes us?

Jesus welcomed sinners. He ate and drank with them. He gave them a second chance. He told them stories about God. He healed and forgave them. When people got to know Jesus, they changed.

LUKE 19:1–10

Zacchaeus

One day Jesus was going through the town of Jericho. The crowds gathered to see him. He did not plan to stop there. Now a man there named Zacchaeus, who was a chief tax collector and also a wealthy man, was seeking to see who Jesus was; but he could not see him because of the crowd, for he was short in stature. So he ran ahead and climbed a sycamore tree in order to see Jesus.

When he reached the place, Jesus looked up and said to him, "Zacchaeus, come down quickly, for today I must stay at your house." Zacchaeus came down quickly and welcomed Jesus to his house with joy.

22

 ## Scripture Background

Lucan themes   This story includes three important themes of Luke's Gospel.

- An outcast receives Jesus with praise and joy and then testifies to the mercy of God at work in his life.

- Jesus is on his way to Jerusalem preaching the Gospel, and challenging his hearers to evaluate their lives.

- Jesus proclaims salvation has come "today" to the house of Zacchaeus.

In the Gospel of Luke, Jesus is often found eating with and speaking to "tax collectors and sinners." (See *Luke 5:30*, *Luke 7:34*, and *Luke 15:1*.) His association with these people is a source of controversy and of rejection on the part of the Jewish religious leaders of the times.

Throughout the Gospel of Luke there is an insistence that it is not people's prejudices or occupations that separate the righteous from sinners but their response to Jesus and to his message.

The people in the crowd were not happy. They said, "He has gone to stay at the house of a sinner." They did not think Jesus should be around sinners.

Zacchaeus told Jesus, "I will give half of my possessions to the poor. If I have taken anything from anyone, I will pay them back four times more."

Jesus said, "Zacchaeus, today God's forgiveness has come to your house."

BASED ON LUKE 19:1–10

❓ Why do you think Jesus decided to stay at Zacchaeus' house?

❓ How would you feel if Jesus came to your house? How would you change?

Faith at Home

Read the Scripture story with your family members. Discuss responses to the questions, and talk about how Zacchaeus changed after he met Jesus. Discuss ways your family welcomes people.

Share

Write a song With a partner or in a small group, write words to the tune of "We Are Marching" that describe what you might do to welcome Jesus into your lives.

_____

_____

_____

_____

23

❓ Invite young people to work with a partner or small group to share their answers to the questions. Possible responses: He wanted to be kind. He rewarded Zacchaeus for going up into the tree. He wanted to get to know Zacchaeus.

❓ Discuss each group's answer to the second question. Accept all reasonable responses.

Share

- Play "We are Marching/Siyahamba" from the *Songs of Celebration* CD, track 2, to help young people recall the melody.

- Point out that song lyrics often rhyme, but they do not have to.

- Allow time for young people to complete the activity.

- Encourage young people as they work.

- Invite volunteers to recite or sing their lyrics to the class.

Activity Master

You may wish to use Activity Master 2 on page CE2 to further integrate the meaning of the Gospel story.

▲ Activity Master 2

Review

- Jesus welcomed sinners.

- The story of Zacchaeus shows that God forgives everyone who is sorry.

✴ Cultural Background

Tax collectors   Absent landlords and oppressive Roman rule made life for the peasant Jews of Israel difficult. "Tax-collectors" came to be regarded as "sinners" because they performed undesirable work for the Romans. Not only did they collect taxes for the enemy but they often took extra profit for themselves. Jewish national pride fed on hopes that someday the Romans would be overthrown and once again, they would maintain their Jewish identity as a people, a nation, and a religion. Collecting taxes for the Romans only postponed Jewish hopes for that reality.

REMEMBER

Objective

To explain how we are welcomed in the Sacrament of Reconciliation

Faith Focus

How are we welcomed in the Sacrament of Reconciliation?

List young people's responses on the board or on chart paper.

Second Chance

- Write the terms *mortal sin*, *venial sin*, *individual celebration*, and *communal celebration* on the board or on chart paper.

- Encourage young people to speculate on the content of the pages by using the Focus Question and the highlighted vocabulary terms as clues.

- List the different names for this sacrament on the board or on chart paper so that young people can recognize them as one sacrament.

- As you work through the material, have a Venn diagram on the board or on chart paper. Use it to highlight similarities and differences between the two types of sins.

✝ Reconciliation Room

- Refer to the illustrated glossary on page 72 to show young people a picture of a Reconciliation room.

- With the young people, visit the Reconciliation room in your parish church, or describe where it is. If you do not visit as a class, encourage young people to visit it when they attend Mass with their families.

Second Chance

REMEMBER

✝ SIGNS OF FAITH

Reconciliation Room

The place where individuals celebrate the Sacrament of Reconciliation is called a **Reconciliation Room**. The room is set up so we can sit face-to-face with the priest, or we may choose to kneel or sit behind a screen while we speak to him. The priest cannot ever tell what we say to him during the Sacrament of Reconciliation.

Faith Focus

How are we welcomed in the Sacrament of Reconciliation?

When God created us, he gave us free will. This is the ability to choose between right and wrong. When we choose to do what we know is wrong, we sin.

One of the ways we can show we are sorry for our sins and ask God's forgiveness is in the **Sacrament of Reconciliation**. We also call this the **Sacrament of Penance**, the Sacrament of Forgiveness, or Confession.

We can celebrate this Sacrament again and again. It is necessary to do so when we choose to completely turn away from God's love and separate ourselves from God's life. This is called a **mortal sin**. For a sin to be mortal, it must be seriously wrong, we must know it is seriously wrong, and we must freely choose to do it anyway. We can also celebrate this Sacrament for less serious sins that weaken our friendship with God. A less serious sin is called a **venial sin**.

24

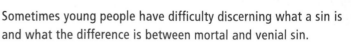

✦ Catechist Background

Sin   Emphasize that an act is sinful when:

- I know something is wrong and I choose to do it anyway.

- I stop and think about whether I should do it and I decide I will do it.

- I actually do it.

Sometimes young people have difficulty discerning what a sin is and what the difference is between mortal and venial sin.

Younger children may judge the seriousness of a sin by how much material damage is done or by how upset significant adults become over the action. This is a developmental issue. As children mature, they will become clearer about distinctions between a serious (mortal) sin and a less serious (venial) sin. It is important to help them clarify when something is a serious matter and what constitutes full consent of will.

Preparation and Welcome

The Church celebrates Penance in two ways. In **individual celebrations** the person seeking forgiveness meets with the priest individually and in private. In **communal celebrations** groups of people gather to listen to God's word and pray together. Then each person tells his or her sins privately to the priest.

In the Sacrament of Reconciliation the priest acts in the place of Jesus. The priest is a sign of God's forgiveness. He prepares to welcome us to the Sacrament of Penance by praying to the Holy Spirit. He asks the Holy Spirit to help him tell us about God's love and forgiveness.

We prepare for the Sacrament by praying to the Holy Spirit and looking at our actions. Whether we celebrate the Sacrament of Penance individually or as a group, we begin with the Sign of the Cross. Then the priest prays words like these:

> "May God who has enlightened every heart, help you to know your sins and trust in his mercy."

We answer, "Amen."

 How will you ask the Holy Spirit to help you look at your life?

Faith at Home

Discuss responses to the question on the page. Ask family members to share how they prepare to celebrate the Sacrament of Reconciliation. When you are at church this week, ask a family member to show you the Reconciliation Room.

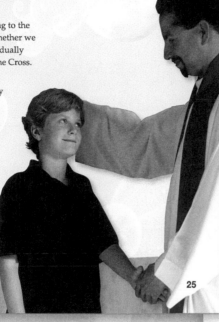

25

Preparation and Welcome

As with the previous page, consider using a Venn diagram on the board or on chart paper to highlight similarities and differences between individual celebrations and communal celebrations of Reconciliation.

- Emphasize that only a priest may hear confessions, and that he may never tell what he has heard in confession.
- Discuss the role of the Holy Spirit in enlightening us about our sins.
- Have volunteers role-play with you the priest's welcome and their response as it is found in the last paragraph.

❓ Invite volunteers to answer the question. Accept all reasonable responses.

Review

- We can receive Reconciliation many times.
- Serious sins are called mortal sins; less serious sins are called venial sins.

✦ Sacrament Background

Confession to a priest   The practice of an individual confessing to a priest developed during the sixth to the ninth centuries within monastic communities where members of the community would talk about their failures and specific sinful actions with a priest who would pray with them and give them a penance.

Earlier, Reconciliation was only celebrated by persons who had committed very serious and public sins, such as murder, adultery, or apostasy. When they had a change of heart, they would confess their sin to the bishop and seek reconciliation with the community and God. The bishop would give them a public penance, which could be very long and severe. After the person had fulfilled their penance and showed signs of conversion, they would be admitted back to the Eucharist.

LIVE

Objective
To reflect on preparing for Reconciliation

Preparing to Celebrate

Respond

- Explain the activity.

- Brainstorm with young people some of the things that they might do to prepare for Reconciliation. Point out that they can use these ideas or other ideas for their sketches.

- Set a time limit.

- Invite volunteers to explain their sketches to the class.

Closing Blessing

- Gather the group into a prayer circle with their books.

- Begin with the Sign of the Cross.

- Read aloud the People of Faith story about Saint Monica.

- Pray the prayer.

- End with *Songs of Celebration* CD, track 2, "We Are Marching/Siyahamba."

Preparing to Celebrate

Respond
Create a sketch In the space below, create a sketch of ways you will prepare to celebrate the Sacrament of Reconciliation.

Closing Blessing

Gather and begin with the Sign of the Cross.

Leader: God, our Gracious Father, you welcome us as your children. Increase our faith and make us strong.

All: Hear us, we pray.

Leader: God, our Gracious Father, you call us to change and grow. Make our light burn brighter for you.

All: Hear us, we pray.

Leader: God, our Gracious Father, help us to know our sins and trust in your mercy.

All: Hear us, we pray.

Sing together.

We are marching in the light of God,
We are marching in the light of God.
We are marching, we are marching in the light of God.
We are marching, we are marching in the light of God.

South African Traditional

People of Faith: A Story

Saint Monica   Monica was a Christian and she was married early in life to a pagan official who had a very violent temper. Monica's married life was not happy. Since Monica was a Christian, she continued to pray and do good works. Her words and example helped many women in her town. Monica and her husband had three children. Monica's husband would not allow them to be baptized. However, Monica continued being a child of the light and, by her prayer and example, her husband became a Christian and her oldest son Augustine turned from a sinful life and became one of the most important leaders in the early Church.

C. 333–387

aith Focus

At Baptism we are called to walk in the light.

Sin is a choice.

The Sacrament of Reconciliation forgives sins committed after Baptism.

itual Focus
enewal of Baptismal romises

he celebration focused on e Renewal of Baptismal romises. You renewed your aptismal promises and were rinkled with holy water. uring the week, use the text pages 18–19 with your mily members, and have em renew their baptismal omises with you.

mily Prayer

oving Father, we give u thanks for all the ways you ake yourself known to us. Help to continue to spread the ght of Christ in our world. We k this in the name of your Son, sus. Amen.

Act

Share Together   Read Luke 19:1–10. Talk about what it must have been like for Zacchaeus to have Jesus come to his house and the changes he made after he met Jesus. Then invite family members to list people whose example caused them to change something in their own lives. Have each person read the names on his or her list. After each name, pray together, "God bless you for being a light in our life."

Do Together   Together, think about and share the names of some people that your family could contribute some light and joy to. Remember that even small things can brighten someone's day. Choose one of the people, and plan what you will do to brighten his or her life.

GO online **www.osvcurriculum.com**
Visit our website for weekly Scripture readings and questions, family resources, and more activities.

27

Faith at Home

Review the five parts of the Faith at Home page with young people.

Encourage them:

- to ask family members to review the Faith Focus statements with them
- to share the **Ritual Focus: Renewal of Baptismal Promises** with family members
- to do at least one of the Act activities with family members
- to pray the **Family Prayer** with their family at times when the family is together
- to encourage their family members to go to **www.osvcurriculum.com** with them and do the activities for this chapter sometime during the week

Looking Ahead

For Chapter 3, you will need:

- a Bible
- a large glass bowl filled with water
- a candle
- a prayer table
- the *Songs of Celebration* CD
- copies of Activity Master 3 on p. CE3 for each young person

Rite of Penance

"The penitents should compare their own life with the example and commandments of Christ and then pray to God for the forgiveness of their sins" (no. 15).

Catechism Connection

To deepen your own background and reflection on the examination of conscience and the Sacrament of Penance, refer to the *Catechism of the Catholic Church, 1454.*

Catechist Resources

How Each Child Learns: Using Multiple Intelligence in Faith Formation

Bernadette Stankard
Twenty-Third Publications

Introduces readers to the theory of multiple intelligences and shows how it can broaden a child's experience of God

Teaching Self-Discipline to Children: 15 Essential Skills

Barbara C. Vasiloff
Twenty-Third Publications

Describes self-discipline skills in the Gospel

Young People's Resources

Close Encounters with the Commandments *(14 min.)*

Videos with Values

An angel helps young people see the significance of the commandments

Catechist Formation

"And now faith, hope, and love abide, these three; and the greatest of these is love."

1 Corinthians 13:13

We Look at Our Lives

When a person looks at something through a prism, the angle at which the prism is held determines the colors that will bath the object being viewed. When Christians review their sins and failures, they are able to view them through the prism of God's love and compassion.

The Rite of Penance confirms this understanding: "The Sacrament of Penance includes the confession of sins, which comes from true knowledge of self before God and from contrition for those sins. However, the inner examination of heart and the outward accusation must be made in the light of God's mercy" (6b). In this sacrament people are able to acknowledge their sinfulness because they understand they will be met by mercy.

Conversion

All the laws and precepts of the Church flow from the great command of Jesus to love God and to love neighbor as onese (*Luke 10:25–28*). Because the love of God is made visible in th love that Christians have for others, sin also becomes visible through the breaks caused in human relationships.

The awareness of sin in one's life is a great opportunity for conversion. When people acknowledge their failure to live th great commandment of love, God's response is always a mor powerful grace that enables a change of heart. There is no rupture between God and humans that God cannot repair.

How does admitting your sins help you to grow?

How does it help to know that the Church is made up of people who are imperfect, like you?

Catechist Prayer

You know me in the depth of my heart, all-loving God; help m to see with the light of Christ and to acknowledge my need fc your help. Amen.

Lesson Planner

www.osvcurriculum.com
Visit our website for additional resources and information.

		OBJECTIVES	LESSON PROCESS	ACTIVITIES	MATERIALS
CELEBRATE	15 minutes Pages 28–29	Ritual Focus *Reverencing the Word* To experience a celebration of the word, including Reverencing the Word	Celebrate the opening prayer.		PROGRAM RESOURCES *Songs of Celebration* CD, track 3 OTHER MATERIALS Bible or lectionary, prayer table, candle, large glass bowl filled with water
	Pages 30–31	To explore the meaning of the ritual action To teach how the Bible is used in liturgy	Complete the activity. ✝ Read about and discuss bowing. Describe how God speaks to us in the Bible. ✝ Read about and become familiar with the Bible and Scriptures.	☀ Reflect Young people make a word collage to reflect on the experience of the celebration and the meaning of Reverencing the Word.	
REMEMBER	30 minutes Pages 32–33	Faith Focus *What is the greatest commandment?* To discuss the commandments	Discuss why laws and commandments are needed. Compare the Ten Commandments and the Great Commandment. 📖 Proclaim the Gospel story. *Luke 10:25–28* Complete the activity.	☀ Share Young people participate in role-plays based on the Great Commandment. ◣ Faith at Home Suggested activities for the home	PROGRAM RESOURCES Copies of Activity Master 3, p. CE3
	Pages 34–35	Faith Focus *What happens during the examination of conscience?* To explain the examination of conscience and the place of Scripture in Reconciliation celebrations	Identify and explain the terms conscience, examination of conscience, and homily. ✝ Read about and discuss the Precepts of the Church. Examine the use of Scripture in Reconciliation celebrations.	◣ Faith at Home Suggested activities for the home	
LIVE	15 minutes Page 36	To reflect on the commandments and their meaning to us	Introduce the activity. Pray the Closing Blessing. Read aloud the People of Faith story about Saint Vincent de Paul.	☀ Respond Young people list ways to keep the commandments.	PROGRAM RESOURCES *Songs of Celebration* CD, track 3
FAITH AT HOME	Page 37	◣ Faith at Home To introduce the different parts of the Faith at Home page	Review the Faith at Home page. Encourage young people to share this page at home.	☀ Act Suggested activities for the home	PROGRAM RESOURCES Reconciliation Family Guide, pp.20–21

CELEBRATE

Objective

To experience a celebration of the word, including Reverencing the Word

Preparation

Familiarize yourself with the movements of the ritual focus for Reverencing the Word on page 29.

Prepare the prayer space ahead of time. You will need:

- a Bible
- a table covered with a white cloth
- a candle and a large glass bowl filled with water on the prayer table

Use the *Songs of Celebration* CD, track 3, to rehearse the suggested song, "Del Señor viene la misericordia," or one of the optional music suggestions on page 29.

Select a young person to carry the Bible in procession.

We Gather

Invite young people to assemble with their books for a procession.

- Direct them to follow you and the young person carrying the Bible.
- As you process, lead young people in singing using the *Songs of Celebration* CD, track 3.
- When all are assembled in the prayer space, light the prayer candle.
- Begin the prayer, and lead young people in the Sign of the Cross.

Follow the order of prayer on pages 28–29.

Ritual Focus: Reverencing the Word

- Invite young people to form a line.
- Have them come forward one by one and reverence the Bible. (See Ritual Background.)
- Conclude the ritual with the prayer.

We Gather

Procession

As you sing, walk forward slowly. Follow the person carrying the Bible.

♪ Sing together.

Misericordia, Señor, show us your mercy, O Lord, hemos pecado, for we have sinned.

© 1998, Bob Hurd. Published by OCP

Leader: Let us pray.

Make the Sign of the Cross together.

Ritual Focus: Reverencing the Word

Come forward one at a time. Bow or place your hand on the Bible.

Leader: [Name], may God's word always enlighten you.

Candidate: Amen.

28

Ritual Background

Bow The bow is a gesture of reverence. When we bow before the altar or genuflect before the Blessed Sacrament in the tabernacle, we honor Jesus' presence. People can bow two ways in the liturgy. A head bow is an inclination of the head forward, with the body kept upright. A profound bow is made from the waist, with the back kept straight and the hands lowered to the knees. The profound bow is a more solemn gesture. It is used during the consecration by people who for a good reason are not able to kneel during the Eucharistic Prayer. An example of the head bow is when we bow our heads to receive a blessing at the end of Mass.

Leader: God, our loving Father, you call us to holiness and goodness. You want us to be united in you. Send us the Holy Spirit so that our minds and hearts will be open to your word and the works of your goodness. We ask this through Jesus Christ our Lord.

All: Amen.

We Listen

Leader: A reading from the holy Gospel according to Luke.

All: Glory to you, O Lord.

Leader: *Read Luke 10:25–28.* The Gospel of the Lord.

All: Praise to you, Lord Jesus Christ.

Sit silently.

Leader: Let us join in the prayer Jesus has taught us.

Pray the Lord's Prayer together.

We Go Forth

Leader: May the Lord bless us, protect us from all evil, and bring us to everlasting life.

All: Amen.

 Sing the opening song together.

29

We Listen

For the proclamation of the Gospel, you may use a Bible or the adapted reading in the *Candidate's Book* on pages 32–33.

You may want to direct young people to page 79 of their books for the words of the Lord's Prayer.

We Go Forth

- Lead the closing prayer.

- As the group processes back to their seats, have them sing *Songs of Celebration* CD, track 3, "Del Señor viene la misericordia," or one of the optional music suggestions.

Optional Music Suggestions:

"Through My Fault,"
© 2011 John Burland, Ovation Music Service

"We Will Journey in Faith,"
© Dan Schutte. Published by OCP

"Grant to Us, O Lord,"
© Lucien Deiss, WLP

✦ Liturgical Background

Processions Liturgical processions provide an orderly way to move people and things from one place to another in worship. However, they do much more than create order. They capture attention, unite people in a shared activity, and express rich symbolism.

- Some processions are commemorative, such as the procession with palms on Palm Sunday when we remember Christ's triumphant entry into Jerusalem.
- Others are devotional, such as processions with the Blessed Sacrament on the feast of Corpus Christi.
- Still others draw us together as a community and express our identity as Church, such as the entrance and communion processions at Mass, wedding processions, or processions of mourners in the Rite of Christian Funerals.

CELEBRATE

Objective

To explore the meaning of the ritual action of Reverencing the Word

To teach how the Bible is used in liturgy

Liturgical Catechesis

The purpose of this section is to help young people reflect on their experiences of the signs, rituals, prayers, and gestures of the celebration and to lead them to express their own meaning of the experiences. Allow young people to share their experiences without commenting on them.

God's Word

- On the board or on chart paper, write the following questions: What did you see? What did you hear? What did you do?

- Guide young people to reflect on the celebration by reviewing what happened in the prayer.

- Invite young people to share their responses to the questions.

☀ Reflect

Make sure young people understand the directions.

- Emphasize that the words for the word collage include feelings about the ritual gesture of reverencing the word as well as those that describe the importance of God's word.

- Invite volunteers to share their responses.

Bowing

- Read aloud the text.

- Encourage young people to watch for the times that the priest and the reader bow during Sunday Mass.

God's Word

SIGNS OF FAITH

Bowing
Bending the head or body forward shows honor and adoration for God. We also bow in prayer when we want to ask for God's blessing. Sometimes we bow our heads to reverence the name of Jesus.

☀ Reflect

Reverencing the word   In the space provided, make a word collage using words that express your feelings about reverencing the Scriptures in the celebration. Also include words that describe the importance of God's word for you in your life.

30

☀ Additional Activity

Play a word game

- On the board or on chart paper, write the phrase, "The word of God is _____."

- Invite young people to write on a separate sheet of paper as many words as they can to describe what the word of God is like for them.

- Encourage them to think of words that begin with different letters of the alphabet.

- After a few minutes, have young people share words beginning with the letter A.

- Have young people explain why they chose each word.

- Continue through the alphabet until you have a word for most of the letters of the alphabet.

God Speaks to Us

We reverence the Bible because it is a holy book. It is God's own word. The Bible tells the story of God's love for his people. The stories of what Jesus said and did are in the Bible.

We hear stories from the Bible every Sunday at Mass. During the Sacrament of Reconciliation, we read or listen to stories from the Bible. These stories may be about God's forgiveness or how we are to live God's laws.

We also use the Bible before we celebrate the Sacrament of Reconciliation to help us look at our lives. We pray to the Holy Spirit to help us know if we are living according to the Ten Commandments, the Beatitudes, the life of Jesus, and Church teachings.

SIGNS OF FAITH

The Bible
The Bible is God's own word. Another name used for the Bible is **Scriptures**. The word *Scriptures* means "writings." God inspired humans to write stories in the Bible about his love and forgiveness. The Bible has two parts, the Old Testament and the New Testament. The Old Testament tells the story of God's love and forgiveness before Jesus came. The New Testament tells us what Jesus and his followers taught about God's love and forgiveness.

31

God Speaks to Us

- Invite young people to offer reasons why we reverence the Bible. Possible responses: It is God's word; it tells the story of Jesus.

- In pairs have young people read the next two paragraphs.

- As they are reading, write the following questions on the board or on chart paper: In the past two weeks what Bible stories have you heard during Mass? What is your favorite Bible forgiveness story?

- Discuss young people's responses to the questions in the large group.

The Bible

- Have volunteers read the text aloud.

- Pass the Bible around the group.

- Allow young people to hold it and look through it.

Teaching Tip

Learn about the Scriptures   Use these activities to help young people become familiar with and appreciate Scripture.

- The young people may be interested to know that we hear the Gospel stories in a three-year cycle. Have them research the current year of the cycle and find out which evangelist wrote the featured Gospel.

- If your parish has liturgy aids, bring those that are available in your church and show young people how to locate the readings for each week in them. Encourage them to read these if they arrive at church early.

- Using the Scripture citation in this chapter as a beginning, show young people how to find books, chapters, and verses in the Bible. Familiarize them with the table of contents and the index. Have groups work with Bibles to find specific books and stories.

Objective

To discuss the commandments

Faith Focus

What is the greatest commandment?
List young people's responses on the board or on chart paper.

Loving God and Neighbor

- Determine what the young people already know about the commandments by asking where the commandments came from and why Jesus taught them to people. If necessary, explain that the commandments are in the Old Testament and Jesus learned and taught them as part of his Hebrew heritage.

- Recall that the commandments are laws from God.

- Discuss the role of laws in guiding our behavior.

 **Scripture**   LUKE 10:25–28

The Great Commandment

- Gather the group into a story circle or in the prayer space. Remind them that they will be hearing the story from the Gospel of Luke again.

- Ask what they remember from hearing the Gospel during the celebration.

- Reread the story aloud.

- Have young people discuss what is happening in the illustration. Jesus is talking to the young man about the commandments.

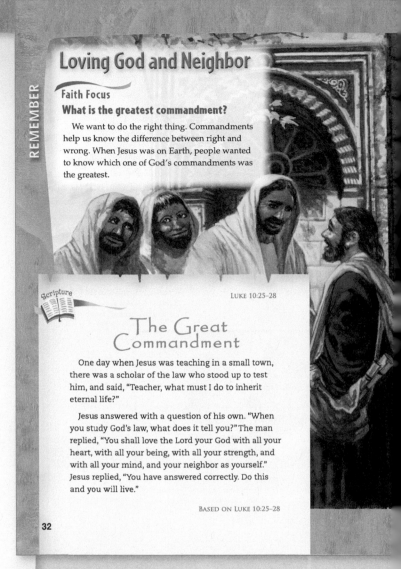

Loving God and Neighbor

Faith Focus

What is the greatest commandment?

We want to do the right thing. Commandments help us know the difference between right and wrong. When Jesus was on Earth, people wanted to know which one of God's commandments was the greatest.

Scripture   LUKE 10:25–28

The Great Commandment

One day when Jesus was teaching in a small town, there was a scholar of the law who stood up to test him, and said, "Teacher, what must I do to inherit eternal life?"

Jesus answered with a question of his own. "When you study God's law, what does it tell you?" The man replied, "You shall love the Lord your God with all your heart, with all your being, with all your strength, and with all your mind, and your neighbor as yourself." Jesus replied, "You have answered correctly. Do this and you will live."

BASED ON LUKE 10:25–28

32

Scripture Background

Love   When the "scholar of the law" questions Jesus about the greatest commandment, Jesus combines two Old Testament passages about law, Deuteronomy 6:5 on love of God and Leviticus 19:18 on love of neighbor. This combination did not originate with Jesus. Jewish rabbis frequently emphasized a correlation between love of God and love of neighbor.

However, some rabbis disputed whether it was possible to identify one or another command as the most important or greatest. They taught that the smallest particle of the law was as great as any other commandment. Jesus is quick to identify and to distinguish love as the greatest commandment. It does not only encompass one's own friends or family, but extends to anyone in need, especially those who might cause us to reexamine our own prejudices and boundaries.

The Ten Commandments sum up for us what is right and wrong. Out of love, God gave the Ten Commandments to the people of Israel and to us. Following the commandments helps people stay close to God.

The Ten Commandments are divided into the two parts of the Great Commandment. The first three commandments show us how we are to love God. The last seven show us how to love ourselves and others. When Jesus told the man he was right, he was telling him and us that the commandment of love is the greatest.

The Ten Commandments show us how to live as God wants us to live. They tell us how to love God, ourselves, and others. They show us the way to real happiness and eternal life.

🔵 What was Jesus trying to tell the man?

🔵 When does following a commandment make you happy?

Faith at Home

Read the Scripture story with your family members. Discuss responses to the questions. Talk about situations in the family, school, or work where family members have to follow laws and rules. Talk about the positive results when everyone follows the laws or rules. Discuss how you as a family can live the Great Commandment.

Share

Role-play With a partner or in a small group, brainstorm ways that young people today keep the Great Commandment. Plan a role-play about one of them, showing how a young person makes a choice to follow the commandment.

33

Cultural Background

Rabbi A rabbi is a teacher and interpreter of the Torah or Jewish Law. Rabbis study the Torah assiduously and try to help the people understand how it applies to daily life.

In Jesus' time rabbis provided an expertise to the common person by handing down authoritative interpretation (*halakah*) of the Law. They determined who properly observed the commandments of God and who did not. There was not, nor is there today among Jews, always a universal interpretation of how the law should be followed.

- Write the term *Great Commandment* on the board or on chart paper. Refer young people back to the Gospel story to find the Great Commandment.

- Point out that the Great Commandment is a summary of all of the other commandments.

- Draw two tablets on the board. After reading the second paragraph aloud, challenge young people to divide the commandments between the tablets. Help them discover the division is three commandments on the left and seven on the right.

- You may want to refer the young people to a more detailed explanation of the Ten Commandments on page 77.

❓ Invite young people to share their responses to the first question. If we love God and our neighbor, we will go to heaven. If you keep these two laws, you will keep all the others.

❓ Ask the second question. Possible responses: when I honor God by praying, when I am kind, when I share, when I obey.

Share

- Divide the group into pairs or small groups.

- Allow time for young people to plan their presentations.

- Circulate and offer assistance as they work.

- Have each group present their role-play to the large group.

Activity Master

You may wish to use Activity Master 3 on page CE3 to encourage young people to share the meaning of the commandments.

▲ Activity Master 3

Review

- The Ten Commandments show us how to live.

- All of God's laws are summarized in the Great Commandment.

Objective

To explain the examination of conscience and the place of Scripture in Reconciliation celebrations

Faith Focus

What happens during the examination of conscience?
List young people's responses on the board or on chart paper.

The Examination of Conscience

- Have young people tell you different meanings of the word *examination*. Possible responses: a test, a doctor's checkup, an investigation, an inspection

- Discuss the meaning of *examination* in the term *examination of conscience*.

- Invite young people to read the first paragraph silently to find out what a conscience is.

- Point out that a conscience is a gift that helps us know right from wrong. It also allows us to learn from our mistakes, makes us want to be better people, and we can strengthen our conscience.

- Call attention to the bulleted questions. Discuss how these types of questions might help them think about their choices.

- Invite them to add questions.

Precepts of the Church

- Use the text to define the precepts of the Church.

- Have the young people briefly review the precepts on page 78.

The Examination of Conscience

SIGNS OF FAITH

Precepts of the Church
Precepts of the Church are helpful laws made by the Church. They help us know the basic things we must do to grow in love of God and neighbor. A list of the precepts is on page 78.

Faith Focus

What happens during the examination of conscience?

When we prepare to receive the Sacrament of Reconciliation, we examine our conscience. Just as God gives us the gift of free will, he also gives us the gift of conscience. **Conscience** helps us know the difference between right and wrong, good and evil. It also helps us know whether something we already did was right or wrong. We strengthen our conscience when we pray for guidance and apply Jesus' teachings to our decision-making. Doing this helps our conscience point us in the right direction.

Here are some questions we ask ourselves during the **examination of conscience**:

- Did I live as Jesus wants me to?
- Did I go to Mass on Sunday?
- Did I love and respect my family members?
- Did I share my time and possessions with others?
- Did I tell the truth, return others' belongings, and treat people fairly?

34

Catechist Background

Family involvement As you discuss the precepts and commandments, some young people may be concerned because their family does not always participate in Mass on Sunday or Saturday evening. This may be because of a parent's work schedule, transportation difficulties, or other situations that seem to be beyond a candidate's control. In such cases, encourage young people to talk to their parents about ways they can arrange to make sure their children will be able to take part in Mass each week.

We Listen to God's Word

When we examine our conscience, we can use Scripture. We often listen to Scripture during the celebration of the Sacrament of Reconciliation. When we receive the Sacrament individually, the priest may read the Scripture. Or he may ask us to read a Scripture story.

When we celebrate the Sacrament with the community, we begin with a Celebration of the Word of God. We listen to one or more readings, and the priest gives a homily. The readings and homily help us hear God's voice. They remind us that God wants to forgive us.

After the homily there is a period of silence. We prayerfully think about our lives.

Faith at Home

Share the Scripture story you chose with family members. Ask them to share one that they might use. Using page 81 of this book, go over the guidelines for the examination of conscience with family members.

❓ **Which Scripture story will you choose for your examination of conscience?**

35

Sacrament Background

Penitential services for children and youth   The Sacrament of Penance was not adapted to the age or specific circumstances of penitents until recently. Modern understanding of the needs and capacities of people led the fathers of the Second Vatican Council to authorize the development of penitential services suited for various groups. These services are meant to strengthen the spirit and virtue of penance and to help people prepare for the celebration of the sacrament. Models for children and youth appear in Appendix II of the *Rite of Penance*, nos. 43–61. Directions are provided if the Sacrament of Penance will be celebrated during these services (Appendix II, no. 4). Adaptation to different age groups is especially important for the examination of conscience. The Rite of Reconciliation for Several Penitents with Individual Confession and Absolution specifically asks that age be taken into account when a priest, deacon, or some other minister helps the assembly to make an examination of conscience.

We Listen to God's Word

Review the terms *examination of conscience*, *commandments*, and *precepts* by writing them on the board or on chart paper and having young people define them and tell how they are related. If they have difficulty, have them review appropriate parts of the text.

- Summarize the role of Scripture in Reconciliation. Point out that receiving this sacrament gives us another chance to learn from Jesus' words to us.

- Add the term *homily* to the vocabulary list.

- Have young people read the text to themselves.

- Ask why there is quiet time after the homily. to give us time to think about the lesson in the scripture reading; to think about our lives

❓ Discuss the question; point out that people may choose different stories. Accept all reasonable responses. Ask young people to share the reason for their choices.

Review

- Conscience helps us know what is right and wrong. In the Sacrament of Reconciliation, we examine our conscience.

- We hear scripture readings and a homily during a communal Reconciliation celebration.

LIVE

Objective

To reflect on the commandments and their meaning to us

Showing Love

Respond

- Explain the activity.
- Distribute writing materials.
- Allow time for personal reflection and for writing.
- Invite students to write some of their suggestions on index cards and pass them to you. Read some of the suggestions to the group.

Closing Blessing

- Gather the group in a prayer circle with their books.
- Begin with the Sign of the Cross.
- Read aloud the People of Faith story about Saint Vincent de Paul.
- Pray the prayer.
- End with *Songs of Celebration* CD, track 3, "Del Señor viene la misericordia," or one of the optional music suggestions on page 29.

LIVE

Showing Love

Respond

Create a reminder In the space provided write ten ways you will keep the commandments this week. You can use a commandment more than once. Keep the list as a reminder for the week.

How I will live the Commandments

1. _____
2. _____
3. _____
4. _____
5. _____
6. _____
7. _____
8. _____
9. _____
10. _____

36

Closing Blessing

Gather and begin with the Sign of the Cross.

Leader: The Lord speaks words of forgiveness and love always. Let us ask him to open our minds and hearts to his love.

All: We pray you, hear us.

Leader: Teach us your ways, O Lord, that we may follow your commandments.

All: We pray you, hear us.

Leader: Open our hearts to your word, that we will learn to follow it and grow ever closer to you.

All: We pray you, hear us.

Sing together.

Misericordia, Señor, show us your mercy, O Lord,
hemos pecado, for we have sinned.

© 1998, Bob Hurd. Published by OCP

✦ People of Faith: A Story

Saint Vincent de Paul   It would be impossible to list all of the good works that Vincent achieved over his lifetime. Love of God and neighbor was the most important thing for him. He took care of children and senior citizens. He worked with the rich and the poor. He started out as a tutor to children. Later he became a parish priest. He founded an order of priests and an order of sisters. No matter how busy he was, Vincent always took time to pray and to take care of the needs of others. He is a good example of someone who lived the Great Commandment. His feast day is September 27th. He is the patron saint of charitable societies.

1580–1660

Faith at Home

Faith Focus

- We prepare for the Sacrament of Reconciliation with an examination of conscience, using the word of God.

- The Holy Spirit guides us in examining our conscience.

- Conscience is the ability to know right from wrong.

Ritual Focus
Reverencing the Word

The celebration focused on Reverencing the Word. You honored God's word by bowing before the Bible or placing your hand on it, while the catechist prayed that God's word would enlighten you. During the week, spend some time each day reading from the Bible. If you do not have a Bible, use the Scripture stories in your book.

Family Prayer

God, our Father, thank you for giving us the gift of conscience. Help us to be kind and helpful to one another. Make us a family that loves you and all the people in our lives. Amen.

Act

Share Together With your family, watch a favorite video, movie, or TV show. Afterward, discuss how the characters were or were not living the Great Commandment. Ask other family members to share examples of people they know who live this commandment in their daily lives.

Do Together Ask your family members to do an examination of conscience together. Read the Scripture reading from this lesson. Invite family members to name times when one of you lived the Great Commandment. Decide one way your family will live out this commandment in the next week. Conclude by praying the Lord's Prayer together.

GO online www.osvcurriculum.com
Visit our website for weekly Scripture readings and questions, family resources, and more activities.

37

Faith at Home

Review the five parts of the Faith at Home page with young people.

Encourage them:

- to ask family members to review the **Faith Focus** statements with them

- to share the **Ritual Focus: Reverencing the Word** with family members

- to do at least one of the ✳ **Act** activities with family members

- to pray the **Family Prayer** with their family at times when the family is together

- to encourage their family members to go to **www.osvcurriculum.com** with them and do the activities for this chapter sometime during the week

Looking Ahead

For Chapter 4, you will need:

- a Bible

- a large glass bowl filled with water

- a candle

- a prayer table

 the *Songs of Celebration* CD

- copies of Activity Master 4 on p. CE4 for each young person

We Are Sorry

CHAPTER 4

Rite of Penance

"Next, through a prayer for God's pardon, the penitent expresses contrition and the resolution to begin a new life" (no. 19).

Catechism Connection

To deepen your own background and reflection on contrition and the Sacrament of Penance, refer to the *Catechism of the Catholic Church, 1450–1453.*

Catechist Resources

God's Word Today: Repentance and Forgiveness

Denise McGonigal
Twenty-Third Publications

Traces the theme of repentance and forgiveness through the Old and New Testaments

The Sacrament of Reconciliation

Rev. David Coffey
The Liturgical Press

Looks to Scripture, tradition, and the practice of the Church to present a good look at the meaning of the celebration of the Sacrament of Reconciliation

Young People's Resources

Reconciliation II: God's Family, Sin, Sacrament of Reconciliation (18 min)

St. Anthony Messenger Press

Shows how we help one another live in peace with God's help in the Sacrament of Reconciliation

Seven Lonely Places, Seven Warm Places

April Bolton
St. Anthony Messenger Press

A book for young people and adults to share, highlighting the seven deadly sins and their opposing virtues

Catechist Formation

"God, be merciful to me, a sinner!"

Luke 18:13

Contrition

No one seeks to be sad. For this reason, many people find it difficult to express sorrow because they associate it with a sadness that they sometimes feel helpless to overcome. The sorrow that Christians have for sin, however, is not a sad feeling. Rather, sorrow for sin is an admission of doing wrong that is accompanied by a desire and decision to do good. Sorrow for sin, called *contrition*, is a moment of growth in the life of a Christian.

"The most important act of the penitent is contrition, which is heartfelt sorrow and aversion for the sin committed along with the intention of sinning no more" (*Rite of Penance, 6*). A genuine sense of sorrow includes the admission and confession of sin, an intention to sin no more, and a willingness to act in a way that makes the presence of God's love concrete in one's life.

Sorrow and Trust

Sorrow is ultimately an expression of great trust in God. When people acknowledge their sin, they recognize that they are wounded and imperfect. Most people find it difficult to express sorrow to someone who does not love them, because they fear being hurt by that person in return. We have no reason to fear God's response. Sorrow for sin becomes a bridge in the relationship that a person has with God. It is a bridge that can be rebuilt over and over again because God's mercy has no limits.

When is it difficult for you to say, "I am sorry"?
How do you know when someone is genuinely sorry?

Catechist Prayer

Holy God, I acknowledge before you my weakness and failure. As you transformed death into life, change my tears of sorrow into the warmth of joyful faith. Amen.

Lesson Planner

GO online www.osvcurriculum.com
Visit our website for additional resources and information.

		OBJECTIVES	LESSON PROCESS	ACTIVITIES	MATERIALS
CELEBRATE	15 minutes Pages 38–39	Ritual Focus *Examination of Conscience and Act of Contrition* To experience a celebration of the word, including the examination of conscience and Act of Contrition	Celebrate the opening prayer.		PROGRAM RESOURCES *Songs of Celebration* CD, track 4 OTHER MATERIALS Bible, prayer table, candle, large glass bowl filled with water
	Pages 40–41	To explore the meaning of the ritual actions To present the importance of asking forgiveness	Complete the activity. ✝ Read about and discuss the meaning of kneeling. Explain reasons for asking forgiveness. ✝ Read about and discuss contrition.	☀ Reflect Young people reflect on the experience of the celebration and the meaning of the examination of conscience and the Act of Contrition by writing a paragraph.	
REMEMBER	30 minutes Pages 42–43	Faith Focus *How do people tell Jesus they are sorry?* To show how people express sorrow for sin	Discuss ways of showing sorrow. 📖 Proclaim the Gospel story. *Luke 7:36–38, 44–48, 50* Complete the activity.	☀ Share Young people write a prayer of sorrow. 🏠 Faith at Home Suggested activities for the home	PROGRAM RESOURCES Copies of Activity Master 4, p. CE4
	Pages 44–45	Faith Focus *Why do we confess our sins?* To explain the role of confession and penance in Reconciliation	Identify and explain confession, contrition, firm purpose of amendment, and penance as part of the Reconciliation celebration. Define confessor and Act of Contrition. ✝ Discuss the meaning of penitent.	🏠 Faith at Home Suggested activities for the home	
LIVE	15 minutes Page 46	To reinforce the idea of contrition for sins	Introduce the activity. Pray the Closing Blessing. Read aloud the People of Faith story about Saint Paul.	☀ Respond Young people make an "I'm sorry" card.	PROGRAM RESOURCES *Songs of Celebration* CD, track 4
FAITH AT HOME	Page 47	🏠 Faith at Home To introduce the different parts of the Faith at Home page	Review the Faith at Home page. Encourage young people to share this page at home.	☀ Act Suggested activities for the home	PROGRAM RESOURCES Reconcilitation Family Guide, pp. 22–23

CELEBRATE

Objective

To experience a celebration of the word, including the examination of conscience and Act of Contrition

Preparation

Familiarize yourself with the movements of the ritual focus for the examination of conscience and Act of Contrition on page 39.

Prepare the prayer space ahead of time. You will need:

- a Bible
- a table covered with a white cloth
- a candle and a large glass bowl filled with water on the prayer table

 Use the *Songs of Celebration* CD, track 4, to rehearse the suggested song, "Remember Your Love," or one of the optional music suggestions on page 39.

Select a young person to carry the Bible in procession.

We Gather

Invite young people to assemble with their books for a procession.

- Direct them to follow you and the young person carrying the Bible.

- As you process, lead young people in singing using the *Songs of Celebration* CD, track 4.

- When all are assembled in the prayer space, light the prayer candle.

- Begin the prayer, and lead young people in the Sign of the Cross.

Follow the order of prayer on pages 38–39.

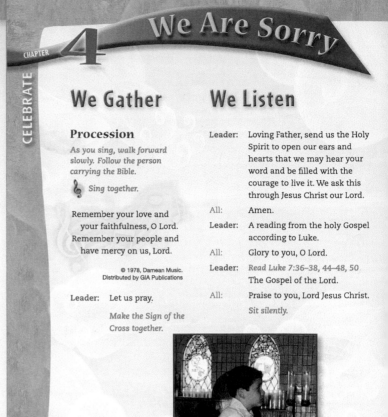

CELEBRATE

We Gather

Procession

As you sing, walk forward slowly. Follow the person carrying the Bible.

 Sing together.

Remember your love and
your faithfulness, O Lord.
Remember your people and
have mercy on us, Lord.

© 1978, Damean Music.
Distributed by GIA Publications

Leader: Let us pray.

Make the Sign of the Cross together.

We Listen

Leader: Loving Father, send us the Holy Spirit to open our ears and hearts that we may hear your word and be filled with the courage to live it. We ask this through Jesus Christ our Lord.

All: Amen.

Leader: A reading from the holy Gospel according to Luke.

All: Glory to you, O Lord.

Leader: *Read Luke 7:36–38, 44–48, 50*
The Gospel of the Lord.

All: Praise to you, Lord Jesus Christ.

Sit silently.

38

Ritual Background

Silence   One of the essential elements of worship is silence.

Silence:

- provides time for interior reflection and prayer

- allows rest

- makes us more attentive

- frames important words and actions

Participation in the liturgy includes moments of silent contemplation. Simply being in the presence of God, without a sound, can be a profound experience of prayer. Worship can also allow time to listen to the voice of our conscience. In certain moments of the liturgy, we attend to "a sound of sheer silence" that tells us we are in the presence of God (*1 Kings 19:12*). Don't be tempted to fill the silence.

Ritual Focus: Examination of Conscience and Act of Contrition

Leader: The sinful woman showed sorrow. Let us think about what we are sorry for.

Use these questions to examine your conscience.

Did I love and honor God?

Did I keep Sunday as a holy day?

Did I obey my parents?

Did I share with others?

Was I kind to others?

Did I tell the truth?

Let us now kneel and pray the Act of Contrition.

All: My God, I am sorry for my sins with all my heart. In choosing to do wrong and failing to do good, I have sinned against you, whom I should love above all things. I firmly intend, with your help, to do penance, to sin no more, and to avoid whatever leads me to sin. Our Savior Jesus Christ suffered and died for us. In his name, my God, have mercy. Amen.

Stand.

We Go Forth

Leader: Lord, our God, you know all things. We want to be more generous in serving you.

All: Amen.

 Sing the opening song together.

39

We Listen

For the proclamation of the Gospel, you may use a Bible or the adapted reading in the *Candidate's Book* on pages 40–41.

Ritual Focus: Examination of Conscience and Act of Contrition

- Invite young people to be quiet and to reflect on the questions for the examination of conscience.
- Have young people kneel.
- Conclude the ritual with prayer.
- Invite young people to stand.

We Go Forth

- Lead the closing prayer.
- As young people process back to their seats, have them sing *Songs of Celebration* CD, track 4, "Remember Your Love," or one of the optional music suggestions.

Optional Music Suggestions:

"Un pueblo camina,"
© Juan Espinosa. Published by OCP

"Give Me Jesus,"
African-American traditional

✦ Liturgical Background

Act of Contrition   The current Rite of Penance (1975) calls this act the "Prayer of the Penitent." There are ten possible formulas for the "Prayer of the Penitent" available in the Rite. The first is based on an "Act of Contrition" that was in general use before Vatican II. After the Second Vatican Council, the Church modified the text to update the language and to include a remembrance of the saving death of Jesus.

This theological addition balances the prayer's emphasis on God's justice and our commitment to reform with a reminder of the unmerited gift we receive through the cross of Christ. The Prayer of the Penitent brings out the mystery of God's love, which is the basis of the sacrament.

CELEBRATE

Objective

To explore the meaning of the ritual actions of the examination of conscience and Act of Contrition

To present the importance of asking forgiveness

Liturgical Catechesis

The purpose of this section is to help young people reflect on their experiences of the signs, rituals, prayers, and gestures of the celebration and to lead them to express their own meaning of the experiences. Allow young people to share their experiences without commenting on them.

Sorrow for Sin

- On the board or chart paper, write the following questions: What did you see? What did you hear? What did you do?

- Guide young people to reflect on the celebration by reviewing what happened in the prayer.

- Invite young people to share their responses to the questions.

Reflect

- Have the young people read the directions silently.

- Point out that there are two parts to their paragraph.

- When the young people are finished, invite volunteers to share what they learned about God, themselves, or the Church.

Kneeling

- Invite young people to share their experience of kneeling.

- Ask young people to read the text to find out how kneeling is a form of prayer.

- Discuss different ways we use our bodies to pray.

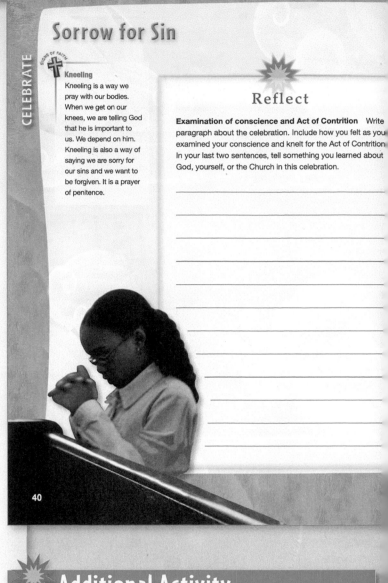

CELEBRATE

Sorrow for Sin

SIGNS OF FAITH

Kneeling

Kneeling is a way we pray with our bodies. When we get on our knees, we are telling God that he is important to us. We depend on him. Kneeling is also a way of saying we are sorry for our sins and we want to be forgiven. It is a prayer of penitence.

Reflect

Examination of conscience and Act of Contrition Write paragraph about the celebration. Include how you felt as you examined your conscience and knelt for the Act of Contrition In your last two sentences, tell something you learned about God, yourself, or the Church in this celebration.

_____

_____

_____

_____

_____

_____

_____

_____

_____

40

Additional Activity

Write a poem Have young people work in pairs to write and illustrate a poem about being sorry. Brainstorm at least three beginning lines and a group of rhyming words that go with each line. Write them on the board or on chart paper.

- Organize young people in pairs.

- Distribute paper and art supplies.

- Direct young people to write a poem and decorate it.

- Have young people share their poems with the larger group.

- Display the poems in your meeting place.

Ask for Forgiveness

When we are unkind to our friends or our family, we hurt our friendship with them, and we feel sorrow or sadness. We wish we did not act that way. We want to make things right. We tell them we are sorry for what we did. We promise not do it again. We make up.

When we sin, we do things that hurt our friendship with God and others. When we examine our conscience, we pray to the Holy Spirit. The Holy Spirit helps us remember how much God loves us. We remember what a good friend Jesus is. We think about the ways we have hurt our friendship with God and others. The Holy Spirit helps us to be sorry for our sins. The Holy Spirit helps us say to God and to others. "I am sorry. Please forgive me."

Signs of Faith

Contrition

Contrition is sorrow for sin. There are different kinds of contrition. Perfect contrition is when we are sorry for our sins because we have ignored or turned away from God. Sometimes we're sorry because of how much we love God.

Other times we are sorry because we are ashamed of what we did. Imperfect contrition is when we are sorry for our sins for reasons other than our love for God, such as fear of punishment.

Both kinds of contrition are gifts of the Holy Spirit. We must have sorrow for our sins to receive the grace of the Sacrament.

41

Ask for Forgiveness

- Invite young people to think about a time when they asked someone to forgive them.

- Ask how it felt to say they were sorry and ask forgiveness.

- Summarize the two paragraphs of text. Use concrete examples from the young people's sharing to explain the text.

✝ Contrition

- Have volunteers read the text aloud.

- Emphasize the importance of genuine sorrow in the process of forgiveness.

💡 Teaching Tip

Prayers of contrition Not all young people will memorize prayers with ease. Some may become concerned if they cannot perfectly recite the Act of Contrition. Encourage them to do as well as they can with memorizing prayers because they are part of our Catholic heritage. Point out that God knows what is in their hearts, and their honest contrition is more important than the precise wording of a prayer.

Also, let the young people know that printed versions of the prayers are available in most Reconciliation rooms. Consider having young people who have trouble with long passages learn a shorter prayer, such as the Jesus Prayer.

Objective

To show how people express sorrow for sins

Faith Focus

How do people tell Jesus they are sorry?
List young people's responses on the board or on chart paper.

Sinners Come to Jesus

- Remind the young people of the Act of Contrition that they prayed in the opening celebration. Point out that this is a well-known prayer because everyone needs to pray it at some time.

- Discuss how we are similar to people in Jesus' time: we want to show we are sorry for our sins, like the woman who was sorry.

 Scripture   LUKE 7:36–38, 44–48, 50

A Woman Who Was Sorry

- Gather the group into a story circle or in the prayer space. Remind them that they will be hearing the Gospel story from Luke again.

- Ask what they remember from hearing the Gospel during the celebration.

- Ask some young people to narrate the story as others act it out.

- With the rest of the group, watch the re-enactment of the story. Ask the young people who acted out the story to tell what they learned from acting it out.

Sinners Come to Jesus

REMEMBER

Faith Focus

How do people tell Jesus they are sorry?

When people heard Jesus' good news about God's love, they were sorry for their sins. They wanted to tell him how sorry they were.

Scripture   LUKE 7:36–38, 44–48, 50

A Woman Who Was Sorry

Simon, a Pharisee, invited Jesus to have dinner with him. So Jesus went to his home and reclined at the table.

Now there was a sinful woman in the city who learned that he was at the table in the house of the Pharisee. Bringing an alabaster flask of ointment, she knelt at his feet weeping and began to bathe his feet with her tears. Then she wiped them with her hair, kissed them, and anointed them with the ointment.

When the Pharisee who had invited him saw this he said to himself, "If this man were a prophet, he would know who and what sort of woman this is who is touching him, that she is a sinner."

42

Scripture Background

Woman at Simon's house   Luke tends to pair people in his stories, contrasting their reactions and inviting the reader to make his or her own judgments. In this story the Pharisee named Simon who had invited Jesus to dinner is contrasted with the unnamed "sinful woman" who anointed Jesus' feet and dried them with her hair (*Luke 7:36–50*).

The woman performs the acts of hospitality usually expected of the host who invited Jesus to eat at his house.

The woman's actions are especially lavish, indicating her respect for Jesus. Simon criticizes Jesus himself for allowing this "sinful woman" to touch him. There is no indication in the story of what the nature of the woman's sin is. In fact, her sinfulness is not important, as Jesus explains to Simon. What is significant is that she shows faith in his forgiveness.

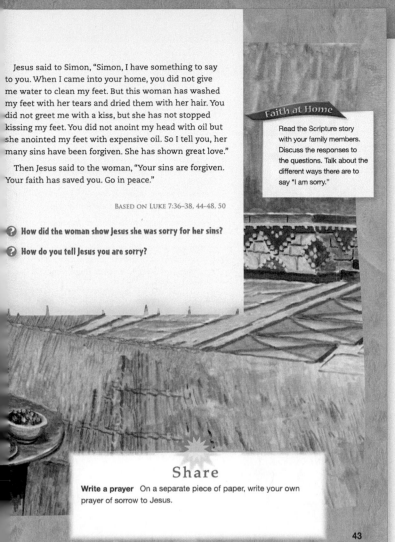

Jesus said to Simon, "Simon, I have something to say to you. When I came into your home, you did not give me water to clean my feet. But this woman has washed my feet with her tears and dried them with her hair. You did not greet me with a kiss, but she has not stopped kissing my feet. You did not anoint my head with oil but she anointed my feet with expensive oil. So I tell you, her many sins have been forgiven. She has shown great love."

Then Jesus said to the woman, "Your sins are forgiven. Your faith has saved you. Go in peace."

BASED ON LUKE 7:36–38, 44-48, 50

❓ How did the woman show Jesus she was sorry for her sins?

❓ How do you tell Jesus you are sorry?

Faith at Home

Read the Scripture story with your family members. Discuss the responses to the questions. Talk about the different ways there are to say "I am sorry."

Share

Write a prayer On a separate piece of paper, write your own prayer of sorrow to Jesus.

43

❓ **Ask the group the first question.** She went to Simon's house. She cried. She wiped Jesus' feet and dried them. She anointed his feet.

❓ **Allow time for personal reflection.** Possible responses: use words, do good things

Share

- Describe the activity to the group.
- Distribute paper and pens or pencils.
- Walk among young people to offer assistance.
- Post the finished prayers on a bulletin board.

Activity Master

You may wish to use Activity Master 4 on page CE4 to further intergrate the meaning of the Gospel story.

▲ Activity Master 4

Review

- There are many ways to show sorrow for sin.
- Jesus will forgive our sins if we are truly sorry.

Cultural Background

Separation of men and women In Jesus' time people were segregated for meals; men ate with their peers, women and children ate together, servants or clients of a household ate separately. The entrance of this unnamed woman into the dining room where men ate suggests that the woman did not care about what others thought of her. The story assumes that she had already encountered Jesus and been so affected by him that she understood she was forgiven. Jesus' comment about her implies that her love was motivated by her awareness that her sins had been forgiven.

REMEMBER

Objective

To explain the role of confession and penance in Reconciliation

Faith Focus

Why do we confess our sins?
List young people's responses on the board or on chart paper.

The Confession of Sin

- Explain that, like the woman in the Gospel story, we want to show that we are sorry for our sins.

- Invite four young people to each read one of the bulleted texts.

- As they read the terms *confession*, *contrition*, *firm purpose of amendment*, and *penance*, write them on the board or on chart paper.

- At the end of the reading, ask the young people to restate the meaning of the terms to assure that they understand them.

- Make a numbered list or diagram on the board or on chart paper to show the progression of events.

✝ Penitent

- Write the word *penitent* on the board or on chart paper. Ask the young people to speculate on what this term means.

- Refer to the illustrated glossary on pages 70–71.

REMEMBER

The Confession of Sin

SIGNS OF FAITH

Penitent
A person who confesses sin during the Rite of Penance is called a **penitent**.

Faith Focus

Why do we confess our sins?

The woman in the Scripture story showed Jesus she was sorry for her sins through her actions. In the Sacrament of Reconciliation, the Church gives us a wonderful way to show our sorrow for our sins. The Sacrament includes each of these four things.

- We admit we have done something wrong. This is called **confession**. We must always confess our mortal sins before going to communion. It is good for us to confess our venial sins often. Confession always helps our friendship with God grow stronger.

- We say "I am sorry." This is called contrition.

- We plan so we will not act unlovingly the next time. This is called a firm purpose of amendment.

- We do the prayer or action the priest tells us to do. This is called doing a **penance**.

44

✦ Catechist Background

Maintaining privacy At this age some young people are willing to discuss their sins with everyone while other young people are reluctant. Emphasize that although everyone sins, a person's sins are private and should not be discussed with just anyone. Assure them that the priest who celebrates the Sacrament of Reconciliation is not allowed to discuss their sins with anyone, not even their family members.

On the other hand, if something the young people have said or done is upsetting them and they would feel better talking to someone about it, they should not hesitate to speak in confidence to a family member or trusted adult.

Sorrow and Penance

In the Sacrament of Reconciliation, we confess our sins to the priest. He is called the **confessor**. The priest acts as God's minister when he listens to our confession. We talk with the priest about how we can make things better.

Then the priest gives us a penance. A penance is a prayer or action that we do to show we are really sorry. The penance may be doing a good act connected to the sin, such as returning stolen property. It may also be an action that shows that we are willing to change, such as being kind. Often it is saying prayers.

Doing the penance helps us take responsibility for our actions. It reminds us to think about how our choices might hurt others.

After we accept our penance, we pray an **Act of Contrition**. The Act of Contrition is a prayer of sorrow. We tell God we are sorry and want to do better. We ask God to help us avoid temptation.

? How does confession help us?

Faith at Home

Discuss your response to the question on this page with family members. Ask them to share their thoughts. Discuss what the difference is between someone just saying the words "I am sorry" and someone showing that they are really sorry. Ask a family member to help you learn the Act of Contrition on page 39.

45

Sorrow and Penance

Recall that the person who confesses sins is called the *penitent*. Contrast this with the term *confessor*, which refers to the priest who hears the confession.

- Write the terms *penance* and *Act of Contrition* on the board or on chart paper.
- Invite young people to write short definitions next to the terms as the other candidates define them, and add them to the list or diagram that was begun with the information on page 44.
- Have individual young people read the text aloud.
- Work with the group to summarize the text.
- **?** Invite volunteers to answer the question. Possible responses: We grow closer to God. We become better people. It helps us change.

Review

- We confess our sins to show that we are sorry.
- The priest gives us a penance to help us change.

✦ Sacrament Background

A place for the sacrament Confession of sin and forgiveness have been celebrated since the time of Jesus and the early Church. But the use of a closed confessional box dates only from the mid-sixteenth century. It was the invention of Saint Charles Borromeo, bishop of Milan. This invention became popular because it protected the anonymity of the penitent.

After the Second Vatican Council, the reformed Rite of Penance included both face-to-face confession and the option of having the penitent and the priest separated by a screen or grille.

Today, a reconciliation chapel normally includes room for either option. It also has a place for the Bible and religious artwork such as a crucifix or some other sacred image conducive to prayer.

LIVE

Objective

To reinforce idea of contrition for sins

Showing Sorrow

Respond

- Explain the activity.
- Distribute art materials.
- Allow time for young people to brainstorm ideas for the card.
- Invite volunteers to share their work with the class.

Closing Blessing

- Gather the group in a prayer circle with their books.
- Begin with the Sign of the Cross.
- Read aloud the People of Faith story about Saint Paul.
- Pray the prayer.
- Lead children in singing using the *Songs of Celebration* CD, track 4, "Remember Your Love," or one of the optional music suggestions on page 39.

Showing Sorrow

LIVE

Respond

Make a card Think about someone to whom you need to say "I am sorry." Use art materials to make a card that expresses your sorrow. Use the space below to brainstorm and to outline how you want to express your sorrow. Decide how and when you will deliver the card.

Closing Blessing

Gather and begin with the Sign of the Cross.

Leader: Lord, look on us and hear our prayer. Give us strength to turn away from sin.

All: Lord, hear our prayer.

Leader: Help us to be sorry for our sins and to change so we can be better followers of Jesus.

All: Lord, hear our prayer.

Leader: Help us to trust in your goodness and to be your generous children.

All: Lord, hear our prayer.

Sing together.

Remember your love and your faithfulness, O Lord.
Remember your people and have mercy on us, Lord.

© 1978, Damean Music.
Distributed by GIA Publications

46

People of Faith: A Story

Saint Paul   Paul did not like the Christians. He punished them for believing in Jesus. One day Paul heard Jesus say, "Why do you persecute me?" Paul knew he had done wrong. He was very sorry. From that time on Paul stopped punishing the Christians. He was baptized, and he went everywhere telling people about Jesus and helping them believe in him. Many people became followers of Jesus because Paul told them about him. The Church celebrates Saint Paul's feast on June 29.

First Century–A.D. 67

Faith at Home

Faith Focus

The Holy Spirit helps us to be sorry for our sins.

Sorrow for sin is very important part of the Sacrament of Reconciliation.

A penance is a prayer or action given by the priest that we do to show we are sorry for what we have done.

Ritual Focus
Examination of Conscience and Act of Contrition

The celebration focused on the Examination of conscience and Act of Contrition. You spent quiet time thinking about your own actions. This week spend some quiet time with a family member, and together use the questions on page 39 to review each day. Begin your quiet time with the prayer to the Holy Spirit on page 80.

Family Prayer

Loving Father, send your Holy Spirit to help us understand when our actions hurt others in our family. Give us the strength to tell God and one another we are sorry and to do better in the future. We ask this in Jesus' name. Amen.

Act

Share Together All of us use the phrase "I'm sorry." It can mean many things. We use it when we bump into someone. We use it when we have hurt someone. We use it when we experience loss. We use it to respond to someone when they tell us something sad. Ask family members to discuss together all the different meanings of the words "I'm sorry." Have family members share stories of how they let people know they were sorry and what happened after they expressed their sorrow.

Do Together Read the Act of Contrition on page 39 with your family members. Discuss each phrase of the prayer and share examples of what each phrase means. Then pray the Act of Contrition together.

GO online **www.osvcurriculum.com**
Visit our website for weekly Scripture readings and questions, family resources, and more activities.

47

Faith at Home

Review the five parts of the Faith at Home page with young people.

Encourage them:

- to ask family members to review the Faith Focus statements with them

- to share the Ritual Focus: Examination of Conscience and Act of Contrition with family members

- to do at least one of the Act activities with family members

- to pray the Family Prayer with their family at times when the family is together

- to encourage their family members to go to **www.osvcurriculum.com** with them and do the activities for this chapter sometime during the week

Looking Ahead

For Chapter 5, you will need:

- a Bible
- a large glass bowl filled with water
- a candle
- a prayer table
- the *Songs of Celebration* CD
- copies of Activity Master 5 on p. CE5 for each young person

We Are Forgiven

Rite of Penance

"Through the sign of absolution God grants pardon to sinners who in sacramental confession manifest their change of heart to the Church's minister; this completes the Sacrament of Penance" (*no. 6d*).

Catechism Connection

To deepen your own background and reflection on the confession of sins and forgiveness, refer to the *Catechism of the Catholic Church, 1455–1460.*

Catechist Resources

 Forgiveness

Pope Saint John Paul II
Andrews McMeel Publishing

A touching collection of the Holy Father's thoughts and reflections on the importance of forgiveness in the human experience

 The Older Brother Returns: Finding a Renewed Sense of God's Love and Mercy

Neal Lozano
Attic Studio

Gives new insights into the story of the returning son

Young People's Resources

 God's Trombones: A Trilogy of African-American Poems *(30 min)*

Billy Budd Films, Inc.

Contains a poetic rendition of the story of the Prodigal Son by James Weldon Johnson

 The Parables of Jesus

Tomie de Paola
Holiday House

This popular young people's author retells parables in a fashion that will be appreciated by all ages

Catechist Formation

"If you forgive the sins of any, they are forgiven them."

John 20:23

Signs of Forgiveness

When two people love each other, they use spoken words, such as "I love you," and concrete signs, such as embracing each other, in order to express their love. If one of the persons stopped using these signs, the other might begin to wonder if he or she was still loved.

In the Sacrament of Penance, God forgives through the words of absolution or forgiveness and the extension of hands upon the penitent. The words of the prayer reveal that this forgiveness comes through the death and Resurrection of Jesus. The cross is a central sign of forgiveness because it shows the depth of God the Father's love; that is, God's willingness to give his only Son and then to raise him up from the dead.

Welcome and Forgiveness

The extension of hands also reflects the way that Jesus welcomed sinners and brought healing to them. This gesture mirrors the welcome given to the prodigal son by his father in the story that Jesus told to his followers in *Luke 15:11–24.*

The forgiveness that God offers to all sinners, no matter how great or small their offenses, is the crowning point of the Sacrament of Penance. It is offered to all so that those who share this gift from God will make his mercy and compassion a part of their own lives. In this way Christians become more committed disciples of Jesus and help to bring reconciliation to the world.

What is it like to experience forgiveness from someone whom you have hurt?
What concrete ways do you show that God's mercy is an important part of your life?

Catechist Prayer

Merciful God, let the power of your love transform my weakness; help me to become a living example of your mercy in every human encounter. Amen.

Lesson Planner

	OBJECTIVES	LESSON PROCESS	ACTIVITIES	MATERIALS
CELEBRATE — 15 minutes — Pages 48–49	Ritual Focus *Prayer over the Candidates* To experience a celebration of the word, including a prayer over the candidates	Celebrate the opening prayer.		PROGRAM RESOURCES *Songs of Celebration* CD, track 5 OTHER MATERIALS Bible, prayer table, candle, large glass bowl filled with water
Pages 50–51	To explore the meaning of the ritual action To present the meaning of reconciliation	Complete the activity. ✝ Read about and discuss laying on of hands. Describe the meaning of reconciliation. ✝ Discuss Heaven.	**Reflect** Young people reflect on the experience of the celebration and the meaning of the prayer over the candidates.	
REMEMBER — 30 minutes — Pages 52–53	Faith Focus *What does Jesus tell us about God's forgiveness?* To reinforce the concept of God's forgiveness	Recall scripture stories of God's forgiveness. 📖 Proclaim the Gospel story. *Luke 15:11–24* Complete the activity.	**Share** Young people create a story about God's forgiveness.	PROGRAM RESOURCES Copies of Activity Master 5, p. CE5 OTHER MATERIALS Writing materials Purple stole
Pages 54–55	Faith Focus *How are sins forgiven in the Sacrament of Reconciliation?* To explain the function of absolution in Reconciliation	Identify how Reconciliation unites people. ✝ Read about and explain the use of the stole. Explain the connection between forgiveness and absolution.	**Faith at Home** Suggested activities for the home	
LIVE — 15 minutes — Page 56	To reinforce the idea of forgiveness in our lives	Introduce the activity. Pray the Closing Blessing. Read aloud the People of Faith story about John Vianney.	**Respond** Young people write about how they will forgive another person.	PROGRAM RESOURCES *Songs of Celebration* CD, track 5
FAITH AT HOME — Page 57	**Faith at Home** To introduce the different parts of the Faith at Home page	Review the Faith at Home page. Encourage young people to share this page at home.	**Act** Suggested activities for the home	PROGRAM RESOURCES Reconciliation Family Guide, pp. 24–25

CELEBRATE

Objective

To experience a celebration of the word, including a prayer over the candidates

Preparation

Familiarize yourself with the movements of the ritual focus for the prayer over the candidates on page 49. You will need:

- a Bible
- a table covered with a white cloth
- a candle and a large glass bowl filled with water on the prayer table

 Use the *Songs of Celebration* CD, track 5, to rehearse the suggested song, "Children of God," or one of the optional music suggestions on page 49.

Select a young person to carry the Bible in procession.

We Gather

Invite young people to assemble with their books for a procession.

- Direct them to follow you and the young person carrying the Bible.

 As you process, lead young people in singing using the *Songs of Celebration* CD, track 5.

- When all are assembled in the prayer space, light the prayer candle.
- Begin the prayer, and lead young people in the Sign of the Cross.

Follow the order of prayer on pages 48–49.

We Listen

For the proclamation of the Gospel, you may use a Bible or the adapted reading in the *Candidate's Book* on pages 50–51.

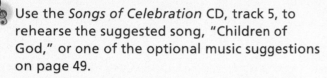

CHAPTER **5** We Are Forgiven

CELEBRATE

We Gather

Procession

As you sing, walk forward slowly. Follow the person carrying the Bible.

🎵 *Sing together.*

Children of God in one
    family,
loved by God in one family.
And no matter what we do
God loves me and God
    loves you.

© 1988, Christopher Walker.
Published by OCP Publications

Leader: Let us pray.

Make the Sign of the Cross.

We Listen

Leader: Good and gracious Father, you who are always ready to forgive us, send us the Holy Spirit. Open our hearts and minds to know your forgiving love. We ask this in the name of your Son, Jesus.

Leader: A reading from the holy Gospel according to Luke.

Leader: *Read Luke 15:11–32.*

The Gospel of the Lord.

All: Praise to you, Lord Jesus Christ.

Sit silently.

48

✦ **Liturgical Background**

Absolution   Historically, the Church has used two formulas for absolving sins. The type from the earliest centuries is a prayer directed to God, such as "May almighty God have mercy on you…" In later centuries, the absolution was formulated in the first person: "I absolve you…" The most recent Rite of Penance, promulgated in 1975, beautifully combines both expressions.

After proclaiming the reconciliation of the world to God through the Paschal mystery and sending of the Holy Spirit, the priest says "…through the ministry of the Church may God give you pardon and peace, and I absolve you from your sins…" The formula for absolution is always said by an ordained priest.

Ritual Focus: Prayer over the Candidates

We Go Forth

Leader: In the Scripture story Jesus told us a story about a father who loved his son very much.

Come forward to the prayer table.

[Name], God loves you and will always forgive you.

Candidate: Thanks be to God.

Leader: Let us ask God our Father to forgive us and free us from evil.

Pray the Lord's Prayer together.

Leader: May the God of peace fill your hearts with every blessing. May he strengthen you with the gift of hope. May he grant you all that is good.

All: Amen.

🎵 *Sing the opening song together.*

49

Ritual Focus: Prayer over the Candidates

- Invite young people to come forward in a single line.
- Place your hands on each young person's head and pray the prayer.
- Pray the Lord's Prayer.
- You may want to refer young people to page 79 of their books for the words of the Lord's Prayer.

We Go Forth

- Lead the closing prayer.

🎵 As young people process back to their seats, have them sing *Songs of Celebration* CD, track 5, "Children of God," or one of the optional music suggestions.

Optional Music Suggestions:

"Savior of the World,"
© John Burland,
Ovation Music Service

"Mi alma está sedienta de ti,"
© Donna Peña. Published by OCP

"Amazing Grace,"
Traditional

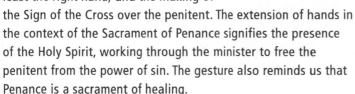

✳ Ritual Background

Extension of hands In the vocabulary of Christian ritual, extension of hands plays an important role. It can signify any of the following, depending on the context:

- calling down of the Holy Spirit
- protection from evil
- healing

In the Rite of Penance, the words of absolution are accompanied by two gestures: an extension of hands (or at least the right hand) and the making of the Sign of the Cross over the penitent. The extension of hands in the context of the Sacrament of Penance signifies the presence of the Holy Spirit, working through the minister to free the penitent from the power of sin. The gesture also reminds us that Penance is a sacrament of healing.

CELEBRATE

Objective

To explore the meaning of the ritual action of the prayer over the candidates

To present the meaning of reconciliation

Liturgical Catechesis

The purpose of this section is to help young people reflect on their experiences of the signs, rituals, prayers, and gestures of the celebration and to lead them to express their own meaning of the experiences. Allow young people to share their experiences without commenting on them.

Reconciliation

- On the board or on chart paper, write the following questions: What did you see? What did you hear? What did you do?
- Guide young people to reflect on the celebration by reviewing what happened in the prayer.
- Invite young people to share their responses to the questions.

Reflect

- Have young people complete the statements.
- Invite volunteers to share their responses.

Laying on of Hands

- Have young people read the text silently.
- Discuss the meaning of the gesture of laying on of hands.

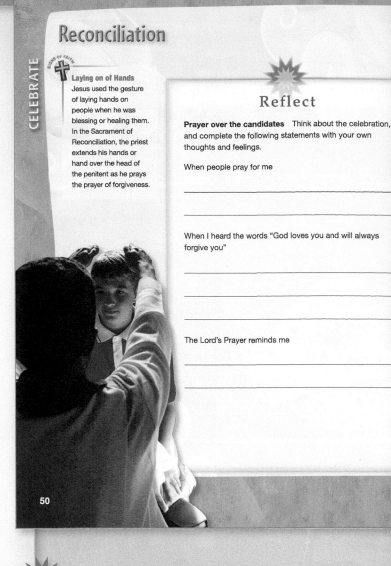

Reconciliation

CELEBRATE

SIGNS OF FAITH

Laying on of Hands
Jesus used the gesture of laying hands on people when he was blessing or healing them. In the Sacrament of Reconciliation, the priest extends his hands or hand over the head of the penitent as he prays the prayer of forgiveness.

Reflect

Prayer over the candidates Think about the celebration, and complete the following statements with your own thoughts and feelings.

When people pray for me

_____

_____

When I heard the words "God loves you and will always forgive you"

_____

_____

_____

The Lord's Prayer reminds me

_____

_____

50

Additional Activity

Make note cards Have young people make note cards with the theme "God loves you and will always forgive you."

- Distribute construction paper or poster board and crayons or colored markers.
- Print the theme "God loves you and will always forgive you" on the board or on chart paper.
- Distribute heavy paper that has been sized to fold and fit into envelopes. Have the young people write the words on the paper and then decorate it.
- Invite young people to use the cards to write to priests, deacons, other parish staff, and parents who have helped them prepare for Reconciliation.

Brought Together Again

When we are unkind to others, we hurt our relationship with them. Our parents, grandparents, teachers, or others in authority trust us to obey them. When we disobey them they are disappointed in us.

Sometimes we do things that hurt our friendship with others and we want to make it better. We say "I am sorry." But we cannot make it better all by ourselves. The people we disobey or hurt have to forgive us. When they say "I forgive you," we are one with them again. We are reconciled. Reconciliation means "to bring together again, or reunite."

In the Sacrament of Penance, God is always ready to forgive us. Through the power of the Holy Spirit we are reconciled with God and one another.

Heaven

God wants us to be one with him. This is why he forgives us. People who do not confess mortal sins will be separated from God forever. God wants us to be happy with him forever in Heaven. So we confess our sins and try to grow in holiness now. People who die in God's friendship will eventually share in the joy of Heaven.

51

Brought Together Again

- Have young people read the first paragraph silently.
- Elicit from the group further examples of how we hurt our relationships with others.
- Ask a volunteer to read the next two paragraphs.
- Discuss why saying "I'm sorry" and being forgiven is important in a relationship.
- Ask volunteers to describe reconciliation in their own words to ensure their understanding.

Heaven

- Have young people read the text silently.
- In pairs have young people share their ideas of heaven.
- Summarize the important points in the text.

🔆 Teaching Tip

A new translation Your students (and their parents) may be wondering why some of the prayers and responses of the Mass changed after the introduction of the revised *Roman Missal* in 2011. In 2000, Pope Saint John Paul II announced a revised version of the *Roman Missal* in Latin. It includes prayers for newly canonized saints, more prefaces for the Eucharist Prayers, some updated rubrics, and more. The English translation of the Third Edition of the Latin *Roman Missal* also includes updated translations of some existing prayers and responses. These translations are closer to the Latin text and show more clearly how our prayers are rooted in Scripture. Parishes in the United States began using the new translations on the first Sunday of Advent in 2011.

You may wish to send home copies of *Catholic Parent Know-How: Revised Roman Missal* (available at **www.osvcurriculum.com**) so parents can understand and familiarize themselves with the changes.

REMEMBER

Objective

To reinforce the concept of God's forgiveness

Faith Focus

What does Jesus tell us about God's forgiveness?
List young people's responses on the board or on chart paper.

God Wants to Forgive

- Ask the young people how Jesus treated sinners. Have them silently read the first paragraph if they cannot remember.

- Tell the young people that Jesus also told stories that showed forgiveness.

 Scripture   LUKE 15:11–24

The Forgiving Father

- Gather the group into a story circle or in the prayer space. Remind them that they will be hearing the Gospel story from Luke again.

- Ask what they remember from hearing the Gospel during the celebration.

- Have the young people view the illustrations and interpret them.

- Invite young people to mime the parts of the story as you read it.

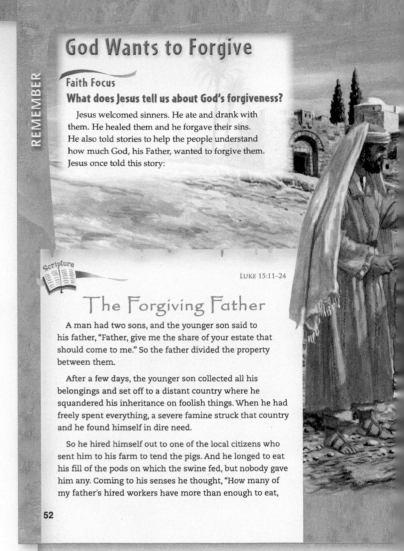

God Wants to Forgive

Faith Focus

What does Jesus tell us about God's forgiveness?

Jesus welcomed sinners. He ate and drank with them. He healed them and he forgave their sins. He also told stories to help the people understand how much God, his Father, wanted to forgive them. Jesus once told this story:

REMEMBER

Scripture

LUKE 15:11–24

The Forgiving Father

A man had two sons, and the younger son said to his father, "Father, give me the share of your estate that should come to me." So the father divided the property between them.

After a few days, the younger son collected all his belongings and set off to a distant country where he squandered his inheritance on foolish things. When he had freely spent everything, a severe famine struck that country and he found himself in dire need.

So he hired himself out to one of the local citizens who sent him to his farm to tend the pigs. And he longed to eat his fill of the pods on which the swine fed, but nobody gave him any. Coming to his senses he thought, "How many of my father's hired workers have more than enough to eat,

52

 ## Scripture Background

Joy in the kingdom   The parable of the Lost Son is the third of three "lost" parables in Luke 15. In response to the complaints of the "Pharisees and scribes" that Jesus welcomes sinners and eats with them (*Luke 15:2*), Jesus tells the stories about the lost sheep, the lost coin, and the lost son. The three stories all have the same purpose: to celebrate with joy the *logic* of the kingdom of heaven, which is very different from the *logic* of the world.

In the kingdom the lost are looked for, sought out, welcomed back, and restored to life. The threefold repetition underscores the reality of the "joy in heaven" (*Luke 15:7*). The third story of the "lost son" best dramatizes the complete reversal and surprise of the fruits of grace. While the story is probably best known as the story of the Prodigal Son, sometimes it is referred to as the story of the Forgiving Father.

ut here am I, dying from hunger. I shall get up and go
o my father and I shall say to him. 'Father, I have sinned
gainst heaven and against you. I no longer deserve to be
alled your son; treat me as you would treat one of your
aired workers.'"

So he got up and went back to his father. While he was
till a long way off, his father caught sight of him, and was
lled with compassion. He ran to his son, embraced him,
nd kissed him. His son said to him, "Father, I have sinned
gainst heaven and against you; I no longer deserve to be
alled your son."

But his father told the servants, "Quickly bring the
nest robe and put it on him; put a ring on his finger and
andals on his feet. Take the fattened calf and slaughter
. Then let us celebrate with a feast, because this son of
nine was dead, and has come to life again; he was lost,
nd has been found." Then the celebration began.

BASED ON LUKE 15:11–24

Faith at Home

Read the Scripture story
with your family members.
Discuss the responses
to both questions. Talk
about why forgiveness is
sometimes difficult.

? What do you think the father will do?

? What does this story tell you about God?

Share

Create a story Jesus' story of the Forgiving Father describes
what God's forgiveness is like. With a partner or small group,
create a modern-day story that describes God's forgiveness.

53

? Read the first question aloud. Possible
response: give him a job

? What does this story tell you about God?
Possible responses: God will always forgive us.
God is happy when we say we are sorry.

Share

- Divide the group into pairs or small groups.

- Allow time for young people to gather ideas.

- Direct young people as they work; circulate to
  offer assistance.

- Have volunteers share their stories with the
  group.

Activity Master

You may wish to use
Activity Master 5 on
page CE5 to further
integrate the meaning
of the Gospel story.

▲ Activity Master 5

Review

- Jesus told stories about forgiveness.

- The story of the Forgiving Father shows that
  God wants to forgive us.

Cultural Background

Patriarchy In a patriarchal system men are regarded as the
authority in the family. Power and possessions are passed on from
father to son. It was a system that Jesus' audience would have
understood and practiced. This story is counter-cultural.

- The son has no claims to an inheritance since he is not the eldest.

- The father has not died, and the son's request would be
  considered outrageous and ungrateful.

- The father's authority and dignity are compromised when he
  extends forgiveness before the son has groveled at his feet.

- The robe, ring, and sandals are symbols of honor and signify the
  complete reconciliation of the son.

The story challenges the cultural thinking of the kind of father God
is. If a parent's love might be limited or conditional in any way, the
parable shows that God's love is not.

Objective

To explain the function of absolution in Reconciliation

Faith Focus

How are sins forgiven in the Sacrament of Reconciliation?
List young people's responses on the board or on chart paper.

The Sacrament of Forgiveness

- Ask the young people to summarize the story of the Forgiving Father and link it to Reconciliation.

- Have volunteers read the bulleted information aloud to show how Reconciliation reunites people with God and one another.

- After each bulleted item is read, ask the group to restate it or give an example to show that they understand its meaning.

Purple Stole

- Write the word *stole* on the board or on chart paper.

- Refer to the illustrated glossary on pages 72–73.

- Bring a stole to class, or have a priest or deacon show one to young people. Remind the group to treat the stole with respect, as they would treat any sacramental.

REMEMBER

The Sacrament of Forgiveness

Purple Stole

A **stole** is a vestment the priest wears when celebrating the Sacraments. It is a sign of his obedience to God and his priestly authority. During the Sacrament of Reconciliation, the priest wears a purple stole around his neck and over his shoulders. The color purple is a sign of penance.

Faith Focus

How are sins forgiven in the Sacrament of Reconciliation?

In the Scripture story, the son tells his father what he has done wrong and asks forgiveness. The father forgives the son and then surprises him. He brings him back into the family. The son is reconciled.

There are many ways we share in God's forgiveness. The most important ways are in the Sacraments, especially the Sacrament of Reconciliation. The Sacrament of Reconciliation does just what it says:

- It forgives our sins.

- It brings us back together with God in friendship.

- It brings us back to the Church and makes us stronger members.

- It brings us peace.

- It heals our relationships.

- It makes us one with all creation.

54

Teaching Tip

Providing practice It is normal for young people to be nervous about celebrating the sacrament for the first time. To help young people feel more comfortable about celebrating the sacrament, take time to role-play the Rite of Penance with them. Invite volunteers to act as penitents. Give them a common "sin" for their age group. Take the part of the priest. Role-play the confession of sins and the acceptance of the penance. Be sure the penance you give is related to the sin confessed.

Make the young person feel as comfortable as possible, allowing for nervous laughter and conversation. Invite other volunteers to role-play with you, if time permits.

Forgiveness and Absolution

God forgives our sins in the Sacrament of Reconciliation through the ministry of the priest. After we confess our sins, accept our penance, and pray an Act of Contrition, the priest extends his hands over us and prays this prayer of forgiveness:

"God, the Father of mercies,
through the death and resurrection of his Son
has reconciled the world to himself
and sent the Holy Spirit among us
for the forgiveness of sins;
through the ministry of the Church
may God give you pardon and peace,
and I absolve you from your sins
in the name of the Father, and of the Son,
and of the Holy Spirit."

RITE OF PENANCE, 55

This prayer is the prayer of **absolution**. *Absolution* means "forgiveness." We receive God's forgiveness through the Church in the Sacrament of Reconciliation.

? What happens in the Sacrament of Reconciliation?

Faith at Home

With your family members, talk about each of the effects of the Sacrament of Reconciliation on page 54. Review your response to the question on this page with them. Ask a family member to review the Rite of Reconciliation with you. Use pages 74–75 in this book.

55

Forgiveness and Absolution

Tell young people that *absolution* comes from words that mean "to free" and "to loosen." Ask how this idea relates to what happens in Reconciliation.

- As you read the first paragraph, invite young people to write the steps on the board or on chart paper.
- Read the prayer of absolution once, pausing at the end of each line to have young people restate its meaning.
- Reread the prayer in its entirety, so that young people will be familiar with it as a whole.
- Write *absolution* = on the board or on chart paper, and challenge the young people to supply the missing word(s). forgiveness, being one, coming together again
- Use the photographs to familiarize young people with the gestures used during absolution.
- **?** Remove the chart paper or erase the steps in Reconciliation from the board, then have volunteers answer the question. confession of sins, acceptance of the penance, praying the Act of Contrition, and absolution of the priest

Review
- Reconciliation brings us back to God and the Church.
- We receive God's forgiveness through the Church during the prayer of absolution.

✦ Sacrament Background

Office and Ministries in Reconciliation of Penitents The *Rite of Penance* (8–10) explains that the Church is an instrument of conversion and that bishops and priests by the power of the Holy Spirit call the faithful to conversion in the name of Christ and grant forgiveness of sins. The Rite of Penance also acknowledges the role of the faith community in bringing sinners to repentance and reconciliation through witness, sharing the word of God, and showing care and interest in their welfare. It places the ministry of bishops and priests in the context of a reconciling community, which is the whole Church.

Confessors are encouraged to prepare for this special role as God's ministers of forgiveness in the Sacrament of Penance through study and prayer, since in the ministry of reconciliation they reflect the image of the Good Shepherd and the heart of God the Father.

LIVE

Objective

To reinforce the idea of forgiveness in our lives

Serving Others

Respond

- Explain the activity.
- Distribute pencils.
- Tell young people how long they will have to complete the activity.
- Point out that forgiveness may happen at school, at home, or at play.
- Invite volunteers to share their work with the group.

Closing Blessing

- Gather children in a prayer circle with their books.
- Begin with the Sign of the Cross.
- Read aloud the People of Faith story about John Vianney.
- Pray the prayer.
- End with *Songs of Celebration* CD, track 5, "Children of God," or one of the optional music suggestions on page 49.

Serving Others

Respond

Be a forgiving person Think of someone you need to forgive. Write what you will do to show him or her forgiveness this week.

_____
_____
_____
_____
_____
_____
_____
_____
_____
_____

Closing Blessing

Gather and begin with the Sign of the Cross.

Leader: God, our Father, in your goodness forgive us our sins.

All: Lord, hear our prayer.

Leader: Jesus, our Savior, welcome us and show us your mercy.

All: Lord, hear our prayer.

Leader: Holy Spirit, fill us with the gift of forgiveness that we may forgive others as we are forgiven.

All: Lord, hear our prayer.

Sing together.

Children of God in one family,
loved by God in one family.
And no matter what we do
God loves me and God
loves you.

© 1998, Christopher Walker.
Published by OCP Publications

56

✦ People of Faith: A Story

John Vianney John was from a family of farmers in France. As a young man he taught other children their prayers. But school was very hard for John. He was a slow learner. He studied very hard to become a parish priest. He loved the people in his parish. John had a gift from God. He used his gift to help sinners who came to celebrate the Sacrament of Reconciliation. People would come many miles to celebrate the sacrament with him. Sometimes he would hear confessions all day long. He helped people know God's forgiving love.

1786–1859

Faith Focus

• In the Sacrament of Reconciliation, God is always ready to forgive us.

• God wants us to be one with him. Reconciliation means "to bring together again, or reunite."

• Through the power of the Holy Spirit and the ministry of the priest, our sins are forgiven.

Ritual Focus
Prayer over the Candidates

The celebration focused on God's love and forgiveness. You came forward and the catechist extended his or her hands and prayed, reminding you that God loves and forgives you. Then you prayed the Lord's Prayer. Every day during the week, take the time to pray the Lord's Prayer slowly, and think about each verse.

Family Prayer

Dear God,
You are so generous in your love for us. You always welcome us back. Help us to be generous in our forgiveness of others. Amen.

Act

Share Together Together read the three stories in Chapter 15 of the Gospel of Luke. Spend a few minutes explaining that Jesus told these stories to show how much God loves sinners and wants to forgive them. Have family members share their responses to the following questions: What is Jesus telling us about God in these stories? Which of the three stories do you like the best? Why?

Do Together As a family group, share some stories of times individual family members experienced being forgiven or forgiving someone else. Talk about times it is hard to forgive others. Prayerfully read Luke 15:11–24. Together write a prayer asking the Holy Spirit to help you to be forgiving to one another. Place the prayer in an area of your home where family members will see it during the next week. Pray the prayer together at appropriate times during the week, such as when you gather for meals, at bedtime, or before a family gathering.

GO online www.osvcurriculum.com
Visit our website for weekly Scripture readings and questions, family resources, and more activities.

57

Faith at Home

Review the five parts of the Faith at Home page with young people.

Encourage them:

• to ask family members to review the Faith Focus statements with them

• to share the Ritual Focus: Prayer over the Candidates with family members

• to do at least one of the ⬥ Act activities with family members

• to pray the Family Prayer with their family at times when the family is together

• to encourage their family members to go to www.osvcurriculum.com with them and do the activities for this chapter sometime during the week

Looking Ahead

For Chapter 6, you will need:

• a Bible

• a prayer table

• a candle

• a large glass bowl filled with water

• a small branch

 the *Songs of Celebration* CD

• copies of the Activity Master on p. CE6 for each young person

Rite of Penance

"The penitent continues the conversion thus begun and expresses it by a life renewed according to the Gospel and more and more steeped in the love of God, for love covers a 'multitude of sins' (*1 Peter 4:8*)" (*no. 20*).

Catechism Connection

To deepen your own background and reflection on the effects of the Sacrament of Penance, refer to the *Catechism of the Catholic Church, 1468–1470*.

Catechist Resources

 Stories of Celebration: Reconciliation*

Rev. Paul Turner and Maureen A. Kelly
Our Sunday Visitor Curriculum Division

Presents the meaning of forgiveness and reconciliation in story and conversation

 Sacrament of Reconciliation

Kathleen Chesto
Twenty-Third Publications

Shows the history and current views of the Sacrament of Reconciliation

Young People's Resources

 Moving On: Responding in the Spirit (*20 min*)

Saint Anthony Messenger Press

Multi-generational story that invites the viewer to consider their responsibility to respond to the Spirit

 My Reconciliation Book*

Our Sunday Visitor Curriculum Division

A helpful keepsake companion guide to the celebration of Reconciliation for both individual and communal contexts

 Understanding the Sacrament of Reconciliation for Young People (*54 min*)

Paulist Press

Part three of this tape tells the story of Jesus' appearance to the disciples behind locked doors and depicts a communal penance service

 GO online **Available at www.osvcurriculum.com*

Catechist Formation

*"If you continue in my word,
you are truly my disciples."*

John 8:31

Living Reconciliation

Every day people engage in some kind of market interchange where goods or services are exchanged for an equal amount of money or other recompense. That is why it is so easy for some people to think of the penance they receive in the Sacrament of Reconciliation as a kind of payment for receiving God's forgiveness. Actually the penance has a two-fold purpose; it serves as an atonement for sin and as a sign of conversion or willingness to change.

When people are sent out from the sacrament, it is with the intention of living their faith in a visible way. The penance they carry out is a sign that they have been embraced by God and are putting into practice the love they have found in celebrating the sacrament. For those who find forgiveness in this sacrament mercy and love characterize their actions and relationships.

Witness

The sacrament restores harmony with God and the Church community, and penitents are strengthened to live more faithfu and to give witness to others about God's abundant love. They are sent out in much the same way people are dismissed at Mas to serve God and one another until the mission of Christ comes to completion. They also have the assurance that, should they fail again, God will not hesitate to welcome them back and offe anew his forgiveness and divine mercy to them.

What changes have occurred in your life as a result of your participation in the Sacrament of Reconciliation?

In what ways can you act as a reconciler in your daily life?

Catechist Prayer

Make me a channel of your peace and healing, O God of compassion. Fill me with the love of Jesus who gave his life on my behalf. Amen.

Lesson Planner

GO online www.osvcurriculum.com
Visit our website for additional resources and information.

		OBJECTIVES	LESSON PROCESS	ACTIVITIES	MATERIALS
CELEBRATE	15 minutes Pages 58–59	Ritual Focus *Sprinkling with Holy Water and the Sign of Peace* To experience a celebration of the word, including sprinkling with holy water and the Sign of Peace	Celebrate the opening prayer.		PROGRAM RESOURCES *Songs of Celebration* CD, track 6 OTHER MATERIALS Bible, prayer table, candle, large glass bowl filled with water, small branch with leaves
	Pages 60–61	To explore the meaning of the ritual actions To explain the effects of conversion	Complete the activity. ✝ Read about and discuss sprinkling with holy water. Describe what conversion means. ✝ Read about and discuss the Sign of Peace.	Reflect Young people reflect on the experience of the celebration and the meaning of bringing Christ's light to others.	
REMEMBER	30 minutes Pages 62–63	Faith Focus *What did Jesus send the disciples to do?* To present the mission of the Church to forgive sins	Discuss how the disciples carried on Jesus' work. 📖 Proclaim the Gospel story. *John 20:19–23* Complete the activity.	Share Young people write slogans about forgiving and reconciling. Faith at Home Suggested activities for the home	PROGRAM RESOURCES Copies of Activity Master 6, p. CE6 OTHER MATERIALS Writing materials Large sheet of paper for collage
	Pages 64–65	Faith Focus *How do we share reconciliation with others?* To encourage young people to share reconciliation with others	Identify how we share the Church's mission of reconciliation and the Holy Spirit's part in it. ✝ Read about how bishops and priests teach us about the Church's mission. Examine the Dismissal Rite.	Faith at Home Suggested activities for the home	
LIVE	15 minutes Page 66	To review what it means to be a reconciler	Introduce the activity. Pray the Closing Blessing. Read aloud the People of Faith story about Blessed Oscar Romero.	Respond Young people complete a graphic organizer about being a reconciler.	PROGRAM RESOURCES *Songs of Celebration* CD, track 6
FAITH AT HOME	Page 67	Faith at Home To introduce the different parts of the Faith at Home page	Review the Faith at Home page. Encourage young people to share this page at home.	Act Suggested activities for the home	PROGRAM RESOURCES Reconciliation Family Guide, pp. 26–27

CELEBRATE

Objective

To experience a celebration of the word, including sprinkling with holy water and the Sign of Peace

Preparation

Familiarize yourself with the movements of the ritual actions of sprinkling with holy water and the Sign of Peace. You will need:

- a Bible
- a table covered with a white cloth
- a candle and a large glass bowl filled with water and a small branch with leaves on the prayer table
- Use the *Songs of Celebration* CD, track 6, to rehearse the suggested song, "Coming Back Together," or one of the optional music suggestions on page 59.

Select a young person to carry the Bible in procession.

We Gather

Invite young people to assemble with their books for a procession.

- Direct them to follow you and the young person carrying the Bible.
- As you process, lead young people in singing using the *Songs of Celebration* CD, track 6.
- When all are assembled in the prayer space, light the prayer candle.
- Begin the prayer, and lead young people in the Sign of the Cross.

Follow the order of prayer on pages 58–59.

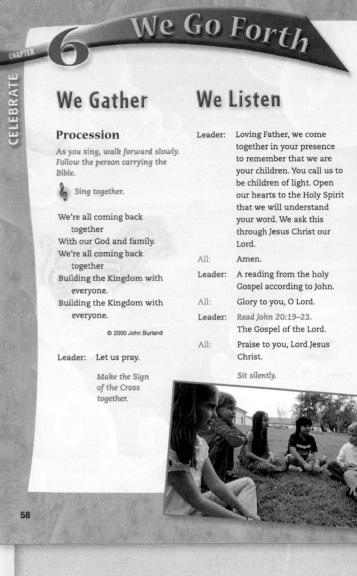

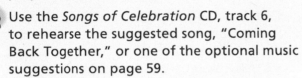

We Gather

Procession

As you sing, walk forward slowly. Follow the person carrying the Bible.

 Sing together.

We're all coming back together
With our God and family.
We're all coming back together
Building the Kingdom with everyone.
Building the Kingdom with everyone.

© 2000 John Burland

Leader: Let us pray.

Make the Sign of the Cross together.

We Listen

Leader: Loving Father, we come together in your presence to remember that we are your children. You call us to be children of light. Open our hearts to the Holy Spirit that we will understand your word. We ask this through Jesus Christ our Lord.

All: Amen.

Leader: A reading from the holy Gospel according to John.

All: Glory to you, O Lord.

Leader: *Read John 20:19–23.*
The Gospel of the Lord.

All: Praise to you, Lord Jesus Christ.

Sit silently.

58

✦ Liturgical Background

Music at the Sprinkling Rite Various songs may be used at the Sprinkling Rite at Sunday Mass. Two chants have traditionally been used. The chant used most of the year is taken from Psalm 51, and its theme is cleansing from sin. It begins with the words "Sprinkle me" or "Asperges me" in Latin, which is why the rite is sometimes called "the asperges," and the tool for sprinkling is called an aspergellum.

The other text, used in Easter time, is the "Vidi aquam," or "I saw water." This chant was inspired by the prophetic vision of *Ezekiel 47:1*, in which Ezekiel sees water flowing from the south side of the temple. Christian interpreters have regarded Ezekiel's temple as a symbol of the Risen Lord, and identify the water flowing from it with the life-giving waters of Baptism flowing from the side of Christ.

Ritual Focus: Sprinkling with Holy Water and the Sign of Peace

Leader: Jesus asks us to forgive others and to bring peace into the world. Through our Baptism and the Sacrament of Reconciliation, we are freed from sin and evil.

All: Amen

Leader: *Sprinkle the candidates with water.*
You have been baptized in Christ and called to bring his light to the world.

All: Amen. Alleluia!

Leader: Let us offer one another the Sign of Peace.

Offer one another a sign of Christ's peace.

Say: The peace of the Lord be with you.

Answer: And with your spirit.

We Go Forth

Leader: God, our Father, send us the Holy Spirit, the giver of peace that we may go forth as a people of peace and forgiveness.

All: Thanks be to God.

 Sing the opening song together.

59

Ritual Background

Sprinkling There are several ways that blessed water is used in the liturgy. In the Sacrament of Baptism, the candidate may be immersed in it or the water may be poured over the candidate.

Outside of Baptism, blessed water may be used to sprinkle objects that are to be blessed, such as ashes or palms. The faithful may also be sprinkled with water to remind them of their Baptism. They are sprinkled after the renewal of baptismal promises at Easter.

A rite of sprinkling can also take place as part of the entrance rites at any Sunday Mass to signify cleansing and spiritual renewal. It is most appropriate during the Easter season.

We Listen

For the proclamation of the Gospel, you may use a Bible or the adapted reading in the *Candidate's Book* on pages 62–63.

Ritual Focus: Sprinkling with Holy Water and the Sign of Peace

- Have young people stand.
- Dip the branch into the water, and then use it to sprinkle young people as you say the prayer.

We Go Forth

- Lead the closing prayer.
- As young people process back to their seats, have them sing *Songs of Celebration* CD, track 6, "Coming Back Together," or one of the optional music suggestions.

Optional Music Suggestions

"It Is Right and Just,"
© John Burland,
Ovation Music Service

"Del Señor viene la misericordia,"
© Bob Hurd. Published by OCP

"Without You,"
© Tom Kendzia and NALR. Published by OCP

CELEBRATE

Objective

To explore the meaning of the ritual actions of sprinkling with water and the Sign of Peace

To explain the effects of conversion

Liturgical Catechesis

The purpose of this section is to help young people reflect on their experiences of the signs, rituals, prayers, and gestures of the celebration and to lead them to express their own meaning of the experiences. Allow young people to share their experiences without commenting on them.

We Share

- On the board or on chart paper, write the following questions: What did you see? What did you hear? What did you do?

- Guide young people to reflect on the celebration by reviewing what happened in the prayer.

- Invite young people to share their responses to the questions.

✦ Reflect

- Have young people read the directions silently.

- Point out that they are to give an example.

- When young people are finished, invite volunteers to share their examples.

✝ Sprinkling with Holy Water

Have young people work in pairs to:

- read the text.

- summarize what the sprinkling means.

- share and compare their summary with another pair.

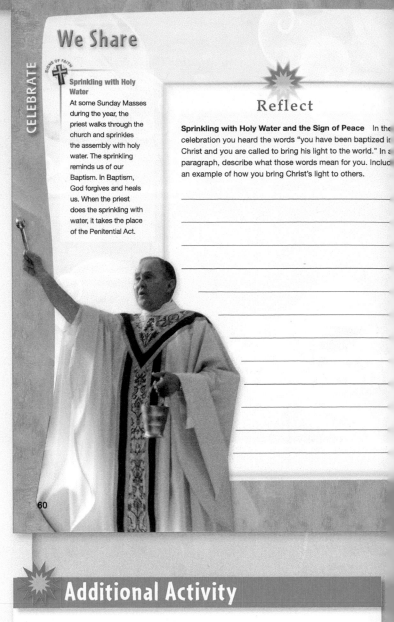

We Share

✝ **Sprinkling with Holy Water**

At some Sunday Masses during the year, the priest walks through the church and sprinkles the assembly with holy water. The sprinkling reminds us of our Baptism. In Baptism, God forgives and heals us. When the priest does the sprinkling with water, it takes the place of the Penitential Act.

60

✦ Reflect

Sprinkling with Holy Water and the Sign of Peace In the celebration you heard the words "you have been baptized in Christ and you are called to bring his light to the world." In a paragraph, describe what those words mean for you. Include an example of how you bring Christ's light to others.

_____

_____

_____

_____

_____

_____

_____

_____

_____

✦ Additional Activity

Make a "We Go Forth" poster Prepare in advance a large cloth with the heading "We Go Forth to Bring God's Light." Have each young person make a fabric flame. On the flame, have young people use indelible markers to write one way they will bring God's light to others. When young people have completed their work, fuse their flames to the larger cloth using fusible webbing available at fabric stores. Display the completed banner in your classroom, a school hallway, or at the First Reconciliation service.

We Are Reconciled

We grow and change when we celebrate the Sacrament of Reconciliation. The Sacrament of Reconciliation is a Sacrament of **conversion**. *Conversion* means "to change or to move away from one thing and toward another."

When we celebrate the Sacrament of Reconciliation, we name the things that have broken or hurt our relationship with God and others. We are sorry and we want to change. We want to move away from the actions that keep us from growing as a child of light. We accept the penance the priest gives us to show that we want to change.

We receive God's forgiveness and peace. Through the action of the Holy Spirit, we are one again with God and others. We are reconciled and at peace.

SIGNS OF FAITH

Sign of Peace
During the Mass we exchange the Sign of Peace before Communion. The Sign of Peace is a sacred action. It is a sign that we are one in the Body of Christ. When we offer each other the Sign of Peace, we remember that we are all one.

61

We Are Reconciled

- Encourage young people to think about and share with the group what it means to grow and change.
- Write the word *conversion* on the board or on chart paper.
- Explain that conversion means to grow and change so we become more like Jesus.
- Write the word *Holy Spirit* on the board or on chart paper.
- Explain that the Holy Spirit helps us grow and change so we become more like Jesus.
- Read the text aloud.

✝ Sign of Peace

- Have volunteers read the text aloud.
- Discuss ways young people can be reconcilers at home and school.
- Practice the Sign of Peace with young people.

💡 Teaching Tip

Accepting responsibility Young people of this age may still find it difficult to accept responsibility for their wrong actions. It is common for them to want to place the blame on others and thus avoid the consequences of their behavior.

Growing in moral responsibility is a lifelong process. Praise young people whenever you witness them accepting responsibility, and be patient with them during the times when they fail to do so.

Part of their moral growth is learning how to accept themselves with all their imperfections. Through your unconditional acceptance of them, they will come to know the infinite love and acceptance of God.

Objective

To present the mission of the Church to forgive sins

Faith Focus

What did Jesus send the disciples to do? List young people's responses on the board or on chart paper.

Hear God's Word

- Call attention to the illustration. Ask young people what is happening in the picture. Jesus is talking to his disciples.

- Summarize the first paragraph.

 Scripture   JOHN 20:19–23

Jesus Appears to the Disciples

- Gather the group into a story circle or in the prayer space. Remind them that they will be hearing the Gospel story from John again.

- Ask what they remember from hearing the Gospel during the celebration.

- Select two young people to read the Gospel passage (one as a narrator and the other as Jesus).

- At the conclusion of the reading, discuss how the disciples might have felt during this appearance. Possible responses: happy, frightened, curious

- Emphasize Jesus' words about the Holy Spirit and the forgiveness of sins.

Hear God's Word

REMEMBER

Faith Focus

What did Jesus send the disciples to do?

While he was alive, Jesus' disciples traveled, preaching and healing in his name. The Risen Jesus wanted his followers to continue to carry on his work of healing and forgiveness.

 JOHN 20:19–23

Jesus Appears to the Disciples

On the evening of that first day of the week, the disciples were in a room with locked doors, for fear of the Jews. Then, Jesus came and stood in their midst and said to them, "Peace be with you."

When he had said this, he showed them his hands and his side. The disciples rejoiced when they saw the Lord.

62

Scripture Background

Resurrection and reconciliation   Despite their betrayal, denial, and inability to remain faithful, the first words of the Risen Jesus to his disciples are, "Peace be with you." John tells us that the Risen Jesus not only speaks a message of peace to his disciples, but also effects that peace in the relationship he has with them.

Jesus' words imply that nothing the disciples could say or do could break the bond established by Jesus between them and God.

Humankind was helpless to heal the breach created by original sin, which affects all of us. But, as John emphasizes more than any other Evangelist, the death of Jesus was victory over sin. The Resurrection of Jesus reconciles us with God and is the source of our reconciliation in the Sacraments of Baptism and Penance.

Jesus said to them again, "Peace be with you. As the Father has sent me, so I send you."

And when he said this, he breathed on them and said to them, "Receive the Holy Spirit.

"Whose sins you forgive are forgiven them, and whose sins you retain are retained."

BASED ON JOHN 20:19–23

❓ What is Jesus sending the disciples to do?

❓ How do you show forgiveness and peace to others?

Faith at Home

Read the Scripture story with your family members. Discuss your responses to the questions. Talk about ways forgiveness brings peace. Use examples from your family's life together.

Share

Write slogans With a partner or a small group, create slogans about living as forgiving and reconciling people. Write your slogan on a large sheet of paper and hang it in a conspicuous place.

63

Cultural Background

Sunday This Resurrection appearance occurs on the "first day of the week" (John 20:19). It seems that from the beginning, Christians commemorated the Resurrection with weekly meetings in homes "on that first day of the week," or Sunday— the day following the Jewish Sabbath.

Acts of the Apostles tells us that the Christians met in homes for the "breaking of the bread," adding this celebration to their ordinary assemblies in the Temple. The early Christians celebrated their agape feasts in honor of Jesus' Last Supper.

As they did so, they began to understand their mission to the world. Eventually, they would not gather in fear, but go out and proclaim the Resurrection by which God reconciled the world to himself.

❓ Ask the first question. to teach people about God the Father, to heal and forgive people

❓ Have young people privately consider answers to the second question, then ask volunteers to answer aloud. Possible responses: I say, "You are forgiven" or "It's OK." Accept all reasonable responses.

Share

• As a group, brainstorm several slogans to help young people understand the activity.

• Divide the group into pairs or small groups.

• Distribute paper and markers or crayons.

• Walk among the groups to offer support.

• Have the groups post their work around the room. Allow time for everyone to circulate and view all of the slogans.

Activity Master

You may wish to use Activity Master 6 on page CE6 to further intergrate the meaning of the Gospel story.

▲ Activity Master 6

Review

• Jesus wanted his disciples to continue his work.

• Jesus told the disciples to forgive sins.

Objective

To encourage young people to share reconciliation with others

Faith Focus

How do we share reconciliation with others? List young people's responses on the board or on chart paper.

Proclamation of Praise and Dismissal

- Ask young people to recall what Jesus asked the disciples to do in the Gospel story. to forgive people

- Summarize the first paragraph of text.

- Have young people write the bulleted items on chart paper, one per page. Allow time for young people to walk around the room and write suggestions on how to do what is written on each page.

- Share some of the suggestions when the young people have returned to their seats.

- After reading the last paragraph, ask how we get the strength to carry out these missions. from the Holy Spirit

Bishops and Priests

- Refer to the illustrated glossary on pages 70–71.

- Name some ways that priests and bishops teach us how to live out the mission of reconciliation.

- Ask how the bishops and priests got their authority to give absolution for sins. from Jesus

---

Proclamation of Praise and Dismissal

SIGNS OF FAITH

Bishops and Priests
In a special way the Church continues Jesus' mission of forgiveness and reconciliation through the ministry of priests and bishops. Like the Apostles, bishops and priests receive from Jesus the authority to absolve people from their sins. They teach us how to live out the mission of reconciliation.

Faith Focus

How do we share reconciliation with others?

Jesus wanted his disciples to know they were forgiven. He wanted them to be at peace. He also wanted them to know they had a special job, a mission. He was sending them to make the world a better place. He wanted them to bring forgiveness and peace to others just as he did in his life. He was calling them to be reconcilers.

The Church continues the mission of reconciliation today. We are reconcilers when we:

- forgive others
- ask for forgiveness
- are fair to others
- act with kindness
- share what we have with those who do not have
- respect all people because they are God's children

The mission of reconciliation is not always easy, but the Holy Spirit gives us strength and courage to carry it out.

64

✦ Catechist Background

Individual and communal celebrations   Most parishes have assigned times for individuals to receive the Sacrament of Reconciliation and consistent times during the year when communal celebrations are offered, such as Advent and Lent. Check with your parish and obtain the necessary information for young people. If possible, put the information on a separate piece of paper so young people can take it home and refer to it. Be sure to encourage young people to continue to celebrate this sacrament during the year.

Go Forth

At the end of the celebration of Reconciliation, we give praise to God for his wonderful gift of forgiveness and reconciliation.

After the prayer of absolution the priest says, "Give thanks to the Lord, for he is good." We respond, "His mercy endures for ever." Then the priest sends us forth. He says this or a similar blessing:

Faith at Home

Review your response to the question with family members and then invite others to share. Go over the meaning of reconciliation on page 72 in this book.

> "Go in peace,
> and proclaim to the world
> the wonderful works of God
> who has brought you salvation."

RITE OF PENANCE, 47

Our sins are forgiven in the Sacrament of Reconciliation. The Holy Spirit remains with us to help us grow and become more like Jesus. This is such a great gift. We want to tell the world about it. The best way we can do that is to be living signs of God's forgiveness and reconciliation to others.

? What can you do to be a living sign of God's forgiveness and mercy?

65

Go Forth

Point out that at the end of every Mass we are told to go and serve God. At the end of Reconciliation, we are to go out and show that we are at peace with God and one another.

- Have a young person read the priest's words after absolution; have the rest of the group say the response.

- Read the priest's words beginning with "Go in peace." Pause after the end of the prayer and ask young people to summarize what it means.

- Summarize the mission of forgiveness by reading the last paragraph aloud.

? Ask the question. Possible responses: Be the first one to say "I am sorry" or "I forgive you." Forgive before the other person says, "I am sorry."

Review
- We are to share reconciliation with others.
- We are meant to be signs of God's forgiveness to others.

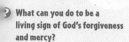

Sacrament Background

Frequency of penance The Code of Canon Law states "the faithful who have reached the age of discretion are bound faithfully to confess their grave sins at least once a year" (989) and the precepts of the Church state "you shall confess your sins at least once a year" (*CCC*, 2042). The Sacrament of Penance was instituted by Christ, so that the contrite sinner could always be reconciled to God's grace and friendship. Since the power of the sacrament restores us to God's grace and joins us in intimate friendship with him and the Church (*CCC*, 1468, 1469), the frequent celebration of the sacrament should be encouraged.

LIVE

Objective

To review what it means to be a reconciler

Being a Reconciler

Respond

- Make a large version of the graphic organizer on the board or on chart paper.
- Work with the young people to fill in the large organizer as a sample.
- Distribute pens or pencils.
- Allow a set time for young people to complete the graphic organizer.
- Invite volunteers to share their ideas with the group.

Closing Blessing

- Gather the group in a prayer circle with their books.
- Begin with the Sign of the Cross.
- Read aloud the People of Faith story about Blessed Oscar Romero.
- Pray the prayer.
- End with *Songs of Celebration* CD, track 6, "Coming Back Together," or one of the optional music suggestions on page 59.

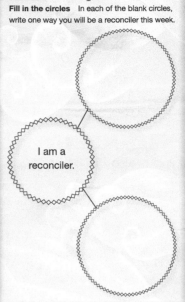

Being a Reconciler

Respond

Fill in the circles In each of the blank circles, write one way you will be a reconciler this week.

I am a reconciler.

Closing Blessing

Gather and begin with the Sign of the Cross.

Leader: God and Father of us al[l] forgive our sins.

All: Thank you for your forgiveness.

Leader: Jesus, our Savior, give u[s] the gift of peace.

All: Thank you for your peace.

Leader: Holy Spirit, give us you[r] strength and courage.

All: Thank you for your strength and courage.

 Sing together.

We're all coming back together
With our God and family.
We're all coming back together
Building the Kingdom with everyone.
Building the Kingdom with everyone.

© 2000 John Burland

66

People of Faith: A Story

Oscar Romero   Oscar was a new bishop in El Salvador when one of his priest friends was murdered for helping the poor. When Oscar went to his friend's funeral, he saw the poor people there. They had no one to help them. The rich people were opressing the poor. They did not treat them fairly. Bishop Oscar decided he would help the poor. Many important people were angry with him for helping. Bishop Oscar knew that they might kill him. He said, "If they kill me, tell them they are forgiven." They did kill him one Sunday while he was giving a homily during Mass.

1917–1980

Faith Focus

The Sacrament of Reconciliation is a Sacrament of conversion.

The mission of reconciliation is to bring forgiveness and peace to others.

The Holy Spirit remains with us to help us grow and become more like Jesus.

Ritual Focus
Sprinkling with Holy Water and the Sign of Peace

The celebration focused on bringing Christ's light and peace into the world. You were sprinkled with water and extended a Sign of Peace to one another. During the week, be aware of situations where you can bring peace to others.

Family Prayer

Gracious God, we give you thanks and praise for the gifts of your mercy and forgiveness. Help us to go out and spread the word of your love to those we meet. Show us how to be reconcilers in our family and with our friends.

Act

Share Together Have family members share their best experiences of the Sacrament of Reconciliation. Read John 20:19–23, and discuss how the disciples must have felt when Jesus appeared to them after the Resurrection. He just says "Peace be with you." Invite family members to share any stories or memories of people they know who forgive like Jesus did. Conclude the sharing with the Prayer of Saint Francis on page 80 of this book.

Do Together For the next week, gather at an appropriate time each day such as at mealtime, before bedtime, or before an evening activity. Light a candle. (This might be a good time to burn your Baptismal candle.) Pray this prayer: We have been baptized in Christ and are called to bring his light to the world. Then have family members share one way they were a light to someone during the day. Together, pray the Prayer to the Holy Spirit on page 80 of this book.

GO online **www.osvcurriculum.com**
Visit our website for weekly Scripture readings and questions, family resources, and more activities.

67

Faith at Home

Review the five parts of the Faith at Home page with young people.

Encourage them:

- to ask family members to review the Faith Focus statements with them
- to share the **Ritual Focus: Sprinkling with Holy Water and the Sign of Peace** with family members
- to do at least one of the Act activities with family members
- to pray the **Family Prayer** with their family at times when the family is together
- to encourage their family members to go to **www.osvcurriculum.com** with them and do the activities for this chapter sometime during the week

Looking Ahead

For Chapter 7, you will need:

- a Bible
- a prayer table
- a candle
- a large glass bowl filled with water
- the *Songs of Celebration* CD
- copies of Activity Master 7 on p. CE7 for each young person

Words of Faith

Words of Faith

absolution The forgiveness of sin that we receive from God through the Church in the Sacrament of Reconciliation.

Baptism The Sacrament that makes the person a child of God and a member of the Church. It takes away Original Sin and all personal sin and makes the person a temple of the Holy Spirit.

communal celebration In a communal celebration, the assembly gathers to pray and hear God's word. Each penitent then confesses his or her sins to a priest, receives a penance, and is absolved individually.

confession Telling our sins to a priest in the Sacrament of Reconciliation. What we confess to the priest is private.

confessor A priest who acts as God's minister when he listens to our confession.

conscience God's gift which helps us know the difference between right and wrong. It also helps us recognize whether an action we already did was right or wrong.

contrition Sorrow for sins and a willingness to do better. Contrition is our first step toward forgiveness. As part of the Sacrament of Reconciliation, we pray an Act or Prayer of Contrition.

conversion A sincere change of mind, will, and heart away from sin and toward God. The Sacrament of Reconciliation is a Sacrament of conversion.

examination of conscience A prayerful way of looking at our lives in light of the Ten Commandments, the Beatitudes, the life of Jesus, and the teachings of the Church. It helps us know whether what we have done is right or wrong.

grace A sharing in God's own life.

Illustrated Words of Faith

This section gives young people a visual reference for the people, places, and things associated with Reconciliation. It contains some of the important words of faith used by the Church to help us understand the mystery of the Sacrament of Reconciliation. Learning these words and their meanings will help young people develop a Catholic vocabulary.

▶ Refer to these pages throughout the sessions to help young people associate liturgical names with the objects and people they describe.

▶ Invite young people to draw their own illustrations for each of the terms.

Holy Trinity The three Persons in one God: God the Father, God the Son, and God the Holy Spirit.

holy water Water blessed by the priest for a religious purpose.

individual celebration In an individual celebration, the penitent meets with the priest in the Reconciliation room. The penitent confesses his or her sins to the priest, receives a penance, and is absolved.

mortal sin A serious sin that separates us from God's life.

Original Sin The name given to the first sin of humans. Because they disobeyed God and turned away from his friendship, Original Sin is passed to all of us.

Paschal candle A candle that is blessed at Easter Vigil and is burned during the Masses of the Easter season. It is also burned at Baptisms and funerals throughout the year.

penance A prayer or good action that we do to show we are sorry for our sins and want to do better. In the Sacrament of Reconciliation, the priest gives us a penance.

penitent The person who confesses his or her sins to the priest in the Sacrament of Reconciliation.

Precepts of the Church Laws of the Church that help us know what we should do to grow in love of God and neighbor.

priest A man who is ordained to serve God and the Church by celebrating the Sacraments, preaching, and presiding at Mass. The priest is the confessor, or minister of the Sacrament of Reconciliation. The stole is a sign of the priest's obedience to God and of his priestly authority.

▶ If possible, take young people on a tour of the church. Ask the sacristan or a parish minister to show young people the vestments and the Reconciliation room used by your parish community. Have young people note how what they see in the parish church is the same as or different from the pictures in the book.

▶ At the end of the first six sessions (Chapters 1–6), go through the glossary word by word, and ask young people to tell when and how each item is used or what each minister does.

R

reconciliation A coming back together.

 Reconciliation room A room or chapel in which the confessor, or priest, hears the penitent's confession of sins. The room is usually furnished with chairs, a kneeler, a table for the Bible, and a candle. A movable screen can also be used as a divider between the priest and the penitent.

 S

Sacrament A holy sign that comes from Jesus and gives us grace, a share in God's life.

Sacrament of Penance Another name for the Sacrament of Reconciliation.

Sacrament of Reconciliation A Sacrament of forgiveness through which the sinner is reconciled with God and the Church.

Scriptures The word of God contained in the Bible. The word *Scripture* means "holy writing." Scripture is used for reflecting on God's love and forgiveness in the Sacrament of Reconciliation. Scripture is proclaimed by a lector or reader, at Mass, at a communal celebration, or in other liturgical celebrations.

 V

venial sin A less serious sin that weakens our friendship with God.

sin The choice to disobey God. Sin is a deliberate choice, not a mistake or accident. We accept God's loving forgiveness for our sins when we show by our sorrow that we are willing to do better.

stole A vestment the priest wears around his neck when celebrating the Sacraments.

▶ Have young people refer to pages 68–73 as the highlighted words of faith appear in each lesson. Have volunteers read the definitions aloud and then use each word in a sentence.

▶ As these words come up in the lessons, have young people make their own set of Words of Faith vocabulary cards. Use index cards. Have them write the word on one side and the definition on the other side. They could also use these cards for a vocabulary word game, either in the session, while they are waiting for the session to begin, or at home with family members.

▶ Take young people on a tour of the Reconciliation room in the church. Help them become comfortable with the furnishings of the room and the procedure before celebration. As you review the procedures, have young people refer to these pages.

Celebrating the Sacrament of Reconciliation

Celebrating the Sacrament

The Communal Rite of Reconciliation

Before celebrating the Sacrament of Reconciliation, take time to examine your conscience. Pray for the Holy Spirit's help.

1. **Introductory Rites**
   Join in singing the opening hymn. The priest will greet the assembly and lead you in the opening prayer.

2. **Celebration of the Word of God**
   Listen to the word of God. There may be more than one reading, with a hymn or psalm in between. The last reading will be from one of the Gospels.

3. **Homily**
   Listen as the priest helps you understand the meaning of the Scriptures.

4. **Examination of Conscience, Litany, and the Lord's Prayer**
   After the homily there will be a time of silence. The priest may lead the assembly in an examination of conscience. This will be followed by a prayer of confession and a litany or song. Then everyone prays the Lord's Prayer together.

5. **Individual Confession, Giving of Penance, and Absolution**
   While you wait to talk with the priest, you may pray quietly or join in singing. When it is your turn, confess your sins to the priest. He will talk to you about how to do better. He will give you a penance and extend his hands over your head and pray the prayer of absolution.

6. **Proclamation of Praise and Dismissal**
   After everyone has confessed individually, join in the prayer or in singing a litany of thanksgiving. The priest or deacon will lead the closing prayer and bless the assembly. Then the priest or deacon will dismiss the assembly.

After celebrating the Sacrament, carry out your penance as soon as possible.

The Individual Rite of Reconciliation

Before celebrating the Sacrament of Reconciliation, take time to examine your conscience. Pray for the Holy Spirit's help.

Wait for your turn to enter the Reconciliation room. You may choose to meet with the priest face-to-face or be separated from the priest by a screen.

1. **Welcome**
   The priest will welcome you and invite you to pray the Sign of the Cross.

2. **Reading of the Word of God**
   The priest may read or recite a passage from the Bible. You may be invited by the priest to read the Scripture yourself.

3. **Confession of Sins and Giving of Penance**
   You tell your sins to the priest. The priest will talk with you about how to do better. Then the priest will give you a penance.

4. **Prayer of the Penitent**
   Pray an Act of Contrition.

5. **Absolution**
   The priest will hold his hand over your head and pray the prayer of absolution. As he says the final words, he will make the Sign of the Cross.

6. **Proclamation of Praise and Dismissal**
   You and the priest praise God for his mercy, and the priest sends you forth.

After celebrating the Sacrament, carry out your penance as soon as possible.

Remember, after you celebrate this Sacrament for the first time, you should receive it often to strengthen your friendship with God. We receive the Sacrament of Reconciliation before we receive Holy Communion for the first time. We are required to celebrate the Sacrament of Reconciliation once a year, if we have committed mortal sin. We cannot receive Holy Communion if we have not received forgiveness for a mortal sin.

Here are some suggested uses for these pages:

These pages describe both communal and individual forms of the Sacrament of Reconciliation. Be sure to find out which form young people will be celebrating for their first reception of the Sacrament.

▶ Use the material on these pages to walk through the Sacrament of Reconciliation celebration.

▶ Refer to the appropriate pages of *Call to Celebrate: Reconciliation and Eucharist* as you go through each chapter of the *Candidate's Book*. Explain and go through all the prayers and actions so the young people become familiar and comfortable with the rite.

▶ Remind young people to keep their books in a handy spot, so they can refer to them when needed.

Sources of Morality

Sources of Morality

The Great Commandment

"You shall love the Lord your God with all your heart, and with all your soul, and with all your strength, and with all your mind; and your neighbor as yourself."

Luke 10:27

The New Commandment

"This is my commandment, that you love one another as I have loved you."

John 15:12

Love of Enemies

"But I say to you, Love your enemies and pray for those who persecute you, so that you may be children of your Father in heaven…."

Matthew 5:44–45

The Beatitudes

"Blessed are the poor in spirit,
   for theirs is the Kingdom of heaven.

Blessed are those who mourn,
   for they will be comforted.

Blessed are the meek,
   for they will inherit the earth.

Blessed are those who hunger and thirst
   for righteousness,
   for they will be filled.

Blessed are the merciful,
   for they will receive mercy.

Blessed are the pure in heart,
   for they will see God.

Blessed are the peacemakers,
   for they will be called children of God.

Blessed are those who are persecuted for
   righteousness' sake,
   for theirs is the kingdom of heaven."

Matthew 5:3–10

The Ten Commandments

1. I am the Lord your God. You shall not have strange gods before me.	Put God first in your life before all things.
2. You shall not take the name of the Lord your God in vain.	Respect God's name and holy things. Do not use bad language.
3. Remember to keep holy the Lord's Day.	Take part in Mass on Sundays and holy days. Avoid unnecessary work on those days.
4. Honor your father and your mother.	Obey and show respect to parents and others who are responsible for you.
5. You shall not kill. Do not hurt yourself or others.	Take care of all life. Avoid anger, fighting, and being a bad example.
6. You shall not commit adultery.	Show respect for marriage and family life. Respect your body and the bodies of others.
7. You shall not steal.	Respect creation and the things that belong to others. Do not cheat. Do not take things that do not belong to you. Do not damage the property of others.
8. You shall not bear false witness against your neighbor.	Tell the truth. Do not gossip. Do not lie or hurt others' good reputation.
9. You shall not covet your neighbor's wife.	Be faithful to family members and friends. Do not be jealous. Avoid impure thoughts and actions.
10. You shall not covet your neighbor's goods.	Share what you have. Do not envy what other people have. Do not be greedy or desire other people's property.

76

77

These pages present the important sources of morality, which young people can use in examining their conscience and making good choices.

The Great Commandment

▶ Review this Scripture quote with young people.

The New Commandment

▶ Read aloud the text.

▶ Ask young people what they think Jesus meant by this commandment.

Love of Enemies

▶ Discuss how it is easy to love those who love us in return, but that Jesus challenges us to love everyone, including our "enemies."

The Beatitudes

▶ Review the Beatitudes with young people. Ask volunteers to suggest ways young people can live these qualities in their daily lives.

▶ Relate the qualities of the People of Faith in the read-aloud story to the Beatitudes.

The Ten Commandments

▶ Review each of the Ten Commandments with young people.

▶ Make a class mural of the Ten Commandments and display it in a place for all to see.

Catholic Prayers

Catholic Prayers

Precepts of the Church

1. Take part in the Mass on Sundays and holy days. Keep these days holy, and avoid unnecessary work.

2. Celebrate the Sacrament of Reconciliation at least once a year if you have committed a serious, or mortal, sin.

3. Receive Holy Communion at least once a year during Easter time.

4. Fast and abstain on days of penance.

5. Give your time, gifts, and money to support the Church.

Works of Mercy

Corporal (for the body)

Feed the hungry.
Give drink to the thirsty.
Clothe the naked.
Shelter the homeless.
Visit the sick.
Visit the imprisoned.
Bury the dead.

Spiritual (for the spirit)

Warn the sinner.
Teach the ignorant.
Counsel the doubtful.
Comfort the sorrowful.
Bear wrongs patiehtly.
Forgive injuries.
Pray for the living and the dead.

The Sign of the Cross

In the name of the Father
and of the Son
and of the Holy Spirit
Amen.

The Lord's Prayer

Our Father, who art in heaven,
hallowed be thy name;
thy kingdom come;
thy will be done on earth as it is in heaven.
Give us this day our daily bread;
and forgive us our trespasses,
as we forgive those who trespass against us;
and lead us not into temptation,
But deliver us from evil.
Amen.

Act of Contrition

My God,
I am sorry for my sins with all my heart.
In choosing to do wrong
and failing to do good,
I have sinned against you
whom I should love above all things.
I firmly intend, with your help,
to do penance,
to sin no more,
and to avoid whatever leads me to sin.
Our Savior Jesus Christ
suffered and died for us.
In his name, my God, have mercy.

Confiteor

I confess to almighty God
and to you, my brothers and sisters,
that I have greatly sinned,
in my thoughts and in my words,
in what I have done and in what I have failed to do,

Gently strike your chest with a closed fist.

through my fault, through my fault,
through my most grievous fault;

Continue:

therefore I ask blessed Mary ever-Virgin,
all the Angels and Saints,
and you, my brothers and sisters,
to pray for me to the Lord our God.

Precepts of the Church

▶ These laws reflect the rights and duties of all Catholics and have existed in some form since the fourth century.

▶ Review the list with young people. Point out how the precepts apply to them.

Works of Mercy

▶ Point out that there are two kinds of Works of Mercy—corporal and spiritual.

The Sign of the Cross

Each of the celebrations begins and ends with the Sign of the Cross. It may be necessary to model the traditional gesture of signing of the cross for young people.

The Lord's Prayer

▶ Show young people the orans posture used when the Lord's Prayer is prayed during the Eucharist. The orans posture is one where the forearms are extended with palms of the hands facing up.

Act of Contrition

▶ Go over the words of the prayer with young people.

Confiteor

▶ Remind young people that this prayer is sometimes used as part of the Penitential Act at Mass. The wording changed when we began to implement the English translation of the Third Edition of the Roman Missal in November 2011.

Prayer of Saint Francis of Assisi

Lord, make me an instrument of your peace.
Where there is hatred, let me show love;
where there is injury, pardon;
where there is doubt, faith;
where there is despair, hope;
where there is darkness, light;
and where there is sadness, joy.

O Divine Master, grant that I may not so much seek
to be consoled as to console;
to be understood as to understand;
to be loved as to love.
For it is in giving that we receive;
it is in pardoning that we are pardoned;
and it is in dying that we are born to eternal life.
Amen.

Prayer to the Holy Spirit

Come, Holy Spirit, fill the hearts of your faithful
And kindle in them the fire of your love.
Send forth your Spirit and they shall be created.
And you shall renew the face of the earth.

An Examination of Conscience

1. You prepare for the Sacrament of Reconciliation by thinking about the things you have done or not done. Think about how you have followed the Beatitudes, the Ten Commandments, and the Great Commandment.

2. Pray to the Holy Spirit to be with you as you think about your choices and actions.

3. Ask yourself:
   • Did I use God's name with respect?
   • Did I show my love for God and others in some way?
   • Did I usually say my daily prayers?
   • Did I always obey my mother and father?
   • Was I kind to those around me or was I mean?
   • Was I fair in the way that I played and worked with others?
   • Did I share my things with others?
   • Did I avoid taking what belongs to someone else?
   • Did I care for my own things and others' things?
   • Did I hurt others by calling them names or telling lies about them?
   • Did I go to Mass and take part in the celebration?

4. Pray for the Holy Spirit's help to change and follow Jesus' example of love.

Prayer of Saint Francis of Assisi

▶ We do not know the author of this prayer. Legend has it that the prayer was found in 1915 in Normandy, written on the back of a card of Saint Francis. But it certainly describes Saint Francis' mission to be an instrument of peace, reconciliation, and redemption in our fallen world.

▶ Go over the prayer with young people. Point out that it describes what it means to be a reconciler and peacemaker.

Prayer to the Holy Spirit

▶ Encourage young people to learn this prayer and to say it anytime they want to call upon the Holy Spirit for help but especially before examining their conscience.

Examination of Conscience

This page provides a sample format for an examination of conscience. Other helpful examples of questions may be found in the *Rite of Penance*, Appendix III.

▶ Review the steps for making an examination of conscience with young people.

▶ Remind young people that this is only an example to work from. Encourage them to make up their own questions for an examination of conscience based on the Ten Commandments, the Beatitudes, and the Precepts of the Church.

CALL to CELEBRATE

EUCHARIST

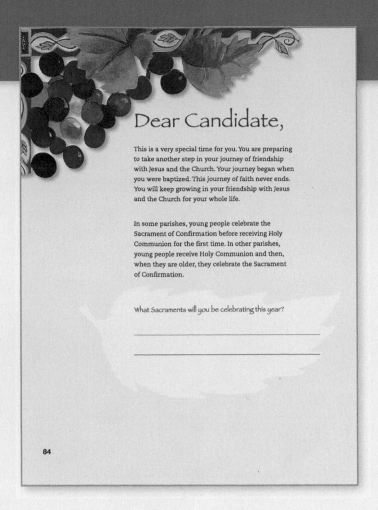

Dear Candidate,

This is a very special time for you. You are preparing to take another step in your journey of friendship with Jesus and the Church. Your journey began when you were baptized. This journey of faith never ends. You will keep growing in your friendship with Jesus and the Church for your whole life.

In some parishes, young people celebrate the Sacrament of Confirmation before receiving Holy Communion for the first time. In other parishes, young people receive Holy Communion and then, when they are older, they celebrate the Sacrament of Confirmation.

What Sacraments will you be celebrating this year?

_____

_____

84

Pages 84 and 85 provide a welcome to the program and the process of preparation.

Dear Candidate

▶ Read aloud the first paragraph.

▶ Discuss ways young people can continue their friendship with Jesus, such as praying, going to Mass, and being kind to others.

▶ Emphasize that when we receive Jesus in Holy Communion, he is very close to us, and going to Communion strengthens our friendship with him.

▶ Summarize the second paragraph.

▶ If your group will be celebrating Confirmation before First Communion or has already celebrated it, spend some time talking about what will or did happen.

▶ Note that all young people receive the Sacrament of Reconciliation before First Communion.

❓ Have young people write their answers in the book. Help them with spelling. Reconciliation, Eucharist (Confirmation, if appropriate)

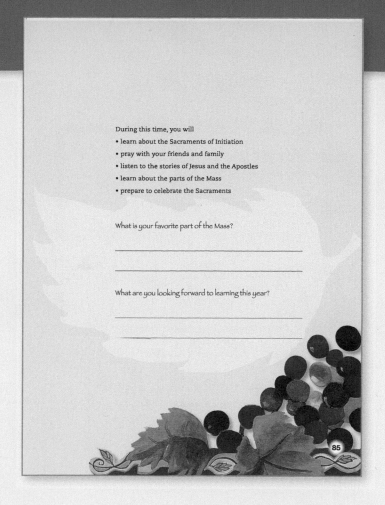

During this time, you will
• learn about the Sacraments of Initiation
• pray with your friends and family
• listen to the stories of Jesus and the Apostles
• learn about the parts of the Mass
• prepare to celebrate the Sacraments

What is your favorite part of the Mass?

_____

_____

What are you looking forward to learning this year?

_____

_____

85

Ask volunteers to read the bulleted text aloud.

Walk young people through the book and show them examples of prayer activities, stories of Jesus, and parts of the Mass.

? Have young people write their responses to the first question. Encourage volunteers to share their responses and the reason they chose that part.

? Read aloud the second question and write young people's responses on the board or on chart paper. Have young people go over the list and choose what they want to write in their books.

My Faith Journey

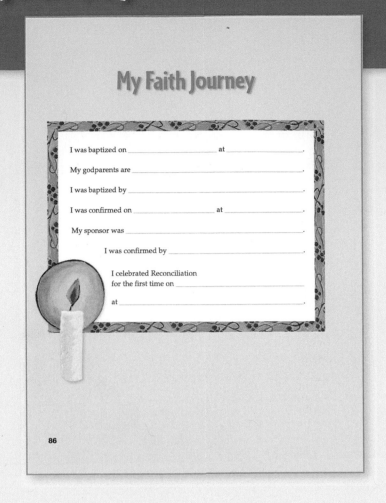

My Faith Journey

These pages in the *Candidate's Book* are meant to be filled in as the young people complete the process.

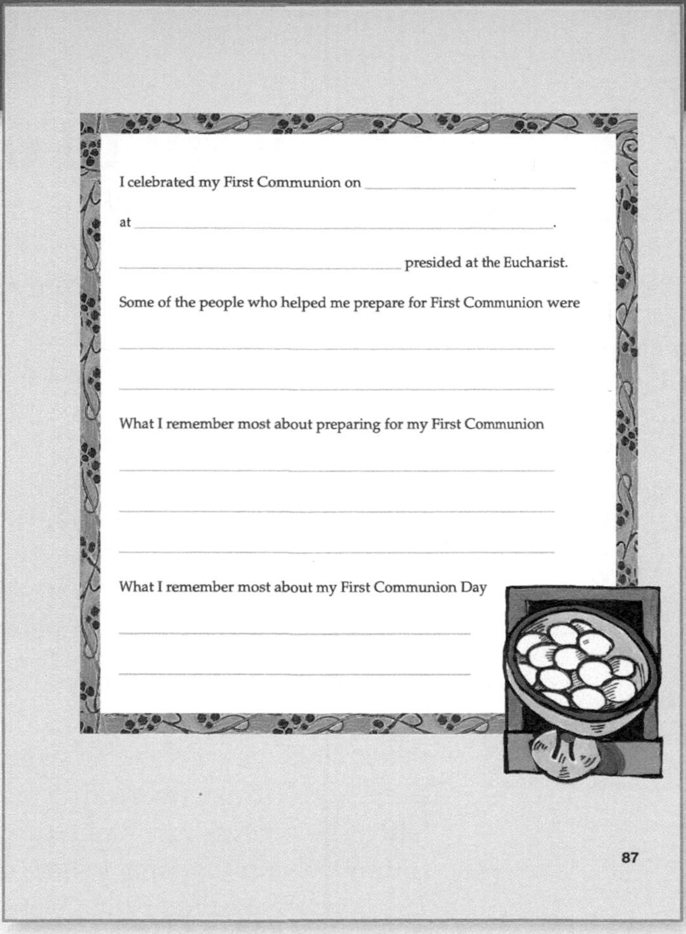

I celebrated my First Communion on _____

at _____ .

_____ presided at the Eucharist.

Some of the people who helped me prepare for First Communion were

_____

_____

What I remember most about preparing for my First Communion

_____

_____

_____

What I remember most about my First Communion Day

_____

_____

Encourage young people to take their books
home and have a family member help them
complete each assignment at the appropriate
time.

We Belong

CHAPTER 7

General Instruction of the Roman Missal

"In the celebration of Mass the faithful form a holy people, a people whom God has made his own, a royal priesthood,... Thus, they are to shun any appearance of individualism or division, keeping before their eyes that they have only one Father in heaven..." *(no. 95)*

Catechism Connection

To deepen your own background and reflection on the Sacraments of Initiation, refer to the *Catechism of the Catholic Church, 1212, 1275–1277, 1285, 1316–1317, 1321–1327.*

Catechist Resources

 The Church Speaks About Sacraments with Children: Baptism, Confirmation, Eucharist, Penance

Mark Searle, Commentator
Liturgy Training Publications

A collection of liturgical and catechetical documents that gives insight into the meaning of the sacrament

Young People's Resources

 Baptism: Sacrament of Belonging *(15 min)*

Franciscan Communications

Tells a story of an orphan boy's need for belonging to make parallels with Baptism

 Parables to Learn by: Based on Stories Told by Jesus

Bob Hartman
Pauline Books & Media, 2001

Updates the lessons told in Jesus' parables; includes Gospel text and questions that help young people apply the lessons in their own lives

Catechist Formation

"You are my friends if you do what I command you."

John 15:14

A Friendship of Faith

Airport terminals are frequently the scene of touching and happy reunions. Family and friends who have been separated for a period of time greet one another and feel a strong sense of belonging. Baptized persons share a similar sense of belonging with one another because they are united in Christ.

The Sacraments of Initiation—Baptism, Confirmation, and Eucharist—join us as members of the Body of Christ. In these sacraments we receive Christ and he receives us. Christians share with Christ, and with one another, a friendship of faith. The profession of faith made at Baptism expresses the common bond Christians share as members of Christ's Body. The deep love of the Father, Son, and Holy Spirit becomes part of the life of Christians when they are baptized in the name of the Trinity.

Sacraments of Initiation

As members of the Catholic family, we are never alone. We belong to Christ and his Church. At Baptism, we receive the Light of Christ to remind us that we are to be a light to the world as Christ is. The gifts of the Holy Spirit are strengthened in us at Confirmation. We are sealed, anointed, and marked as totally belonging to Christ. We are strengthened to show the love of Christ to the world and to send a message that all are invited to belong to God's family. In the Eucharist, we share the Body and Blood of Christ and celebrate this communion of belonging and friendship that helps us grow stronger as a family.

When you think of Jesus as a friend, what qualities come to mind?
Why is being part of a faith community important to you?

Catechist Prayer

God, our Father, draw me into the circle of love that you share with your Son and the Holy Spirit; help me express and celebrate that love with others. Amen.

Lesson Planner

GO online www.osvcurriculum.com
Visit our website for additional resources and information.

		OBJECTIVES	LESSON PROCESS	ACTIVITIES	MATERIALS
CELEBRATE	15 minutes Pages 88–89	Ritual Focus *Renewal of Baptismal Promises* To experience a celebration of the word, including the Renewal of Baptismal Promises	Celebrate the opening prayer.		PROGRAM RESOURCES *Songs of Celebration* CD, track 7 *And With Your Spirit* CD, track 6
	Pages 90–91	To explore the meaning of the ritual action To explain that through Baptism, we belong to God and the Church forever	Complete the activity. ✝ Read about and discuss water. Describe the Church as the Body of Christ, and discuss Baptism, the Holy Spirit, and Christian. ✝ Read about and discuss the Paschal candle.	☀ Reflect Young people reflect on the experience of the celebration and the meaning of renewing Baptismal Promises.	OTHER MATERIALS Bible, prayer table, candle, large glass bowl filled with water
REMEMBER	30 minutes Pages 92–93	Faith Focus *What does Jesus tell us about belonging to God?* To understand what it means to belong to God	Discuss the meaning of the vine and the branches. 📖 Proclaim the Gospel story. *John 15:1–12* Complete the activity.	☀ Share Young people draw pictures that show our connection to Jesus. ◢ Faith at Home Suggested activities for the home	PROGRAM RESOURCES Copies of Activity Master 7, p. CE7
	Pages 94–95	Faith Focus *Which sacraments are signs of belonging?* To describe the Sacraments of Initiation	Identify the Sacraments of Initiation Explain the terms , Baptism, , , chrism, Holy Communion. ✝ Read about and discuss the .	◢ Faith at Home Suggested activities for the home	
LIVE	15 minutes Page 96	To help young people express that they are followers of Christ	Introduce the activity. Pray the Closing Blessing. Read aloud the People of Faith story about Blessed Carlos Manuel Rodríguez.	☀ Respond Young people complete a list of ways to keep Baptismal Promises and choose one to practice.	PROGRAM RESOURCES *Songs of Celebration* CD, track 7
FAITH AT HOME	Page 97	◢ Faith at Home To introduce the different parts of the Faith at Home page	Review the Faith at Home page. Encourage young people to share this page at home.	☀ Act Suggested activities for the home	PROGRAM RESOURCES Eucharist Family Guide, pp.16–17

CELEBRATE

Objective

To experience a celebration of the word, including the Renewal of Baptismal Promises

Preparation

Familiarize yourself with the movements of the ritual focus for the Renewal of Baptismal Promises on pages 88–89. You will need:

- a Bible
- a table covered with a white cloth
- a candle and a large glass bowl filled with water on the prayer table
- Use the *Songs of Celebration* CD, track 7, to rehearse the suggested song, "Yes Lord, I Believe!" or one of the optional music suggestions on page 89.

Select a young person to carry the Bible in procession.

We Gather

Invite young people to assemble with their books for a procession.

- Direct them to follow you and the young person carrying the Bible.
- As you process, lead young people in singing using the *Songs of Celebration* CD, track 7.
- When all are assembled in the prayer space, light the prayer candle.
- Begin prayer, and lead young people in the Sign of the Cross.

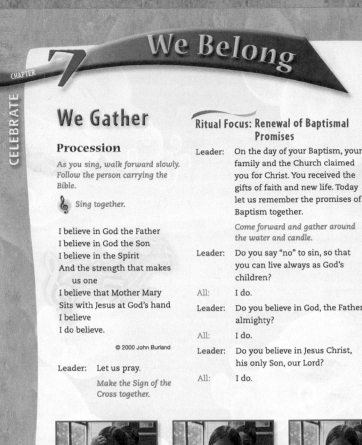

CHAPTER **7** We Belong

CELEBRATE

We Gather

Procession

As you sing, walk forward slowly. Follow the person carrying the Bible.

🎵 *Sing together.*

I believe in God the Father
I believe in God the Son
I believe in the Spirit
And the strength that makes us one
I believe that Mother Mary
Sits with Jesus at God's hand
I believe
I do believe.

© 2000 John Burland

Leader: Let us pray.

Make the Sign of the Cross together.

Ritual Focus: Renewal of Baptismal Promises

Leader: On the day of your Baptism, your family and the Church claimed you for Christ. You received the gifts of faith and new life. Today let us remember the promises of Baptism together.

Come forward and gather around the water and candle.

Leader: Do you say "no" to sin, so that you can live always as God's children?

All: I do.

Leader: Do you believe in God, the Father almighty?

All: I do.

Leader: Do you believe in Jesus Christ, his only Son, our Lord?

All: I do.

88

Liturgical Background

Baptismal Promises   Three questions make up the profession of faith in the Sacrament of Baptism and the Renewal of Baptismal Promises. The questions are derived from the three sections of the Apostles' Creed, which had its beginnings in the ancient baptismal liturgy. The questions for the profession of faith express our faith in the Father, Son, and Holy Spirit.

We consider this profession of faith to be a promise. It commits us to something in the future. When the profession of faith is made in Baptism, it implies that with God's help we will continue to believe and live according to the faith we have professed. The baptismal rite includes a rejection of sin before the profession of faith. The threefold rejection of sin parallels the threefold profession of faith.

Yes, I believe

Leader:	Do you believe in the Holy Spirit, the holy catholic Church, the communion of saints?
All:	I do.
Leader:	This is our faith. This is the faith of the Church. We are proud to profess it in Jesus Christ.
All:	Amen.

BASED ON RITE OF BAPTISM FOR CHILDREN, 144–146

| Leader: | Let us come to the water and thank God for the gift of our Baptism. |

One at a time, make the Sign of the Cross with the water.

| Leader: | [Name], you are the light of Christ. |
| Candidate: | Amen. |

We Listen

Leader:	God, our Father, open our hearts to the Holy Spirit as we remember our Baptism. We ask this through Jesus Christ our Lord.
All:	Amen.
Leader:	A reading from the holy Gospel according to John.
All:	Glory to you, O Lord.
Leader:	*Read John 15:1–17.* The Gospel of the Lord.
All:	Praise to you, Lord Jesus Christ.

Sit silently.

We Go Forth

| Leader: | Loving God, we thank you for the gift of Baptism. Send us forth to bring your love to others. We ask this through Jesus Christ our Lord. |
| All: | Amen. |

 Sing the opening song together.

89

Ritual Focus: Renewal of Baptismal Promises

- Follow the order of prayer on pages 88–89.

We Listen

For the proclamation of the Gospel, you may use a Bible or the adapted reading in the *Candidate's Book* on pages 92–93.

We Go Forth

- Lead the closing prayer.

- As the group processes back to their seats, have them sing *Songs of Celebration* CD, track 7, "Yes Lord, I Believe!" or one of the optional music suggestions.

Optional Music Suggestions:

"Pan de vida,"
© Jaime Cortez. Published by OCP

"Taste and See,"
James Moore © GIA Publications

✳ Ritual Background

Blessing with holy water Catholics make the Sign of the Cross with holy water when they enter and leave a church. The purpose of this gesture is to recall their identity as baptized Christians. The Sign of the Cross and the blessed water are a reminder that every person is solemnly signed with the cross and claimed for Christ in the Sacrament of Baptism.

Water is the central symbol of the Sacrament of Baptism. It signifies

- cleansing
- life
- rebirth
- God's grace

Every time we touch the blessed water, it is an opportunity to remember the mystery of God's life within us.

CELEBRATE

Objective

To explore the meaning of the ritual action of Renewal of Baptismal Promises

To explain that through Baptism, we belong to God and the Church forever

Liturgical Catechesis

The purpose of this section is to help young people reflect on their experience of the signs, rituals, prayers, and gestures of the celebration and to lead them to express their own meaning of the experiences. Allow young people to share their experiences without commenting on them.

New Life

- On the board or on chart paper, write the following questions: What did you see? What did you hear? What did you do?

- Guide young people to reflect on the celebration by reviewing what happened in the prayer.

- Encourage young people to share their responses to the questions.

- Invite young people to share stories or details they know about their own Baptism.

Reflect

- Explain the activity to the young people.

- Give young people time to work in pairs to discuss possible responses.

- Ask young people to write their own response in the book.

- Invite volunteers to share their responses.

Water

- Discuss the life-giving effects of water.

- Invite a young person to read the text aloud.

New Life

Water

Water gives life. It cleans and makes things like new. The water used at Baptism is blessed. The blessed water is a sign that God the Father gives us his life and cleanses us from all sin. Through the waters of Baptism, we have new life in Jesus. Every time we go into a church, we make the sign of the cross with holy water. We remember our Baptism.

90

Reflect

Renewal of baptismal promises Imagine that an unbaptized friend was watching as you renewed your baptismal promises and sent you this e-mail message. Write a response to explain.

Hey, what were you doing in that ceremony? Heard you say "I do," "I do," "I do." What ARE you DO - ING?

Additional Activity

Make a mural   Place a large sheet or sheets of paper in a location (such as on the floor, the wall, or tables) where young people can gather in a group or groups to draw.

- Discuss the many ways water and light help us in our daily life.

- Distribute crayons or markers.

- Invite young people to draw one way that water or light helps them.

When the mural is complete, help young people connect the meanings expressed in the mural to the symbols of water and light in Baptism.

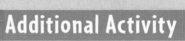

The Body of Christ

Baptism makes us children of God and members of the Church, the **Body of Christ**. At Baptism we are given new life with Jesus Christ. **Original Sin** and all personal sins are forgiven. At Baptism we receive the light of Christ and become his followers. People who follow Jesus are called disciples. Another name for a follower of Christ is *Christian*.

Baptism makes us members of the Church. When we are baptized we belong to the Church and become special friends of God. We need Baptism to have life with God forever. In Baptism God the Holy Spirit comes to live in us.

The Holy Spirit:

- helps us believe and have faith
- shows us how to pray
- guides us to be the light of Christ for others and makes us holy
- helps us follow God's law

SIGNS OF FAITH

Paschal Candle
Sometimes this candle is called the Easter candle. Every year at the Easter Vigil, a new candle is lit from the Easter fire. The deacon or priest carries it through the darkness. He sings, "Light of Christ," and the people sing, "Thanks be to God." The candle is lit at all the Masses during the Easter season and at all Baptisms and funerals. During Baptisms the priest or deacon lights the candles for those being baptized from the **Paschal candle**.

91

The Body of Christ

- Ask young people to read silently the first two paragraphs and underline or circle all the things that happen when we are baptized.
- Discuss the role of the Holy Spirit using the bulleted items.
- Ask young people to give examples of when the Holy Spirit might do these things.

Paschal Candle

- Invite several young people to read the text aloud.
- Point out the picture of the Paschal candle on this page.

Additional Activity

Explore Original Sin   Using the song and lyrics for "Incarnate One" (track 6) provided with the *And With Your Spirit* music CD, help your students explore the concept of Original Sin:

- Print each verse of "The Incarnate One" on a separate sheet of paper. Make the letters large enough that the young people can easily read the words from their desks.
- Tape verses across the board (or wall) in consecutive order.
- Provide paper and markers and have young people work in groups of two to illustrate one of these stories:
  - God makes the world
  - God makes Adam and Eve
  - Adam and Eve choose to eat from the tree
  - Mary and Baby Jesus
  - Jesus on the cross
- Attach pictures under the appropriate verses.
- Recount the story of salvation by reminding the young people that God made us to be with him forever. We chose sin. But God saved us from Original Sin by sending his Son (true God and true man) to save us.

And With Your **SPIRIT**
Songs for Deepening Children's Understanding of the Mass

JOHN BURLAND

REMEMBER

Objective

To understand what it means to belong to God

Faith Focus

What does Jesus tell us about belonging to God?

List young people's responses on the board or on chart paper.

We Belong to God

Call attention to the Scripture illustration. Point out that it illustrates the Gospel story from the celebration.

- Explain the natural relationship between a vine and a branch.

- Summarize the first paragraph of text.

- Remind the young people that we read the Bible today to remind us that we belong to God in a special way.

 Scripture   JOHN 15:1–12

The Vine and the Branches

- Gather the group into a story circle or in the prayer space. Remind them that they will be hearing the Gospel story from John again.

- Ask what they remember from hearing the Gospel during the celebration.

- Read the story aloud.

- Have volunteers explain the meaning of the story in their own words.

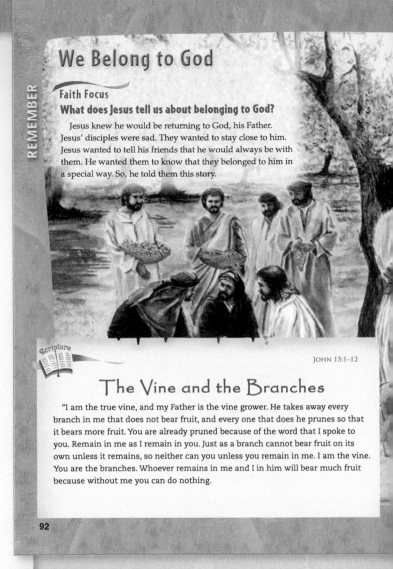

We Belong to God

Faith Focus

What does Jesus tell us about belonging to God?

Jesus knew he would be returning to God, his Father. Jesus' disciples were sad. They wanted to stay close to him. Jesus wanted to tell his friends that he would always be with them. He wanted them to know that they belonged to him in a special way. So, he told them this story.

Scripture   JOHN 15:1–12

The Vine and the Branches

"I am the true vine, and my Father is the vine grower. He takes away every branch in me that does not bear fruit, and every one that does he prunes so that it bears more fruit. You are already pruned because of the word that I spoke to you. Remain in me as I remain in you. Just as a branch cannot bear fruit on its own unless it remains, so neither can you unless you remain in me. I am the vine. You are the branches. Whoever remains in me and I in him will bear much fruit because without me you can do nothing.

92

Scripture Background

The Gospel of John   The Gospel according to John does not have the kinds of story parables that are in the Gospels of Matthew, Mark, and Luke. Instead, images such as the vine and the branches serve a similar purpose as the parables do in the other Gospels. In John, Jesus begins this speech with the words, "I am," identifying himself with images familiar to his disciples.

Elsewhere in the Gospel of John, Jesus says, "I am the bread of life," "I am the way and the truth and the life," and "I am the good shepherd."

The images are used to make a point and to challenge the listener to think beyond the ordinary.

"As the Father loves me, so I also love you. Remain in my love. If you keep my commandments, you will remain in my love. This is my commandment: love one another as I love you. No one has greater love than this, to lay down one's life for one's friends. You are my friends if you do what I command you. I have told you everything I have heard from my Father. You did not choose me. I chose you and appointed you to go forth and bear fruit that will remain, so that whatever you ask the Father in my name he may give you. This I command you: love one another."

BASED ON JOHN 15:1–17

Faith at Home

Read the Scripture story with your family members. Answer the questions and discuss everyone's responses. Decide one action you can take as a family to strengthen your friendship with Jesus.

 Name three things Jesus is telling his friends in this story.

 Describe your friendship with Jesus.

Share

Draw a picture With a partner think about and discuss other images, similar to the vine and branches, which could be used to show our connection to Jesus. Choose one of the images, and draw it on a large sheet of poster paper. Share your image with the whole group. Explain why it is similar to the vine and branches image.

93

? Ask the first question. Possible answers: They should bear fruit; they are his friends; if they love one another, they will stay close to him.

? Allow time for personal reflection on the second question. Have young people list words that describe their relationship with Jesus on a separate sheet of paper. Invite volunteers to share their words with the group. Accept all reasonable responses.

Share

- Divide young people into pairs.
- Explain the activity.
- Walk among the pairs, offering suggestions and supportive observations.
- Ask volunteers to share their pictures and explain the images.

Activity Master

You may wish to use Activity Master 7 on page CE7 to further integrate the meaning of the Gospel story.

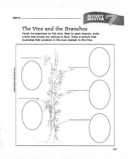

▲ Activity Master 7

Review

- We belong to God.
- Jesus commands us to love one another.

Farewell addresses The reading about the vine and the branches is part of a longer speech in John 14–17 sometimes described as the "Farewell Address." It was customary in Jewish tradition that at the time of his impending death, a father or leader would summon his heirs or disciples to review his legacy to them. In these farewell addresses, the speaker charges his heirs or disciples to carry on his life's mission and warns them of the dangers they will face in his absence. He cautions them to be faithful.

There are several examples of this tradition in the Scriptures. In the Old Testament, references are found for Jacob (*Genesis 49*), Moses (most of the *Book of Deuteronomy*), and Joshua (*Joshua 24*). In the New Testament, Jesus (*John 13–17*) is pictured as speaking about his death and what the disciples can expect after he is gone.

Objective

To describe the Sacraments of Initiation

Faith Focus

Which sacraments are signs of belonging? List young people's responses on the board or on chart paper.

The Sacraments of Initiation

- Point out that *initiation* means to join, or to become a member.
- Ask a volunteer to read the text aloud.

Baptism

- Ask the young people to recall the Baptismal promises made during the prayer service.
- As you read and discuss the major points in the text, make notes about Baptism on the board or on chart paper.

The Holy Trinity

- Write the words *Trinity, Creator,* and *Savior* on the board or on chart paper.
- Draw a triangle, shamrock, or other symbol of the Trinity. Have a volunteer explain why it is an appropriate symbol of the Trinity.
- Explain that the Holy Trinity is one of the mysteries of our faith. It is difficult for us to understand, but we must believe in it.

The Sacraments of Initiation

REMEMBER

SIGNS OF FAITH

The Holy Trinity
God the Father, God the Son, and God the Holy Spirit are the three Persons in one God. The three Persons act together in all they do, but each Person also has a special role. We sometimes call God the Father the Creator because he made everything. Jesus Christ is the Son of God and our Savior. God the Holy Spirit makes us holy. When we make the Sign of the Cross, we show our belief in the Trinity.

Faith Focus

Which Sacraments are signs of belonging?

A Sacrament is an effective sign that comes from Jesus and gives us grace, a share in God's life. Baptism, Confirmation, and Eucharist are called **Sacraments of Initiation**. We are joined closely to Christ and made full members of the Catholic Church through these Sacraments. They are signs that we belong to God and to the Church.

Baptism

In Baptism the priest or deacon pours water over our head three times or lowers us into the water three times. As he does this he says, "I baptize you in the name of the Father, and of the Son, and of the Holy Spirit." Then he rubs blessed oil on our heads. This is called an anointing. In Baptism we receive the Holy Spirit. We may only be baptized once. As a sign of our new life in Christ, we receive a white garment. Then the priest or deacon gives our parent or godparent a lighted candle as a sign of faith. He prays that we will walk as children of the light and follow Jesus' example.

94

✦ Catechist Background

Sacraments   A sacrament is an outward sign of an invisible reality—that is, something we cannot see. The invisible reality of a sacrament is God's presence and action. Here are important things to know about sacraments:

- Sacraments give grace, a sharing in God's own life and friendship.
- The sacraments are actions of God and the Church.
- God the Father, God the Son, and God the Holy Spirit are always at work in the sacraments.
- There are seven sacraments: three Sacraments of Initiation (Baptism, Confirmation, and Eucharist); two Sacraments of Healing (Reconciliation and Anointing); and two Sacraments at the Service of Communion (Holy Orders and Matrimony).

Confirmation

The Sacrament of **Confirmation** strengthens God's life in us. Confirmation completes our Baptism and helps us grow as followers of Jesus. In the Sacrament, the bishop or priest puts his hand out and prays:

"Send your Holy Spirit upon them to be their Helper and Guide."

Then the bishop or priest lays his hand on our heads and anoints us with the holy oil of **chrism**. Oil is a sign of strength. He says:

"Be sealed with the Gift of the Holy Spirit."

These words tell us that we receive the Holy Spirit in a special way during Confirmation. Both Baptism and Confirmation mark us with a special character that shows we belong to Jesus forever.

Eucharist

The Sacrament of the **Eucharist** joins us in a very special way to Jesus. It is a sacred meal of thanksgiving in which Jesus shares his own Body and Blood with us in Holy Communion.

You already participate in the Eucharist by coming to Mass with your family.

? In what ways are the Sacraments of Initiation signs of belonging?

Ask family members to share stories and pictures of your Baptism with you. Tell them about renewing your baptismal promises in the celebration. Show them your e-mail response on page 90. Invite family members to share anything they would add to your e-mail message.

95

Confirmation

Have several volunteers read the text aloud.

- Challenge students to find similarities between Baptism and Confirmation. Possibilities include: They are both Sacraments of Initiation, both involve anointing, and both mark us with a special character.

- Stress the role of the Holy Spirit in Confirmation.

Eucharist

As you read the information about the Eucharist aloud, summarize it.

- Emphasize that as young people get ready to receive Communion, they will be learning about Mass which is another name for the Eucharist.

? Invite volunteers to answer the question. They make us members of the Church.

Review

- Baptism, Confirmation, and Eucharist are the Sacraments of Initiation.

- These sacraments make us full members of the Church.

- These sacraments are signs that we belong to God.

✦ Sacrament Background

Initiation and Conversion   The process of initiation and the celebration of the Sacraments of Initiation have undergone a process of change and development over the centuries. The Acts of the Apostles documents deep and immediate conversions and baptisms (*Acts 2:14–41, 8:26–39*). Baptism marked a change of heart and conversion to a way of life that was lived in community. Later the process of initiation took on a more structured approach in the development of the baptismal catechumenate where those who were looking to become a Christian were apprenticed to the community for a period of time. They were baptized when they exhibited they were living for Christ. Inititation into the community took place with the celebration of Baptism, Confirmation, and Eucharist in one ceremony.

LIVE

Objective
To help young people express that they are followers of Christ

Children of Light

Respond

- Explain the activity and divide the group into smaller groups.
- Distribute pencils or other writing materials.
- Set a time limit.
- Invite volunteers to share their ideas.

Closing Blessing

- Gather the group in a prayer circle with their books.
- Begin with the Sign of the Cross.
- Read aloud the People of Faith story about Blessed Carlos Manuel Rodríguez.
- Pray the prayer.
- End with *Songs of Celebration* CD, track 7, "Yes Lord, I Believe!" or one of the optional music suggestions on page 89.

Children of Light

Respond

Brainstorm choices In a small group, brainstorm ways that young people can keep their baptismal promises and be children of the light. Jot down each of the ideas below. Choose one that you will promise to practice this week. Circle it.

_____

_____

_____

_____

_____

_____

_____

Closing Blessing

Gather and begin with the Sign of the Cross.

Leader: God, our Father, we praise and thank you for choosing us to be your children.

All: Amen.

Leader: Jesus, the Son, we praise and thank you for showing us how to live and love.

All: Amen.

Leader: Holy Spirit, giver of God's gifts, we praise and thank you for guiding us on our way.

All: Amen.

♪ *Sing together.*

I believe in God the Father
I believe in God the Son
I believe in the Spirit
And the strength that makes us one
I believe that Mother Mary
Sits with Jesus at God's hand
I believe
I do believe.

© 2000 John Burland

People of Faith: A Story

Blessed Carlos Manuel Rodríguez Blessed Carlos Manuel Rodríguez was born in Puerto Rico on November 22, 1918. His friends called him "Charlie." He wanted to help people do things to make the world more Christian. During his life he spent a lot of time gathering people into study groups. He thought it was important for all baptized people to be involved in spreading the faith. He also spent time translating English liturgy into Spanish so that the members of the Church in Puerto Rico could pray in their own language. Charlie's belief in the Resurrection of Jesus was very important to his life. Because of this, the Easter Vigil was an important celebration for him.

Faith at Home

Faith Focus

- A Sacrament is an effective sign that comes from Jesus and gives us grace.

- Baptism, Confirmation, and Eucharist are called Sacraments of Initiation.

- The Sacraments of Initiation make us full members of the Church.

Ritual Focus
Renewal of Baptismal Promises

The celebration focused on the renewal of baptismal promises. During the week, use the text on pages 88–89 with your family members and have them renew their baptismal promises with you.

Family Prayer

God our Father, thank you for making us your children. We believe in you and we belong to you. We ask you to keep us close to you. Show us how to love each other as you have loved us. Amen.

Act

Share Together Read John 15:1–17. Talk about what actions show we are friends of Jesus. Use a shoe box to create a "Friends of Jesus" box. Invite family members to look for examples of how others are acting as friends of Jesus. Have them write the examples on pieces of paper during the week and place them in the box. At the end of the week, read the slips of paper and share what you have learned.

Do Together Discuss what you and your family can do to help babies who are born into families that do not have money for food or clothing. Decide one thing you might do to help. (Suggestions: Buy baby food or diapers for a homeless shelter, or pray for these children at a specific time every day.)

GO online **www.osvcurriculum.com**
Visit our website for weekly Scripture readings and questions, family resources, and more activities.

97

Faith at Home

Review the five parts of the Faith at Home page with young people.

Encourage them:

- to ask family members to review the **Faith Focus** statements with them

- to share the **Ritual Focus: Renewal of Baptismal Promises** with family members

- to do at least one of the **Act** activities with family members

- to pray the **Family Prayer** with their family at times when the family is together

- to encourage their family members to go to **www.osvcurriculum.com** with them and do the activities for this chapter sometime during the week

Looking Ahead

For Chapter 8, you will need:

- a Bible

- a prayer table

- a candle

- a large glass bowl filled with water

- the *Songs of Celebration* CD

- copies of Activity Master 8 on p. CE8 for each young person

We Belong **97**

General Instruction of the Roman Missal

"Their purpose (the rites preceding the Liturgy of the Word) is to ensure that the faithful who come together as one establish communion and dispose themselves to listen properly to God's word and to celebrate the Eucharist worthily" (no.46).

Catechism Connection

To deepen your own background and reflection on the Introductory Rites, refer to the *Catechism of the Catholic Church, 1153, 1156–1158.*

Catechist Resources

The Breaking of the Bread: The Development of the Eucharist According to Acts

Eugene Laverdiere
Liturgical Training Publications

Presents an understanding of the Eucharist by examining the life of the early Church

Saving Signs, Wondrous Words

David Philippart
Liturgical Training Publications

Explains twenty-five words, actions, gestures, signs, and symbols of the liturgy in short essays

Young People's Resources

The First Christians: The Acts of the Apostles for Young people

Marigold Hunt
Sophia Institute Press, 2004

Describes the lives and times of the early Christians

Catechist Formation

> "For where two or three are gathered in my name, I am there among them."
>
> Matthew 18:20

The Importance of Gathering

The difference between an anonymous crowd on a street and sports fans in a football stadium is that the sports fans are gathered with a common purpose: to cheer on their team. Similarly, when Catholics gather for Mass, they gather as one family who shares a common faith and purpose.

The purpose of the entrance song is twofold: "to foster the unity of those who have been gathered" and "to introduce their thoughts to the mystery of the liturgical season or festivity" (*General Instruction of the Roman Missal, 47*). The procession expresses that we are a "pilgrim people."

The opening prayer of the Mass is called the collect. The priest gathers together or collects the petitions of the community and offers them to God. The prayer also prepares people to listen attentively to God's word and to give thanks to God for all that he has accomplished throughout history.

The Presence of Christ

The gathering of the assembly at Mass is one of the signs that Christ is truly present. This presence of Christ is also seen in the priest who presides, the word proclaimed, and, most especially, in the consecrated bread and wine, which is the Body and Blood of Jesus. By gathering as the Body of Christ, the members of the assembly are strengthened to live faithfully following the examples of the Christian communiti (*Acts 2:42–47*).

What signs do you see in your parish that the community is truly gathering as one?

What role do you have in helping the community to gather for prayer?

Catechist Prayer

Holy God, lead me to be one with my brothers and sisters in May our gatherings of prayer help me see you in our midst. A

Lesson Planner

GO online www.osvcurriculum.com
Visit our website for additional resources and information.

	OBJECTIVES	LESSON PROCESS	ACTIVITIES	MATERIALS
CELEBRATE 15 minutes Pages 98–99	**Ritual Focus** *Procession and Gloria* To experience a celebration of the word, including a Procession and the singing of the Gloria	Celebrate the opening prayer.		**PROGRAM RESOURCES** *Songs of Celebration* CD, track 8 *And With Your Spirit* CD, track 3
Pages 100–101	To explore the meaning of the ritual actions To teach about the ways the community comes together and prays during the Mass	Complete the activity. ✝ Read about and discuss the role of the assembly. Read about and discuss gathering for worship and forms of prayer within the Mass. ✝ Describe how processions are part of our worship.	☀ Reflect Young people reflect on the experience of the celebration by writing a rhyming poem.	**OTHER MATERIALS** Bible, prayer table, candle, large glass bowl filled with water
REMEMBER 30 minutes Pages 102–103	**Faith Focus** *What is a community of faith?* To understand the qualities of a community of faith	Discuss why we are a community of faith. 📖 Proclaim the Scripture/Bible story. *Acts 2:42–47* Complete the activity.	☀ Share Partners perform a pantomime. ✎ Faith at Home Suggested activities for the home	**PROGRAM RESOURCES** Copies of Activity Master 8, p. CE8 *And With Your Spirit* CD, track 3
Pages 104–105	**Faith Focus** *What happens when we gather as a community of faith?* To describe the Introductory Rites	Examine why we worship together. Discuss the importance of the Introductory Rites. ✝ Read about and discuss the importance of prayer and singing.	✎ Faith at Home Suggested activities for the home	
LIVE 15 minutes Page 106	To choose ways of praising God	Introduce the activity. Pray the Closing Blessing. Read aloud the People of Faith story about Sister Thea Bowman.	☀ Respond Young people write letters to God.	**PROGRAM RESOURCES** *Songs of Celebration* CD, track 8
FAITH AT HOME Page 107	✎ Faith at Home To introduce the different parts of the Faith at Home page	Review the Faith at Home page. Encourage young people to share this page at home.	☀ Act Suggested activities for the home	**PROGRAM RESOURCES** Eucharist Family Guide, pp. 18–19

CELEBRATE

Objective

To experience a celebration of the word, including a Procession and the singing of the Gloria

Preparation

Familiarize yourself with the movements of the ritual focus for the Procession and Gloria on pages 98–99.

Prepare the prayer space ahead of time. You will need:

- a Bible
- a table covered with a white cloth
- a candle and a large glass bowl filled with water on the prayer table
- Go to www.osvcurriculum.com for a Gloria that reflects the revised Roman Missal wording: "Glory to God," © 2007, 2009 Daniel L. Schutte. Published by OCP. Rehearse the suggested song, "Glory to God," or the optional music suggestion on page 99.

Select a young person to carry the Bible in procession.

We Gather

Invite young people to assemble with their books for a procession.

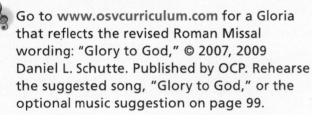

Ritual Focus: Procession and Gloria

- Direct young people to follow you and the young person carrying the Bible.
- As you process, lead them in singing "Glory to God," noted above.
- When all are assembled in the prayer space, light the prayer candle.
- Begin prayer, and lead young people in the Sign of the Cross.

Follow the order of prayer on pages 98–99.

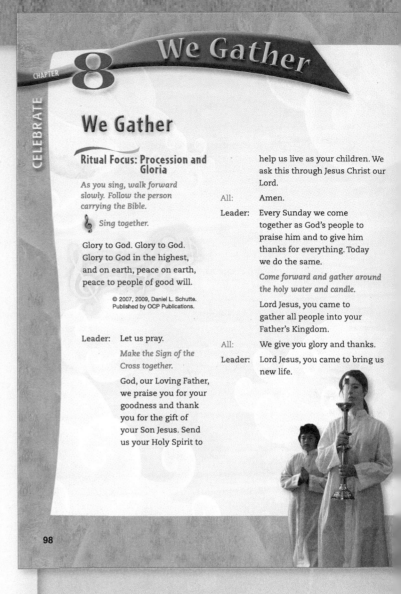

CELEBRATE

CHAPTER **8** We Gather

We Gather

Ritual Focus: Procession and Gloria

As you sing, walk forward slowly. Follow the person carrying the Bible.

Sing together.

Glory to God. Glory to God. Glory to God in the highest, and on earth, peace on earth, peace to people of good will.

© 2007, 2009, Daniel L. Schutte. Published by OCP Publications.

Leader: Let us pray.
Make the Sign of the Cross together.
God, our Loving Father, we praise you for your goodness and thank you for the gift of your Son Jesus. Send us your Holy Spirit to help us live as your children. We ask this through Jesus Christ our Lord.

All: Amen.

Leader: Every Sunday we come together as God's people to praise him and to give him thanks for everything. Today we do the same.
Come forward and gather around the holy water and candle.
Lord Jesus, you came to gather all people into your Father's Kingdom.

All: We give you glory and thanks.

Leader: Lord Jesus, you came to bring us new life.

98

✦ Liturgical Background

The Gloria The first historical record of the Gloria is found in Greek and Syrian sources. It began as an Easter hymn, which became a regular part of Morning Prayer in the Eastern churches.

The Eastern churches were those that looked to Constantinople rather than Rome as their center. Churches that looked to Rome as their center are called the Western churches.

In the sixth century the Gloria entered the Roman Rite. Only the bishops sang it as they presided on Sundays and at the feasts of martyrs. However, priests sang the Gloria at the Easter Vigil. It was not until the eleventh century that the Gloria became a regular part of the Sunday liturgy for all.

It remains a regular part of the liturgy today. The Gloria, which has a revised English translation in the Third Edition of the *Roman Missal*, is sung only on Sundays, solemnities, and special feasts, except in Advent and Lent.

All: We give you glory and thanks.

Leader: Lord Jesus, you came to save us.

All: We give you glory and thanks.

Leader: Let us give thanks and praise.

🎵 *Sing the opening song together.*

We Listen

Leader: God, our Father, you alone are holy. You give us life and all good things. We ask you to help us be grateful children who always remember your glory. We ask this through Jesus Christ our Lord.

All: Amen.

Leader: A reading from the Acts of the Apostles.

Read Acts 2:42–47.

The word of the Lord.

All: Thanks be to God.

Sit silently.

We Go Forth

Leader: God, the Holy Spirit, we praise you and thank you for your gifts. May we act in ways that show your gifts to others. We ask this through Jesus Christ our Lord.

All: Amen.

 🎵 *Sing the opening song together.*

99

We Listen

For the proclamation of the Scripture, you may use a Bible or the adapted reading in the *Candidate's Book* on pages 102–103.

We Go Forth

- Lead the closing prayer.

🎵 As the group processes back to their seats, have them sing the "Glory to God," or the optional music suggestion.

Optional Music Suggestion:

"Pan de vida,"
© Jaime Cortez. Published by OCP

✳ Ritual Background

Sung parts of the Mass   Some parts of the liturgy are intended to be sung by the people. The Church does not consider singing at the liturgy to be only for those who have special musical talents, but rather it is a profound way for the entire people to express their prayer.

Singing fosters communal prayer and raises the heart to God. According to Saint Augustine, "Singing is for one who loves." There is a difference between singing songs and hymns at Mass and singing the parts of the Mass.

Although both are important, the Church gives greater priority to singing the parts of the Mass, such as the Gloria; the Gospel Acclamation; the Holy, Holy, Holy; the Mystery of Faith; the Amen that concludes the Eucharistic Prayer; and the Lamb of God *(Agnus Dei)*. By singing, we intensify our participation in the Eucharist.

CELEBRATE

Objective

To explore the meaning of the ritual actions of procession and the singing of the Gloria

To teach about the ways the community comes together and prays during the Mass

Liturgical Catechesis

The purpose of this section is to help young people reflect on their experiences of the signs, rituals, prayers, and gestures of the celebration and to lead them to express their own meaning of the experiences. Allow young people to share their experiences without commenting on them.

Gathered Together

- On the board or on chart paper, write the following questions: What did you see? What did you hear? What did you do?

- Guide young people to reflect on the celebration by reviewing what happened in the prayer.

- Encourage young people to share their responses to the questions.

Reflect

- Read the directions and give some examples of a rhyme.

- Walk among the group to offer assistance.

- Invite volunteers to share their rhymes with the group.

Assembly

- Read aloud the text.

- Talk about the different times people come together.

- Ask young people to name what happens when people come together. They are friendly; they do things together.

- Point out that when we come together as people who believe in Jesus, we do many of the same things.

Gathered Together

Assembly

Many different people come together at Mass. Each person comes to praise and give thanks to God and to ask for his blessing. When we gather together to give God thanks and praise, we are an **assembly** of people who believe in Jesus. When the assembly gathers, the Holy Trinity is there.

Reflect

Procession and Gloria Write a rhyming poem about ways you gather with friends. Include ways you gather at church.

_____
_____
_____
_____
_____
_____
_____
_____
_____
_____
_____
_____

100

Additional Activity

Write a cinquain Explain to young people that a cinquain is a poem made up of five lines. Together with young people, write a cinquain about: the Gloria or the procession.

- Prepare a large sheet of paper or a space on the board.

- Mark off five lines.

- On the first line, write a one-word title.

- Ask young people for two descriptive words about the title, and place them on the second line.

- Repeat the process for three action words about the title. Place them on the third line.

- Repeat the process for a four-word phrase about the subject. Place it on the fourth line.

- Repeat the process for one or two words that describe the title. Place them on the fifth line.

Have young people recite the cinquain together.

We Come Together

Every time we gather as a group, we come together to pray. When we begin to form the procession for our celebration, we are gathering for prayer. **Prayer** is talking and listening to God. The procession gathers us as a community ready for prayer.

During the Mass, we pray in many different ways. When we stand, we pray a prayer of reverence. Prayers can be said. We can say the Lord Have Mercy (*Kyrie, eleison*). We can ask for God's help. Prayers can be sung. We can sing the Gloria in Mass. We pray in silence during the Mass, too. One time we do this is during the silence after the Gospel reading.

SIGNS OF FAITH

Procession

A **procession** is a group of people moving forward as part of a celebration. Processions at Mass remind us that we are walking forward with God and that God is walking with us. At Mass the priest and other ministers come into the church in a procession. People bring the gifts to the altar in a procession. We walk in a procession to receive Jesus in Holy Communion.

101

We Come Together

- Write the word *prayer* on the board or on chart paper.
- Ask young people to define prayer in their own words.
- Summarize the first paragraph.
- Have young people read the second paragraph silently to identify the different ways we pray at Mass.
- Point out that the gesture of standing and silence are forms of prayer.

✠ Procession

- Invite a young person to read the text aloud.
- Identify the different processions that occur during the Mass.
- Invite young people to pay attention to the processions during Sunday Mass.

Teaching Tip

Greeting in the classroom Use the Introductory Rites as a model for greeting young people as they arrive. Arrive early and stand by the door. As young people enter the classroom, try to engage them by:

- greeting them as individuals
- giving them time to greet one another
- asking them to assist you with preparing the room for class
- having a gathering activity prepared
- clearly showing when class is beginning with a special gesture or phrase

Objective

To understand the qualities of a community of faith

Faith Focus

What is a community of faith?
List young people's responses on the board or on chart paper.

We Gather as God's People

- Ask a volunteer to define the word *community*. Discuss with the group the different communities to which they belong.

- Invite the group to list similarities and differences between the early Christian gatherings and our gatherings today. Use a Venn diagram to record responses on the board or on chart paper.

- As you summarize the text, emphasize that early Christians were drawn together because of their faith in Jesus.

 Scripture   ACTS 2:42–47

The Early Christians

- Gather the group into a story circle or in the prayer space. Remind them that they will be hearing the Scripture story from Acts again.

- Ask what they remember from hearing the story during the celebration.

- Read the scripture story aloud.

- Pause occasionally during the story, asking young people to connect the images in the illustrations with the ideas in the story.

- Invite young people to speculate on why others would join the Christians every day. Possible responses: because others saw how happy the Christians were, because others came to have faith in Jesus.

REMEMBER

We Gather as God's People

Faith Focus
What is a community of faith?

The early followers of Jesus gathered often to pray and to remember him. They were like a family. Their faith in Jesus made them a community of faith.

ACTS 2:42–47

The Early Christians

The early Christian community gathered together over and over again. They devoted themselves to the teaching of the Apostles and to the communal life, to the breaking of the bread and to prayers. Awe came upon everyone, and many wonders and signs were done through the Apostles. All who believed were together and had all things in common; they would sell their property and possessions and divide among all according to each one's need.

102

Scripture Background

Breaking of the Bread   The reading in Acts describes the relationships and life of the early Christian community. The description of the early Christians gathering together in their homes for the "breaking of the bread" shows that they wanted to remain faithful to Jesus' command "Do this in memory of me" and the importance of Sunday as "the first day of the week."

According to Luke (*Luke 24:35; Acts 2:42; 20:11*), the Christians called this meal the "breaking of the bread." Paul refers to this celebration as the "Lord's Supper" (*1 Cor. 11:20*) and warns the Christians in Corinth not to let their household gatherings for food and drink do "more harm than good." He reminds them that the reason for their gathering was primarily to observe the Lord's Supper in memory of what Jesus did the night before he died. From then until now we continue to celebrate the Sacrament of the Eucharist throughout the whole Church with the same fundamental structure.

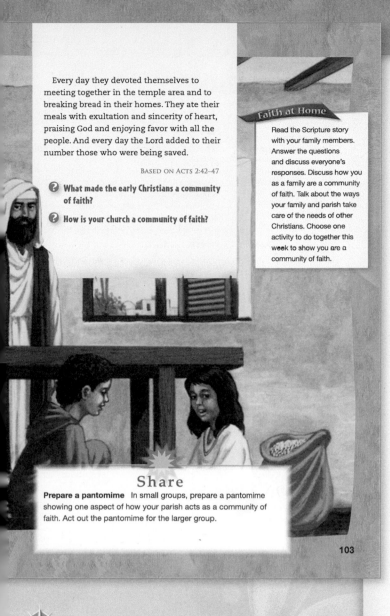

Every day they devoted themselves to meeting together in the temple area and to breaking bread in their homes. They ate their meals with exultation and sincerity of heart, praising God and enjoying favor with all the people. And every day the Lord added to their number those who were being saved.

BASED ON ACTS 2:42–47

❓ What made the early Christians a community of faith?

❓ How is your church a community of faith?

Faith at Home

Read the Scripture story with your family members. Answer the questions and discuss everyone's responses. Discuss how you as a family are a community of faith. Talk about the ways your family and parish take care of the needs of other Christians. Choose one activity to do together this week to show you are a community of faith.

Share

Prepare a pantomime In small groups, prepare a pantomime showing one aspect of how your parish acts as a community of faith. Act out the pantomime for the larger group.

103

❓ Invite volunteers from the group to answer the question. They believed in Jesus.

❓ Have young people work in small groups to answer the second question. Accept all reasonable responses.

Share

- Invite young people to use their answer to the second question as a starting place for their pantomime.

- Walk among the groups to offer assistance.

- Encourage each group to perform in front of the larger group.

Activity Master

You may wish to use Activity Master 8 on page CE8 to further intergrate the meaning of the Gospel story.

▲ Activity Master 8

Review

- Early Christians met in communities of faith.
- We belong to a community of faith.

✦ Cultural Background

Separation In the society of Jesus' day, only people of the same social status shared meals with one another. Men ate separately from women, freedmen separated from slaves, Jews from Gentiles, rich from poor. Even the food that they ate distinguished social classes.

Paul emphasizes that there ought not to exist among Christians the divisions that ordinary society tolerated and sometimes even encouraged (*1 Corinthians 11:17–34*).

- Christians represented a whole new society, different from anything previously known.

- In the "new creation" called the Church, all are one "in Christ." There is neither "Jew nor Greek, there is no longer slave or free, there is no longer male and female" (*Galatians 3:28*).

- Such distinctions were not to characterize Christians or Christian assemblies.

Objective

To describe the Introductory Rites

Faith Focus

What happens when we gather as a community of faith?
List young people's responses on the board or on chart paper.

The People Gather

- Ask volunteers to read the text aloud.

- Emphasize the reasons for worshiping as a community each Sunday.

- Have young people recall what happens when we gather for Mass. We greet one another, sing, and pray.

- Recall that the celebration at the beginning of the session began with a procession. Point out that our Saturday night or Sunday Masses begin with a procession, too.

✠ Prayer and Singing

- Read aloud the text.

- Discuss the meaning of singing at celebrations such as birthday and Christmas parties. Invite volunteers to mention other times that they sing with family or friends.

- Consider passing out hymnals for young people to appreciate the range of choices available to music ministers.

- You may also want to invite your music minister to talk about how music is chosen for Mass, or invite young people to participate in a young people's choir, if your parish has one.

REMEMBER

The People Gather

✠ Prayer and Singing

Singing is a way to pray. When we sing during Mass, we lift our minds, hearts, and voices to praise God in a special way. The whole assembly sings songs and hymns. Sometimes the choir sings and the assembly listens. The priest sometimes sings parts of the Mass.

Faith Focus

What happens when we gather as a community of faith?

Like the first Christians, we celebrate the Eucharist with a community, too. Our faith community is our Church family. During Mass we come together as the Body of Christ. Every Sunday or Saturday evening we gather with our parish community for the celebration of Mass.

Sunday is an important day for Christians because Jesus rose from the dead on Easter Sunday. It is so important that the Church requires us to participate in Sunday Mass.

We come together as an assembly
- to give God thanks and praise
- to listen to God's word
- to remember Jesus' death, Resurrection, and Ascension
- to share the Lord's Body and Blood
- to be sent forth to live as Jesus' followers

When we gather for Mass, we greet one another. We share our joy as we sing and pray.

104

✦ Additional Activity

Filled with Praise Use the song and lyrics for "When We Praise You" (track 3) provided with the *And With Your Spirit* music CD to help your students understand the actions behind the words praise, adore, glory, and bless, and how they help us honor God:

- Read through each verse separately, explaining:

Praise:	When we acknowledge God for who he is, even beyond what he does.
Adore:	When we acknowledge, with wonder and awe, God as Creator.
Glory:	When we honor God through our words and actions.
Bless:	When we recognize that God has first blessed us, blessing him acknowledges him as source of all things.

Introductory Rites

The prayers and actions that begin the Mass are called the Introductory Rites. The Introductory Rites help us turn our hearts and minds to the great celebration of the Eucharist. The priest leads the assembly in the celebration of the Mass. Mass begins when he walks in procession to the altar. All of us in the assembly stand and sing.

The priest greets us. He often says, "The Lord be with you," or similar words. We answer, "And with your spirit." We know that God the Father, his Son Jesus, and the Holy Spirit are with us. We believe Jesus is present in every part of the Mass. Together we thank God for his goodness.

Faith at Home

Ask your family members how they would answer the question. Discuss their responses. Invite them to tell which of the songs sung during Mass are their favorites. Sing some of them together. If you have the *Songs of Celebration* CD for this program, spend some time listening to the songs.

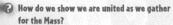 How do we show we are united as we gather for the Mass?

105

Introductory Rites

Write *Introductory Rites* on the board or on chart paper. Explain that this is the term for the actions at the beginning of Mass.

- Point out that the word *Introductory* means "beginning" and *Rites* are "official prayers of the Church."

- Emphasize that God is with us as we begin to worship.

❓ Invite volunteers to answer the question. We stand and sing, we greet one another, we pray together.

Review
- The Introductory Rites begin the Mass.
- We pray and sing together as Mass begins.

✴ Sacrament Background

Structure of the Mass   Roman Catholic worship has its roots in Judaism and the New Testament. From earliest times the focus of liturgy was the assembly gathering to remember the celebration of Jesus' Last Supper. These gatherings always had some structure but not as formal a structure as we experience today.

Over the centuries the Mass developed different forms and was affected by the architecture of churches and the influx of different cultures.

In the sixteenth century the Council of Trent revised the Roman liturgy and made it uniform for the whole Western Church. The structure of the Mass, which developed from this reform, was maintained until the Second Vatican Council (1962), which called for a renewal of all the rites of the Church. Some of the changes in the Mass included the priest facing the people, more participation of the people, the use of vernacular language, and a renewed emphasis on Scripture.

The revised *Roman Missal* changes introduced in 2011 reflect the wording of the Third Edition of the *Roman Missal* in Latin (2002).

LIVE

Objective
To choose ways of praising God

Give Praise and Thanks

Respond

- Explain the activity.
- Distribute paper and writing implements.
- Set a time limit; young people who finish early may decorate their letters.
- Invite volunteers to post their letters on a bulletin board.

Closing Blessing

- Gather the group in a prayer circle with their books.
- Begin with the Sign of the Cross.
- Read aloud the People of Faith story about Sister Thea Bowman.
- Pray the prayer.
- End with the "Glory to God," available at **www.osvcurriculum.com** or the optional music suggestion on page 99.

Give Praise and Thanks

LIVE

Respond

Write a letter In the space below, write a letter to God. In the letter tell how you will give him praise and thanks during the week.

_____
_____
_____
_____
_____
_____
_____
_____
_____
_____

Closing Blessing

Gather and begin with the Sign of the Cross.

Leader: God, our Father, we praise and thank you for gathering us as your children. Send us your Holy Spirit to increase our faith and make our community strong. We ask this in the name of Jesus Christ our Lord.

All: Amen.

Leader: Go in peace.

All: Thanks be to God.

Sing together.

Glory to God. Glory to God. Glory to God in the highest, and on earth, peace on earth, peace to people of good will.

© 2007, 2009, Daniel L. Schutte. Published by OCP Publications.

106

People of Faith: A Story

Sister Thea Bowman   Thea was born in Canton, Mississippi. Her grandfather was a slave, and her father was a doctor. She was the first African American woman to receive her doctorate in theology from Boston College. Using song, dance, poetry, and stories, Sister Thea helped African American Catholics, both children and adults, plan celebrations of the Mass that expressed the life, joy, and story of their culture.

1937–1990

Faith Focus

- The Church is the People of God and the Body of Christ.

- The Eucharist, or Mass, is the Church's most important action of praise and thanks.

- The Introductory Rites gather us as a community of faith.

Ritual Focus
Procession and Gloria

The celebration focused on the Procession and Gloria. You sang the Gloria and prayed a litany of glory and praise to God. During the week, pray and talk about the meaning of the verses of the Gloria found on page 98.

Family Prayer

Loving God, we are your people. Thank you for the gift of faith. Help us to grow closer as a family. Strengthen our faith in you. Amen.

Act

Share Together Read Acts 2:42–47. Talk about what it must have been like for the early Christians to live as a community of faith. Emphasize the sharing of their possessions and their prayer life. With your family members, choose one way your family can continue to live as a community of faith, such as going to Mass or sharing your time and talent with others.

Do Together Together with your family members make a list of all the things you want to thank God for. Read the list as a litany. One person prays, "For sun and rain," and everyone responds, "We thank you, God." During the weeks ahead, select appropriate times to pray this thanksgiving prayer with your family or by yourself.

Litany

GO online **www.osvcurriculum.com**
Visit our website for weekly Scripture readings and questions, family resources, and more activities.

107

Faith at Home

Review the five parts of the Faith at Home page with young people.

Encourage them:

- to ask family members to review the Faith Focus statements with them

- to share the Ritual Focus: Procession and Gloria with family members

- to do at least one of the ✸ Act activities with family members

- to pray the Family Prayer with their family at times when the family is together

- to encourage their family members to go to www.osvcurriculum.com with them and do the activities for this chapter sometime during the week

Looking Ahead

For Chapter 9, you will need:

- a Bible

- a prayer table

- a candle

- a large glass bowl filled with water

- the *Songs of Celebration* CD

- copies of Activity Master 9 on p. CE9 for each young person

General Instruction of the Roman Missal

"Then the priest invites those present to take part in the Act of Penitence, which, after a brief pause for silence, the entire community carries out through a formula of general confession. The rite concludes with the priest's absolution, which, however, lacks the efficacy of the Sacrament of Penance..." (no.51).

Catechism Connection

To deepen your own background and reflection on the Entrance Rites, refer to the *Catechism of the Catholic Church*, 1153, 1156–1158.

Catechist Resources

A Eucharist Sourcebook

J. Robert Baker and Barbara Budde
Liturgical Training Publications

Gathers poetry and prose, hymns, and prayers for a reflection on the Eucharist

We Shall Go Up with Joy: The Entrance Rite
(30 min)

Liturgical Training Publications
Shows how the Entrance Rite unifies a community as the liturgy begins

Young People's Resources

I Meet Jesus: He Tells Me "I Love You"

Jean Vanier
Paulist Press, 1981

The message of Christianity is simply taught in a way that will appeal to young people and adults

Pope John Paul II Breaking Barriers

Jill C. Wheeler
Abdo & Daughters Publishing

Tells the story of the Pope's life from his childhood to his papacy

Catechist Formation

> "... I desire mercy, not sacrifice.' For I have come to call not the righteous but sinners."
>
> Matthew 9:13

Penitential Act: Ritual of Unity

Most people have had experiences when things are just not right between them and another person. It may be something as trivial as the way the other person uses a tube of toothpaste, or as serious as a betrayal of trust. Whatever the cause, the relationship is disrupted. But then something happens—an unexpected kind word, or a tragedy and a sense of shared humanity, and unity is recovered.

Whenever a community gathers for the Eucharist, the members share the need for God's mercy and love. We are a Church of sinners, and we know it. We come to the Eucharist with a sense of our imperfection. We know that in our human condition, we are in need of God's grace and help—in need of having things right again with God and one another.

God's Mercy

The Introductory Rites of the Mass include the Penitential Act, during which the assembly joins in a general confession and to ask for God's mercy. The whole assembly recalls that God is a loving God who constantly extends to us his mercy and salvation and who unites us. The primary focus of the Penitential Act is upon God's gift of mercy, not upon human sinfulness. We confess our sinfulness knowing that the Lord is merciful. This belief and realization unites us as an assembly.

What comes to mind when you realize you are not alone as a sinner? How does the assurance of God's forgiveness help you?

Catechist Prayer

Merciful Lord, look kindly upon me, especially when I fail. Unite me with all my brothers and sisters. May your compassion strengthen me to follow the path of Jesus Christ with devotion and hope. Amen.

Lesson Planner

GO online www.osvcurriculum.com
Visit our website for additional resources and information.

		OBJECTIVES	LESSON PROCESS	ACTIVITIES	MATERIALS
CELEBRATE	15 minutes — Pages 108–109	Ritual Focus *Penitential Act* — To experience a celebration of the word, including the Penitential Act	Celebrate the opening prayer.		PROGRAM RESOURCES *Songs of Celebration* CD, track 9 — *And With Your Spirit* CD, track 2
	Pages 110–111	To explore the meaning of the ritual actions — To teach the relationship between forgiveness and unity	Complete the activity. — ✝ Read about and discuss the Penitential Act, including the Lord Have Mercy (*Kyrie, eleison*). — ✝ Describe unity. — Read about and discuss silence.	☀ Reflect — Young people reflect on the experience of the celebration and the meaning of the Confiteor.	OTHER MATERIALS Bible, prayer table, candle, large glass bowl filled with water
REMEMBER	30 minutes — Pages 112–113	Faith Focus *Why did Jesus eat with sinners?* — To explain that Jesus is a friend to sinners	Discuss Jesus' attitude toward sinners. — 📖 Proclaim the Gospel story. *Matthew 9:9–13* — Complete the activity.	☀ Share — Young people participate in a role-playing activity. — Faith at Home — Suggested activities for the home	OTHER MATERIALS Large glass bowl filled with water, small branch — PROGRAM RESOURCES Copies of Activity Master 9, p. CE9
	Pages 114–115	Faith Focus *What happens during the Penitential Act?* — To explain why we pray for forgiveness at Mass	Identify reasons for asking forgiveness. — ✝ Read about and discuss sprinkling with holy water. — Examine the Penitential Act and Confiteor.	Faith at Home — Suggested activities for the home	
LIVE	15 minutes — Page 116	To integrate and review signs and prayers of forgiveness	Introduce the activity. — Pray the Closing Blessing. — Read aloud the People of Faith story about Pope Saint John Paul II.	☀ Respond — Young people make a bulletin board about forgiveness at Mass.	PROGRAM RESOURCES *Songs of Celebration* CD, track 9
FAITH AT HOME	Page 117	Faith at Home — To introduce the different parts of the Faith at Home page	Review the Faith at Home page. — Encourage young people to share this page at home.	☀ Act — Suggested activities for the home	PROGRAM RESOURCES Eucharist Family Guide, pp. 20–21

CELEBRATE

Objective

To experience a celebration of the word, including the Penitential Act.

Preparation

Familiarize yourself with the movements of the ritual focus for the Penitential Act on pages 108–109. You will need:

- a table covered with a white cloth
- a Bible
- a candle and a large glass bowl filled with water on the prayer table

 Use the *Songs of Celebration* CD, track 9, to rehearse the suggested song, "Create in Me," or one of the optional music suggestions on page 109.

We Gather

- Gather young people in a prayer circle.
- When all are assembled in the prayer space, light the prayer candle.

 Lead young people in singing using the *Songs of Celebration* CD, track 9.

- Begin prayer, and lead young people in the Sign of the Cross.

Follow the order of prayer on pages 108–109.

Ritual Focus: Penitential Act

- Invite young people to sit as they reflect.
- Ask young people to stand for the Confiteor.

We Gather

Ritual Focus: Penitential Act

Sing together.

Create in me a clean heart,
    O God.
A clean heart, O God,
    create in me.

© 1998, Tom Kendzia. Published by OCP

Leader: Let us pray.

Make the Sign of the Cross together.

Leader: Every week we come together as a community of faith. God wants us to be united with him and with one another as one family. Let us be quiet now and think about the times we have not been united to God or others.

Sit silently.

Leader: Let us pray for God's forgiveness and mercy.

Confiteor

Come forward, and gather around the holy water and candle.

All: I confess to almighty God and to you, my brothers and sisters, that I have greatly sinned, in my thoughts and in my words, in what I have done and in what I have failed to do,

Gently strike your chest with a closed fist.

All: through my fault, through my fault, through my most grievous fault;

Continue:

All: therefore I ask blessed Mary ever-Virgin, all the Angels and Saints, and you, my brothers and sisters, to pray for me to the Lord our God.

Leader: May God forgive our sins and make us united with him and one another.

All: Amen.

108

 Liturgical Background

The Penitential Act The Introductory Rites of the Mass include three options for a Penitential Act. One of these is the prayer called the Confiteor, which is the Latin word for "I confess."

To understand the Confiteor, we need to see how this prayer fits into the whole action of the Penitential Act. First, the priest invites the people into a spirit of recollection and a moment of silence. Then the Confiteor is prayed by all. The people must be given time to reflect before they can pray this prayer of confession. Finally, the priest says the absolution. (See Third Edition of *The Roman Missal*.) It is not a sacramental absolution, as we find in the Sacrament of Penance, but a simple invocation of God's mercy.

The Penitential Act assures that whenever we gather for Mass we are called to enter into a spirit of recollection. We are sinners asking forgiveness, we realize our need for God, who is generous and merciful.

The wording used in this lesson's ritual matches the Third Edition of the *Roman Missal*, which we began to use in November 2011.

We Listen

Leader: God, our loving Father, you call us to forgiveness and peace. You want us to be united in you. We ask you to help us forgive others as you forgive us. We ask this through Jesus Christ our Lord.

All: Amen.

Leader: A reading from the holy Gospel according to Matthew.

All: Glory to you, O Lord.

Leader: *Read Matthew 9:9–13.*
The Gospel of the Lord.

All: Praise to you, Lord Jesus Christ.

Sit silently.

We Go Forth

Leader: Let us offer each other the Sign of Peace.

Give the Sign of Peace to one another.

Say: The peace of the Lord be with you.

Answer: And with your spirit.
Go forth united in God's love.

All: Amen.

 Sing the opening song together.

109

We Listen

For the proclamation of the Gospel, you may use a Bible or the adapted reading in the *Candidate's Book* on pages 112–113.

We Go Forth

- Lead the closing prayer.

As young people go back to their seats, have them sing *Songs of Celebration* CD, track 9, "Create in Me," or one of the optional music selections.

Optional Music Suggestions

Salmo 50: "Oh Dios, crea en mi,"
© Eleazar Cortés. Published by OCP

"Loving and Forgiving,"
© Scott Soper. Published by OCP

✴ Ritual Background

General Confession   The Confiteor is not addressed to God alone, but also "to you, my brothers and sisters." It is a general prayer of confession for each person to acknowledge publicly, before God and the community, that he or she is a person who needs forgiveness. This act of humility creates a bond among those who join together in worship. We admit, as Saint Paul did, that "all have sinned and fall short of the glory of God" (*Romans 3:23*).

At the conclusion of the Confiteor, in another gesture of solidarity, we ask our brothers and sisters to pray for us. The prayers of Mary, the saints in heaven, and our Church family help us to approach God with confidence in his mercy.

CELEBRATE

Objective

To explore the meaning of the ritual action of praying the Confiteor

To teach the relationship between forgiveness and unity

Liturgical Catechesis

The purpose of this section is to help young people reflect on their experiences of the signs, rituals, prayers, and gestures of the celebration and to lead them to express their own meaning of the experiences. Allow young people to share their experiences without commenting on them.

God's Forgiveness

- On the board or on chart paper, write the following questions: What did you see? What did you hear? What did you do?

- Guide young people to reflect on the celebration by reviewing what happened in the prayer.

Reflect

- Organize the group in pairs.

- Read the directions aloud.

- Give examples of hand motions.

- Walk among the pairs to offer assistance.

- Ask volunteers to share their illustrations.

Lord Have Mercy

- Have several volunteers take turns reading aloud the text.

- Tell young people that God is always ready to show us his mercy.

God's Forgiveness

CELEBRATE

SIGNS OF FAITH

Lord Have Mercy (Kyrie, eleison) Sometimes in the Mass, during the Penitential Act, we say the prayer, "Lord Have Mercy (Kyrie, eleison)." These are the words that people say to Jesus when they ask him to heal them. When we pray these words at Mass, we ask Jesus to heal and forgive our sins and the sin of the world. We want everyone to be forgiven and united to God and one another forever.

Reflect

Confiteor In the celebration you prayed the Confiteor. With a partner, talk about what that prayer means to each of you. From your conversation develop three or four hand motions that could be used to express the meaning of the prayer as you pray it. Illustrate those hand motions and write the words that express what they mean next to the illustrations.

110

Additional Activity

Choosing to Do Good   Use the song and lyrics for "Through My Fault" (track 2) provided with the *And With Your Spirit* music CD to teach your students about making choices that please God.

- Write "It's my fault that I…" on the board or on chart paper.

- Have the young people finish the sentence by calling out things someone their age might say. Record their reponses.

- Review the completed list and place check marks next to the ones that are an intentional choice.

- Explain to students that sin is an intentional choice to disobey God, but that God is always willing to forgive us if we are sorry.

- Draw a happy face on the board or on chart paper to reinforce that happiness comes from doing what God wants.

We Are One

Just like our parents want our families to be united, or joined together, God wants us to be united to him. He wants us to love and care for others, but we know that sometimes we do not show love to others and we are not always caring.

At the beginning of the Mass, we confess our sinfulness to God and one another in the Confiteor. When the assembly prays the Confiteor together, we are united in our sinfulness and in our need for God's forgiveness and mercy.

SIGNS OF FAITH

Silence

There are special times of quiet at Mass. These times of silence unite us to God. During the silent times we can listen or speak to God in our hearts. We keep our minds and hearts open to what God may be sharing with us.

111

We Are One

- Ask young people to share what "being united" or "being together" means to them.

- Have volunteers read aloud the first paragraph.

- Summarize the second paragraph.

- Review the Confiteor on page 108 with young people.

- Explain that confessing our sins to God and one another is a sign that we want to be united at the Eucharist.

Silence

- Ask young people how it felt to be silent during the celebration.

- Read aloud the text and talk about the different times that young people can be silent and talk to God in their hearts.

Teaching Tip

Keep it hypothetical   Whenever you discuss various experiences of sin with young people, be sure to distance the examples from individuals. Do not mention specific young people's names or use situations that actually occurred within the group.

If young people try to bring up actions of a classmate or a family member, remind them that this is a private issue between the person and God. Emphasize that we should not judge other people's actions as sins.

REMEMBER

Objective

To explain that Jesus is a friend to sinners

Faith Focus

Why did Jesus eat with sinners?

List young people's responses on the board or on chart paper.

Jesus Calls Sinners

- Ask the group about ways that they convince others of the truth.

- Point out that Jesus wanted people to know about God's love for them and that Jesus used different ways of teaching about God's love.

 Scripture   MATTHEW 9:9–13

The Call of Matthew

- Gather the group in a story circle or in the prayer space. Remind them that they will be hearing the Gospel story from Matthew again.

- Ask what they remember from the Gospel during the celebration.

- Read the story aloud, pausing to have young people interpret the meaning of Jesus' words.

- Call attention to the illustration. Have the young people point out the various people who are mentioned in the story.

- Have young people summarize how Jesus felt about Matthew and the people he was eating with.

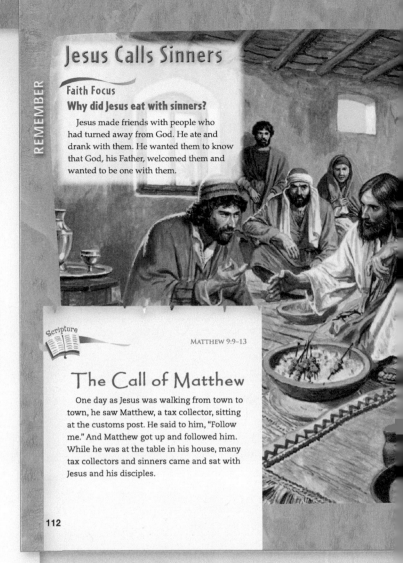

REMEMBER

Jesus Calls Sinners

Faith Focus

Why did Jesus eat with sinners?

Jesus made friends with people who had turned away from God. He ate and drank with them. He wanted them to know that God, his Father, welcomed them and wanted to be one with them.

MATTHEW 9:9–13

Scripture

The Call of Matthew

One day as Jesus was walking from town to town, he saw Matthew, a tax collector, sitting at the customs post. He said to him, "Follow me." And Matthew got up and followed him. While he was at the table in his house, many tax collectors and sinners came and sat with Jesus and his disciples.

112

 ## Scripture Background

Matthew or Levi   All three synoptic Gospels include the story of the tax collector who was called to follow Jesus and left everything to do so. Only in the Gospel of Matthew is the tax collector named Matthew. In the Gospels of Mark and Luke, he is named Levi (*Mark 2:14–17; Luke 5:27–32*). This observation illustrates that the very early Christians identified with certain stories that started off as historical events in the life of Jesus and became exemplary stories of faith, even though the names or other details of the story may have changed as the story was passed on. In the Gospel according to Matthew, the author inserts this event into a series of miracle stories, implying that people are healed by Jesus, not only from physical ailments and diseases, but also from sin.

The Pharisees, who were Jewish leaders and teachers, saw Jesus eating with sinners and tax collectors, and they said to Jesus' disciples, "Why does your teacher eat with tax collectors and sinners?" When Jesus heard their question, he said, "Those who are well do not need a physician, but the sick do. Go and learn the meaning of the words, 'I desire mercy, not sacrifice.' I did not come to call the righteous but sinners."

BASED ON MATTHEW 9:9–13

Faith at Home

Read the Scripture story with your family members. Discuss situations where people in your family or school feel left out. Talk about ways you can reach out to them.

❓ Why did Jesus eat with sinners?

❓ How do you feel about Jesus eating with sinners?

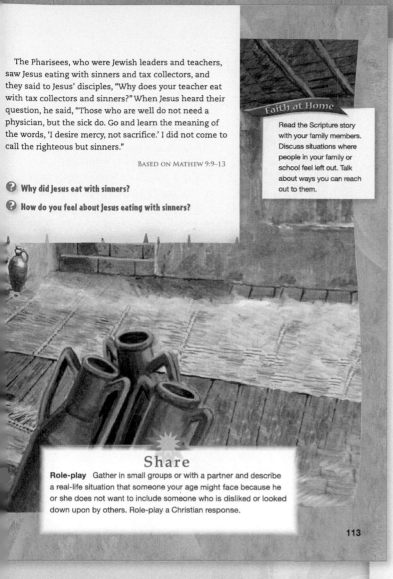

Share

Role-play Gather in small groups or with a partner and describe a real-life situation that someone your age might face because he or she does not want to include someone who is disliked or looked down upon by others. Role-play a Christian response.

113

❓ **Invite volunteers to share responses to the first question.** Possible answers: He wanted to forgive them, tell them about the Father's love, or help them.

❓ **Allow time for personal reflection on the second question, and then have volunteers answer it.** Accept all reasonable responses.

Share

• Organize the large group into smaller groups.

• Allow time for young people to brainstorm situations and solutions.

• Circulate among the groups to offer assistance where needed.

• Have the groups perform their situations.

• Discuss which solutions would work best in real life, and encourage young people to use them when appropriate.

Activity Master

You may wish to use Activity Master 9 on page CE9 to further integrate the meaning of the Gospel story.

▲ Activity Master 9

✦ Cultural Background

The Pharisees   The Pharisees were strict observers of Jewish Law and custom. They were students and teachers of the Law, and their role was to help the Jewish people interpret the Law in a way that would preserve their Jewish identity in the midst of a non-Jewish government and economic system.

The Pharisees considered it an abomination to eat or socialize with non-Jews or sinners. They considered tax collectors to be sinners because some of them were dishonest and inflated the amount of the tax in order to pocket the difference. Whether they were honest or not, tax collectors collaborated with the pagan Roman government and supported it by collecting taxes. Pharisees viewed support of the Romans as an obstacle to having their own nation and religious identity.

Review

• Jesus made friends with many people.

• Jesus wanted sinners to know that God welcomed them.

• We are called to listen to God's word and follow it.

REMEMBER

Objective

To explain why we pray for forgiveness at Mass

Faith Focus

What happens during the Penitential Act? List young people's responses on the board or on chart paper.

Penitential Act

- Recall that the Sacrament of Reconciliation forgives our sins.

- Point out that our venial sins can also be forgiven during the Mass. Note that *Penitential* and *penance* come from a Latin word meaning "to be sorry."

- Summarize the text, emphasizing that God knows that we are not perfect. The Eucharist gives us ways to become one with God after we have sinned.

✝ Sprinkling with Holy Water

- Assist young people in recalling when the sprinkling rite is used in your parish.

- Ask young people why this would remind us of our Baptism.

- If possible, borrow the items used by the priest during this rite and explain how they are used.

Penitential Act

✝ SIGNS OF FAITH

Sprinkling with Holy Water
During some Sunday Masses, the priest walks through the Church and sprinkles the assembly with holy water. The sprinkling reminds us of our Baptism. When the priest does the sprinkling with holy water, it takes the place of the Penitential Act.

Faith Focus

What happens during the Penitential Act?

Like the sinners in Jesus' time, sometimes we need Jesus to call us back to loving our Father:

- We may do things that hurt other people's feelings.
- We may fail to do things for people who need our help.
- We may not follow God's law and instead choose to do what we know is wrong.

When we do these things, we are not at one with God or others. When we come to Mass to share a meal with Jesus, Jesus welcomes us. It is a time to become one again with God and others. The Eucharist is a Sacrament of forgiveness and unity. However, anyone who has not confessed mortal sins must first receive the Sacrament of Penance before going to Holy Communion.

114

✶ Catechist Background

Unity Unity is an essential element of the Church. We are one because:

- we are children of the same Father
- our founder, Jesus, reconciled all of us through his death on the cross
- the same Holy Spirit dwells in the hearts of all the faithful and guides us to unity
- we have the same pope
- we celebrate the same sacraments
- we have the same Scripture and Church Tradition

Sin and its consequences disrupt the unity in the Church. We are reminded of this at the beginning of every Eucharist as we reflect on sin and its consequences, and we pray for God's mercy. The Penitential Act reminds us of who we are before God and what God is calling us to become through this celebration.

We Are Sorry

After the opening song and greeting, we pray together for God's forgiveness during the Penitential Act. We ask God to make us one again. The priest invites us to confess our sins to God and one another.

We pray the Confiteor, a prayer of sorrow that begins with the words "I confess." Sometimes we pray the Lord Have Mercy (*Kyrie, eleison*). When we do this, the priest prays three prayers to Jesus, and we answer him. We pray, "Lord have mercy, Christ have mercy, Lord have mercy" or "Kyrie, eleison, Christe, eleison, Kyrie, eleison." At the end of the Penitential Act, the priest says this prayer:

"May almighty God have mercy on us, forgive us our sins, and bring us to everlasting life."

After the Penitential Act, the Holy Spirit continues to unite us as an assembly. We are now ready to listen to God's word.

Faith at Home

With family members, remember times when each of you said you were sorry and asked forgiveness of one another. Then talk about how expressing sorrow and asking forgiveness can help your relationships with one another grow and become stronger. Use pages 108–109 to learn the responses and prayers for the Penitential Act.

? Why is the Penitential Act important for the assembly?

115

We Are Sorry

Explain that the priest has choices for the Penitential Act. List the options on the board or on chart paper as you work through the text.

- Point out that the Confiteor and the Lord have Mercy (*Kyrie, eleison*) both show sorrow for sin. Remind young people that the Confiteor was part of the opening prayer service.

- Read and summarize the text.

- Discuss how the options are the same and are different.

? Invite volunteers to answer the question. The assembly confesses its sinfulness and prepares to listen to God's word.

Review

- During the Penitential Act, we recall our sins.
- During the Penitential Act, God unites us with himself and others.

Sacrament Background

The Confiteor The prayer we say today is one of the oldest elements in the Introductory Rites. Although its form has changed over the centuries, its essential parts have remained until today.

- It began in Rome during the seventh and eighth centuries as a moment of quiet prayer by the pope as he prostrated himself on the floor before coming to the altar in papal liturgies.

- Gradually, the period of silence developed into a prayer and confession spoken in a dialogue by or between the priests and deacons and the people. As the practice of confessing one's sins developed, so did the prayers for God's mercy and absolution.

- With the Third Edition of the *Roman Missal* changes instituted in 2011, revised wording was introduced and the gesture of striking the breast during certain parts of the Confiteor has been restored.

LIVE

Objective
To integrate and review signs and prayers of forgiveness

We Forgive

Respond

- Explain the activity.

- Distribute prayer books or refer young people to the first three chapters in this book.

- Have young people write prayers or draw pictures of forgiveness at Mass.

- Invite volunteers to help you display the work on a bulletin board.

Closing Blessing

- Gather the group in a prayer circle with their books.

- Begin with the Sign of the Cross.

- Read aloud the People of Faith story about Pope Saint John Paul II.

- Pray the prayer.

- End with *Songs of Celebration* CD, track 9, "Create in Me," or one of the optional music suggestions from page 109.

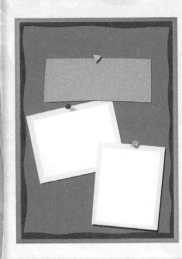

We Forgive

Respond

Make a bulletin board Display ways you forgive at home, school, or at church. Use words and drawings.

Closing Blessing

Gather and begin with the Sign of the Cross.

Leader: God, our Father, we praise and thank you for being a God who forgives.

All: Amen.

Leader: Jesus, our Savior, we praise and thank you for welcoming sinners and showing us how to live and love.

All: Amen.

Leader: Holy Spirit, giver of God's gifts, we praise and thank you for giving us courage to say I am sorry and to forgive others.

All: Amen.

Sing together.

Create in me a clean heart, O God.
A clean heart, O God, create in me.

© 1998, Tom Kendzia. Published by OCP

116

People of Faith: A Story

Pope Saint John Paul II   John Paul II was born in Poland. When he was growing up, he observed anti-semitism among Catholics. Very few people would help the Jews, not even some Church people. Later, when he became pope, John Paul wrote a letter to the people who were Jewish. He expressed sorrow for the way Christians had treated them and asked for forgiveness.

Another time, a man attempted to kill Pope Saint John Paul II. The police caught the man who had shot the pope and put him in jail. When the pope recovered from his wounds, he went to the jail to meet the man who had shot him. He forgave him. Pope Saint John Paul II showed us how to say "I'm sorry" and "I forgive you."

1920–2005

Faith Focus

The Eucharist is a Sacrament of unity and forgiveness.

Sin keeps us from being one People of God.

During the Penitential Act we confess our sinfulness and ask God's forgiveness.

Ritual Focus Penitential Act

The celebration focused on the Penitential Act. You prayed the Confiteor. This week at bedtime, pray the Confiteor before going to sleep.

Family Prayer

God of Mercy, thank you for always forgiving us. By the power of the Holy Spirit, help us change and become more like your Son, Jesus. Make us one in love with you and all the people in our lives. Amen.

Act

Share Together Saying "I'm sorry" and "I forgive you" are important moments in the life of a family. Asking for and giving forgiveness can strengthen relationships. Sometimes we seek forgiveness in indirect ways by doing something special for the person we hurt. Have each family member draw a picture of one way they have seen a family member forgive another. Invite family members to share the story behind the picture.

Do Together Admitting we have hurt one another and saying "I am sorry" are not always easy things to do. Choose a time for family members to gather for prayer. Open with the prayer Come, Holy Spirit on page 191 of this book. Invite family members to ask for, give, and receive forgiveness for the times they may have hurt one another during the week.

GO online **www.osvcurriculum.com**
Visit our website for weekly Scripture readings and questions, family resources, and more activities.

117

Faith at Home

Review the five parts of the Faith at Home page with young people.

Encourage them:

- to ask family members to review the Faith Focus statements with them
- to share the **Ritual Focus: Penitential Act** with family members
- to do at least one of the Act activities with family members
- to pray the **Family Prayer** with their family at times when the family is together
- to encourage their family members to go to **www.osvcurriculum.com** with them and do the activities for this chapter sometime during the week

Looking Ahead

For Chapter 10, you will need:

- a Bible
- a prayer table
- a candle
- a large glass bowl filled with water
- the *Songs of Celebration* CD
- copies of Activity Master 10 on p. CE10 for each young person

Teaching Tip

A new translation Your students (and their parents) may be wondering why some of the prayers and responses of the Mass changed after the introduction of the revised Third Edition of the *Roman Missal* in 2011. In 2000, Pope Saint John Paul II (who was canonized in 2014) announced a revised version of the *Roman Missal* in Latin. It includes prayers for newly canonized saints, more prefaces for the Eucharist Prayers, some updated rubrics, and more. The English translation of the Third Edition of the Latin *Roman Missal* also includes updated translations of some existing prayers and responses. These translations are closer to the Latin text and show more clearly how our prayers are rooted in Scripture. Parishes in the United States began using the new translations on the first Sunday of Advent in 2011.

You may wish to send home copies of *Catholic Parent Know-How: Revised Third Edition of the Roman Missal* (available at **www.osvcurriculum.com**) so parents can understand and familiarize themselves with the changes.

General Instruction of the Roman Missal

"When the Sacred Scriptures are read in the Church, God himself speaks to his people, and Christ, present in his own word, proclaims the gospel.

"Therefore, all must listen with reverence to the readings from God's word, for they make up an element of greatest importance in the Liturgy…." (no.29)

Catechism Connection

To deepen your own background and reflection on the word of God, refer to the *Catechism of the Catholic Church, 101–104, 136, 141, 1154, 1190, 1349, 1408.*

Catechist Resources

Listening to God's Word: Activities and Stories

Eileen Drilling and Judy Rothfork
Liturgy Training Publications

Stories, questions, games, prayers, and blessings for the entire liturgical year

Threshold to God's Word (23 min)

Stephen J. Bing
Twenty-Third Publications

How to read the Bible as a basis for prayer

Young People's Resources

What Do We Do at Mass? (17 min)
Liturgical Training Publications

Young people (ages 7–13) provide wonderful insights into the Mass that will inspire their peers.

God Speaks to Us in Feeding Stories (God Speaks to Us Series)

Mary Ann Getty-Sullivan,
Marygrace Dulski Antkowski
Liturgical Press

Scripture stories with meal themes

Catechist Formation

> "Your word is a lamp to my feet and a light to my path."
>
> Psalm 119:105

Feasting on God's Word

Readers of good books know what it means to say a book is "delicious." At times, people use the expression, "I devoured that book." In daily life good books nurture and provide sustenance. They teach lessons. They make other worlds real. So, too, does the Bible.

When one reflects on "feasting" in reference to the Mass, the focus is usually on bread and wine, table and communion. However, "feasting" at the Eucharist is celebrated from two tables, the table of God's Word and the table of the Lord's Supper. Just as readers of good books find nourishment and transformation from the words and stories, so do we as we listen to the inspired word of God proclaimed and alive in our midst. The breaking open and sharing of God's word is a primary part of our liturgical celebration. Christ, the Word of God, is present in the Scriptures as he is in the sacred bread and wine, which is the Body and Blood of Christ.

Liturgy of the Word

We are called both to listen attentively and to respond to the Scriptures during the Liturgy of the Word. What we see and hear during this part of the Mass is a dialogue between God and his people. Within each of us is another dialogue, one that is not necessarily seen or shared with others at the time. It is the internal dialogue inspired by the Holy Spirit that occurs as we listen to God's word; we are inspired by its meaning and respond to whatever call or challenge we may hear.

When have you experienced the power of God's word in your life? Which scripture story do you find particularly nurturing or challenging?

Catechist Prayer

Dear God, nourish me with your word. Empower me to be a living witness of your Son, Jesus, in my daily life. Amen.

Lesson Planner

www.osvcurriculum.com
Visit our website for additional resources and information.

	OBJECTIVES	LESSON PROCESS	ACTIVITIES	MATERIALS
CELEBRATE — 15 minutes — Pages 118–119	Ritual Focus *Signing* To experience a celebration of the word, including the signing before the proclamation of the Gospel	Celebrate the opening prayer.		PROGRAM RESOURCES *Songs of Celebration* CD, track 10 *And With Your Spirit* CD, track 13
Pages 120–121	To explore the meaning of the ritual action To explain that God is present in the word	Complete the activity. ✝ Read about and discuss The Sign of the Cross. Describe the Bible as God's word. ✝ Read about the Bible. Find the differences between the Old and New Testament.	☀ Reflect Young people reflect on the experience of the celebration and the meaning of signing.	OTHER MATERIALS Bible, prayer table, candle, large glass bowl filled with water
REMEMBER — 30 minutes — Pages 122–123	Faith Focus *Why do we listen to God's word?* To explain why it is important to listen to God's word	Discuss how Jesus' stories were good news for people. 📖 Proclaim the Gospel story. *Matthew 13:1–23* Complete the activity.	☀ Share Young people write a modern day story about the seed. ◤ Faith at Home Suggested activities for the home	OTHER MATERIALS Lectionary and/or Book of the Gospels PROGRAM RESOURCES Copies of Activity Master 10, p. CE10
Pages 124–125	Faith Focus *What happens during the Liturgy of the Word?* To describe the parts of the Liturgy of the Word	Identify the two parts of the Mass. Examine each part of the Liturgy of the Word. ✝ Read about and discuss ambo, lectionary, Book of the Gospels.	◤ Faith at Home Suggested activities for the home	OTHER MATERIALS Lectionary and/or Book of the Gospels
LIVE — 15 minutes — Page 126	To encourage young people to express how they will show God's word alive in their lives	Introduce the activity. Pray the Closing Blessing. Read aloud the People of Faith story about Jean Donovan.	☀ Respond Young people make posters about God's word alive today.	PROGRAM RESOURCES *Songs of Celebration* CD, track 10 OTHER MATERIALS Magazines, newspapers, poster board, paste, scissors
FAITH AT HOME — Page 127	◤ Faith at Home To introduce the different parts of the Faith at Home page	Review the Faith at Home page. Encourage young people to share this page at home.	☀ Act Suggested activities for the home	PROGRAM RESOURCES Eucharist Family Guide, pp. 22–23

CELEBRATE

Objective

To experience a celebration of the word, including the signing before the proclamation of the Gospel

Preparation

Familiarize yourself with the movements of the ritual focus for the signing before the Gospel on pages 118–119.

Prepare the prayer space ahead of time. You will need:

- a Bible
- a table covered with a white cloth
- a candle and a large glass bowl filled with water
- Use the *Songs of Celebration* CD, track 10 to rehearse the suggested song, "Open My Eyes" or one of the optional music suggestions on page 119.
- Select a young person to carry the Bible in procession.

We Gather

Invite young people to assemble with their books for a procession.

- Direct them to follow you and the young person who is carrying the Bible.
- As you process, lead young people in singing using the *Songs of Celebration* CD, track 10.
- When all are assembled in the prayer space, light the prayer candle.
- Begin prayer, and lead young people in the Sign of the Cross.

Follow the order of prayer on pages 118–119.

CHAPTER 10 **We Listen**

CELEBRATE

We Gather

Procession

As you sing, walk forward slowly. Follow the person carrying the Bible.

 Sing together.

Open my ears, Lord.
Help me to hear your voice.
Open my ears, Lord.
Help me to hear.

© 1998, Jesse Manibusan.
Published by OCP Publications

Leader: Let us pray.

Make the Sign of the Cross together.

We Listen

Leader: Father, send the Holy Spirit to open our ears and hearts that we may hear and live your word. We ask this in Jesus' name.

All: Amen.

Leader: A reading from the holy Gospel according to Matthew.

All: Glory to you, O Lord.

Ritual Focus: Signing

Leader: Loving Father, we want to live by your word. May your word be in our minds.

Trace the Sign of the Cross on your forehead.

118

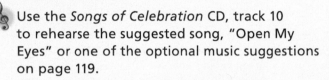 **Liturgical Background**

Reverence   Reverence is a form of respect given to someone or something that we care deeply about. We reverence the word of God because we believe that God is present in it. At Mass the Church shows reverence for the word of God by carrying it in procession, incensing it, and bowing before it.

We also show reverence when we:

- listen attentively to the word proclaimed
- apply the word to our own lives
- act on the word

Leader:	May your word be on our lips.
	Trace the Sign of the Cross on your lips.
Leader:	May your word be in our hearts.
	Trace the Sign of the Cross on your heart.
Leader:	We ask this through Jesus Christ our Lord.
All:	Amen.
Leader:	*Read Matthew 13:1–23.* The Gospel of the Lord.
All:	Praise to you, Lord Jesus Christ.
	Sit silently.

We Go Forth

Leader:	Loving God, we thank you for your word. Help us remember and share it. We ask this through Jesus Christ our Lord.
All:	Amen.

 Sing the opening song together.

119

We Listen

Ritual Focus: Signing

- Sign yourself reverently and slowly as you pray the words.
- Allow time for everyone to sign themselves.

For the proclamation of the Gospel, you may use a Bible or the adapted reading in the *Candidate's Book* on pages 122–123.

We Go Forth

- Lead the closing prayer.
- As the group processes back to their seats, have them sing *Songs of Celebration* CD, track 10, "Open My Eyes" or one of the optional music suggestions.

Optional Music Suggestions

"Abre mis ojos" (Open My Eyes)
© Jesse Manibusan. Published by OCP

"Jesus, Bread of Life," (refrain)
© 2000-Dvorak/Schaubel. Published by WLP

✦ Ritual Background

Signing   The gesture of the signing of forehead, lips, and heart evolved in the ninth through the eleventh centuries, as the Church placed a stronger emphasis on honoring the Gospel. At that time the Signing of the Cross was also done at the close of the Gospel. Its meaning was connected to the scriptural verse about the evil one coming to steal away the word of God from those who did not understand it (*Matthew 13:19*) and the power of the cross to overcome evil.

Other meanings of the signing are:

- a readiness to respond to God's word with courage as expressed in the Letter to the Romans. "For I am not ashamed of the gospel; it is the power of God for salvation to everyone who has faith…" (*Romans 1:16*)

- an expression of the assembly's desire to take in the word of God and make it their own

CELEBRATE

Objective

To explore the meaning of the ritual action of the signing before the Gospel

To explain that God is present in the word

Liturgical Catechesis

The purpose of this section is to help the group reflect on how they experienced the signs, rituals, prayers, and gestures of the celebration and to lead them to express their own meaning of the experience.

At this point in the lesson, your role as a catechist is to listen. Allow individuals to share their experience without commenting on it.

God's Word

- On the board or on chart paper, write the following questions: What did you see? What did you hear? What did you do?

- Guide the group to reflect on the celebration by reviewing what happened during the prayer.

- Have volunteers share any feelings or thoughts they had as they signed themselves before the Gospel reading.

☀ Reflect

- Invite the young people to quiet themselves for a few minutes and then to complete the activity. You may wish to play *Songs of Celebration* CD, track 10, "Open My Eyes" or one of the optional music suggestions as background while they write.

- Encourage volunteers to share their responses.

✝ The Sign of the Cross

- Have the group read the text silently.

- Ask why the Sign of the Cross helps us remember our Baptism.

- Make a list of the times people make the Sign of the Cross.

CELEBRATE

God's Word

✝ SIGNS OF FAITH

The Sign of the Cross
Each of us is signed with the Sign of the Cross at our Baptism. The Sign of the Cross marks us as followers of Jesus. Every time we sign ourselves with the Sign of the Cross, we remember our Baptism. In Baptism we are called to be disciples who follow God's word.

☀ Reflect

Signing In the celebration, you traced the Sign of the Cross on your forehead, lips, and heart. You prayed that God's word would be in your mind, on your lips, and in your heart. Write paragraph explaining what this means for you.

_____
_____
_____
_____
_____
_____
_____
_____
_____
_____

120

☀ Additional Activity

Lamb of God   Use the song lyrics for "Under My Roof" (track 13) provided with the *And With Your Spirit* music CD to explore with young people what we mean when we say, "Lord I am not worthy that you should come under my roof" during the *Agnus Dei* (Lamb of God) at Mass.

The Bible

We know that the **Bible** is God's own word. Another name for the Bible is Scriptures. *Scripture* means "writings." God inspired humans to write stories of his love and friendship. At Mass we listen to and remember those stories. The good news of the Sacred Scriptures is the same good news that Jesus taught.

God the Father, Jesus his Son, and the Holy Spirit are with us when we pray for God's word to be in our minds, on our lips, and in our hearts. They help us hear the good news and share it with others.

SIGNS OF FAITH

The Bible
The Bible has two parts. The parts of the Bible are the Old Testament and the New Testament. The Old Testament tells stories of the friendship between God and his people before the birth of Jesus. The New Testament tells the stories of Jesus and the people in the early Church.

121

The Bible

- Point out the picture on page 121. Ask what the young man is doing. Reading the Bible.

- Discuss when and why people read the Bible. Possible responses: to pray, learn about Jesus, get ready for Sunday Mass.

- Invite volunteers to read aloud the first paragraph.

The Bible

- Have the group read the text silently to find what the differences are between the Old and New Testament. Possible responses: The Old Testament is about the time before Jesus; the New Testament is about Jesus. Jesus' stories are in the New Testament but not in the Old Testament.

- Together prayerfully read aloud the last paragraph.

- Emphasize that when we sign ourselves before the reading of the Gospel, we ask God to be with us.

Teaching Tip

Signs of God's presence   Bear in mind that sometimes in today's world young and old alike are so busy and easily distracted that they may miss God's word and presence in daily life. Make it a point periodically during the sessions to:

- allow some quiet time to reflect

- pray the prayer, "Let us remember the presence of God"

- point out experiences and events which are signs of God's presence as they happen over the course of the year. Some examples: the change of seasons or the birth of a baby

REMEMBER

Objective

To explain why it is important to listen to God's word.

Faith Focus

Why do we listen to God's word?
List young people's responses on the board or on chart paper.

Hear God's Word

Together study the scripture illustration. Point out that it illustrates the Gospel story from the celebration.

- Write the terms *Gospel* and *Good News* on the board or on chart paper. Summarize the first paragraph.
- Ask volunteers to share their favorite Jesus stories.
- Ask how those stories were good news for people.

 Scripture   MATTHEW 13:1–23

The Sower

- Gather the group in a story circle or in the prayer space. Remind them that they will be hearing the Gospel story from Matthew again.
- Ask what they remember from hearing the Gospel during the celebration.
- Have a volunteer reread the story aloud.
- Review the images described in the parable.

REMEMBER

Hear God's Word

Faith Focus

Why do we listen to God's word?

Jesus was a storyteller, and he told many stories about God. We find his stories in the Gospels. The word *gospel* means "good news." Many of Jesus' stories are parables, which are short stories that make a point and help us think about our relationship with God. They help us listen to and understand Jesus' message of good news.

One day Jesus told a parable about a sower. A sower is a person who puts seeds on the ground so they can grow.

Scripture   MATTHEW 13:1–23

The Sower

"A sower went out to sow. And as he sowed, some seed fell on the path, and birds came and ate it up. Some fell on rocky ground, where it had little soil. It sprang up at once because the soil was not deep, and when the sun rose it was scorched, and it withered for lack of roots. Some seed fell among thorns, and the thorns grew up and choked it. But some seed fell on rich soil, and produced fruit, a hundred or sixty or thirtyfold. Whoever has ears ought to hear."

122

Scripture Background

Parables This story marks the beginning of a whole section of parables in the Gospel according to Matthew. A parable is a literary form that uses a fictional story to make a point. In the parable of the sower, Jesus is proclaiming the reign of God and the rich harvest that will be accomplished by the actions of those who hear and understand God's word.

There are two possible reasons Jesus spoke in parables:

- Most of the people Jesus taught could not read or write. Using stories was a way to help them understand and remember.
- Many of the parables have surprising endings. Jesus used them to challenge the people to look at beliefs they took for granted.

The disciples approached him and said, "Why do you speak to them in parables?" Jesus answered, "because they look but do not see and hear but do not listen or understand."

Jesus went on to explain the story. He said, "Hear then the parable of the sower. The seed sown on the path is the one who hears the word of the kingdom without understanding it, and the evil one comes and steals away what was sown in his heart. The seed sown on rocky ground is the one who hears the word and receives it at once with joy. But he has no root and lasts only for a time. When some tribulation or persecution comes because of the word, he immediately falls away. The seed sown among thorns is the one who hears the word, but then worldly anxiety and the lure of riches choke the word and bears no fruit. But the seed sown on rich soil is the one who hears the word and understands it, who indeed bears fruit and yields a hundred or sixty or thirtyfold."

BASED ON MATTHEW 13:1–23

Faith at Home

Read the Scripture story with your family members. Answer the questions, and discuss everyone's responses. Discuss the examples Jesus gives and how they relate to each of you. Decide one way your family can help each other listen to God's word and follow it.

? Which of Jesus' descriptions applies to young people today?

? What steps can you take to hear and understand God's word?

Share

Write a modern-day story In small groups, choose one of the people Jesus was talking about in the parable. Make up a modern-day story of what might happen to that person when the "seed" falls on them.

123

? Discuss the question. Accept all reasonable responses.

? Organize the group into smaller groups of three or four to respond to the second question. Have a volunteer from each small group summarize the discussion. Accept all reasonable responses.

Share

- Keeping the same groups, explain the activity.
- Set a time limit.
- Circulate around the groups to be sure they understand what to do.
- Invite each group to read or act out their story.

Activity Master

You may wish to use Activity Master 10 on page CE10 to further intergrate the meaning of the Gospel story.

▲ Activity Master 10

Review

- *Gospel* means "good news."
- We are called to listen to God's word and follow it.

Cultural Background

Agriculture Jesus used many agricultural images in his teachings because the majority of the people he taught were members of a peasant society. Agricultural production was an important source of income. About 90 percent of the people were peasants. The other 10 percent would be considered the elite or upper class. This division led to a society in which:

- many of the peasants were exploited through taxation and land rent
- the upper class controlled the economic and religious lives of the peasants
- the good news of Jesus' teachings was a freeing experience for many and an unwelcome challenge for others

Objective
To describe the parts of the Liturgy of the Word

Faith Focus
What happens during the Liturgy of the Word?
List young people's responses on the board or on chart paper.

The Liturgy of the Word

- Ask the group to remember the meanings they wrote about on page 120. Explain that during the Liturgy of the Word at Mass, we listen to God's word. Summarize the first paragraph. Emphasize that the Liturgy of the Word is one of two important parts of the Mass, and Jesus is present in God's word.

- Together look at the photographs on pages 124–125, and discuss what is happening in them.

Gospel

- Through reading and discussion, work through the next two paragraphs with the group, and make an outline on the board or on chart paper that lists the important parts of the first part of the Liturgy of the Word.

✝ The Readings

- Write the words *ambo*, *lectionary*, and *Book of the Gospels* on the board or on chart paper.

- Have the group read the text silently and then write a question that could be answered with one of the three words on the board.

- If you were able to obtain a lectionary or a Book of the Gospels, show it to the group, and allow them to look at and carefully handle it.

REMEMBER

The Liturgy of the Word

SIGNS OF FAITH ✝
The Readings
The readings are read from a place called the **ambo**. The reader reads the first and second readings from a special book called the **lectionary**. The lectionary has all the Bible readings for every Sunday in it. The Gospel is read from the **Book of the Gospels**, which is carried in procession during the Introductory Rites to show the importance of the four Gospels.

Faith Focus
What happens during the Liturgy of the Word?

The Mass has two very important parts. The first part is the Liturgy of the Word. The second part is the Liturgy of the Eucharist. In the Liturgy of the Word, we feast on Jesus' presence in the word. In the Liturgy of the Eucharist, we feast on Jesus' presence in his Body and Blood.

During the Liturgy of the Word, we listen to three readings from the Bible. The first reading is usually from the Old Testament. The second reading is from the New Testament and tells more about the story of the early followers of Jesus. Between the first two readings, we sing or pray a psalm from the Old Testament. The psalm is a response, or answer, to God's word. It is called the Responsorial Psalm.

Gospel

The third reading always comes from one of the four Gospels. Each Gospel tells the story of the life, death, and Resurrection of Jesus. They are the heart of the Scriptures because they tell the good news of Jesus.

During the Mass we stand and greet the Gospel reading with joy. Most Sundays, except during Lent, we say or sing "Alleluia," which means "Praise the Lord." Sometimes the priest or deacon will incense the Book of the Gospels before the Gospel is proclaimed.

124

✦ Catechist Background

Scripture in liturgy
The word of God proclaimed in the Liturgy of the Word:

- helps form us into a community

- announces to us the good news of our salvation, beginning in the Old Testament

- teaches us how to live as followers of Jesus and children of God

- opens us up to listen to God in our everyday lives

Our Response

After the readings the priest or deacon gives a homily to help us understand and follow God's word we have just heard. There is a period of silence after the homily when we think about how to live the word in our lives.

We respond to God's word when we stand and pray the Creed. In the Creed we proudly profess what we believe about the Trinity and the Church. Feasting on God's word makes us want to share with others who are hungry for good news. We close the Liturgy of the Word by praying together for the needs of the Church and for all people around the world. These special prayers are called the Prayer of the Faithful, Universal Prayer, or Bidding Prayers.

Faith at Home

Before going to Mass this weekend, remind family members to listen carefully to the readings and homily. Spend some time after Mass discussing how the readings or the homily relates to your family life.

❓ What do we call the part of the Mass when we listen to God's word?

125

Our Response

Explain that during the Liturgy of the Word, we not only listen, but also respond to God's word.

- Summarize the page by writing the terms *homily*, *the Creed*, *Prayer of the Faithful*, *Universal Prayer*, *and Bidding Prayers* on the board or on chart paper.
- Invite volunteers to read the sentence from the text that describes each term.
- Discuss each of these parts.
- ❓ Invite volunteers to answer the question. the Liturgy of the Word

Review

- The Liturgy of the Word is one of the two important parts of the Mass.
- After we listen to God's word, we pray for the needs of the Church and people around the world.

✦ Sacrament Background

Jewish roots The Liturgy of the Word has its origins in Jewish synagogue worship, which is centered on the word of God in prayers and Scriptures, especially the Torah, the first five books of the Bible. For the Jewish people the synagogue is both the building itself and the community of people who assemble to pray, to read the Scriptures, and to hear teachings based on the Scriptures.

During his public life, Jesus went to the synagogue (*Matthew 4:23; Mark 1:21; Luke 4:16–28*) to pray, to teach, and to hear the Scriptures proclaimed. After the Resurrection the early Church continued to gather to hear the word and break bread together.

LIVE

Objective

To encourage young people to express how they will show God's word is alive in their lives.

Share God's Word

Respond

- Explain the activity.
- Distribute newspapers, magazines, poster board, scissors, and paste.
- Set a time limit.
- Invite volunteers to share their posters and responses.

Closing Blessing

- Gather the group in a prayer circle with their books.
- Begin with the Sign of the Cross.
- Read aloud the People of Faith story about Jean Donovan.
- Pray the prayer.

 End with *Songs of Celebration* CD, track 10, "Open My Eyes" or one of the optional music suggestions on page 119.

Share God's Word

Respond

Make a poster   Using newspapers and magazines, cut out stories and pictures that show God's word alive today in people and events. Paste the pictures on poster board. Choose one of the stories or pictures, and tell why you chose it. Describe how you are going to do something similar this week to show that God's word is alive in your own life.

Closing Blessing

Gather and begin with the Sign of the Cross.

Leader: We praise and thank you, Lord, for the gift of your word.

All: Alleluia.

Leader: Help us to go forth and listen for your word in all we do. Show us how to speak your good news to others.

All: Amen.

Sing together.

Open my ears, Lord.
Help me to hear your voice.
Open my ears, Lord.
Help me to hear.

© 1998, Jesse Manibusan.
Published by OCP Publications

126

People of Faith: A Story

Jean Donovan   Jean Donovan was a young Catholic American woman who listened to God's word. She showed that God's word was in her heart. She loved people and she loved life. As a college student, Jean began visiting the sick and elderly. She even cooked meals for them. The more she worked with the poor, the more she knew that she did not need a lot of things to make her happy. She could be happy by serving others. Later, Jean became a missionary in Central America and gave up her life for her faith.

1953–1980

Faith at Home

Faith Focus

- The Bible is God's word written in human words.

- We listen to the word of God during the Liturgy of the Word.

- When we listen to God's word, we want to share it with others.

Ritual Focus
Signing

The celebration focused on Signing and listening to God's word. You prayed by signing yourself with the Sign of the Cross on your forehead, lips, and heart before the Gospel was proclaimed. You prayed that God's word would be with you. At appropriate times during the week, pray the signing prayer on pages 118–119 with your family.

Family Prayer

Jesus, bless us as we listen for your word this week. Open our eyes, our hearts, and our minds that we will become more faithful followers and have the courage to spread your word to all those we meet. Amen.

Act

Share Together Have your family members name people in your neighborhood or the world who are in need of seeing God's word alive today. Create a family prayer of the faithful, and pray it this week during times you are together.

Do Together Read Matthew 13:1–23, and talk about the question, "How can we bring the word of God to someone in need this week?" Check in your parish bulletin for the names of those who might appreciate a get-well card or a card of encouragement. Have family members include their favorite verses in the card.

Mom
Dad
Sheila
Aunt Kathy
Uncle Bill

GO online **www.osvcurriculum.com**
Visit our website for weekly Scripture readings and questions, family resources, and more activities.

127

Faith at Home

Review the five parts of the Faith at Home page with young people.

Encourage them:

- to ask family members to review the **Faith Focus** statements with them
- to share the **Ritual Focus: Signing** with family members
- to do at least one of the **Act** activities with family members
- to pray the **Family Prayer** with their family at times when the family is together
- to encourage their family members to go to **www.osvcurriculum.com** with them and do the activities for this chapter sometime during the week

Looking Ahead

For Chapter 11, you will need:

- a Bible or a lectionary
- a prayer table
- a candle
- a large glass bowl filled with water
- the *Songs of Celebration* CD
- a large cross or crucifix
- copies of Activity Master 11 on p. CE11 for each young person

General Instruction of the Roman Missal

"...Even though the faithful no longer bring from their own possessions the bread and wine intended for the liturgy...the rite of carrying up the offerings still retains its force and its spiritual significance.

"It is well also that money or other gifts for the poor or for the Church, brought by the faithful or collected in the church, should be received..." (*no. 73*).

Catechism Connection

To deepen your own background and reflection on the signs of bread and wine, refer to the *Catechism of the Catholic Church, 1333–1136*.

Catechist Resources

The Mystery and Meaning of the Mass

Rev. Joseph Champlin
The Crossroad Publishing Company

A very basic theology of the Mass with easy to find answers to specific questions

The Bread of God: Nurturing a Eucharistic Imagination

Tony Kelly C.Ss.R.
Liguori Publications

Examines a way of thinking that helps integrate the Eucharist into daily living

Young People's Resources

Maximilian Kolbe: Saint of Auschwitz

Elaine Murray Stone
Paulist Press

A biography of the martyr that is based on first-hand information

A Bible Way of the Cross for Young people

Gwen Costello
Twenty-Third Publications

Guides young people through this traditional devotion

Catechist Formation

> "This is my body, which is given for you..."
>
> Luke 22:19

Preparing Through Thanksgiving

Many families begin their meals together by praying the grace before meals in which they give thanks to God for the gifts they will be sharing at the table. In the same way, as Catholics prepare to celebrate the Liturgy of the Eucharist, they give thanks to God for the gifts they have, especially the bread and wine, which will become their spiritual food and drink.

Through the power of the Holy Spirit and the words and actions of the priest, this bread and wine will become the Body and Blood of Christ. Those gathered at Mass recognize that after the consecration, Christ is present under the appearances of bread and wine. As the community celebrates the sacramental presence of Christ, it also celebrates the sacrifice that Christ made on behalf of all through his suffering and death on the cross.

The Cross

Because the Mass is a re-presentation of Jesus' sacrifice on the cross, the cross always has a prominent place near the altar. Frequently, it is carried in procession so that the assembly will remember they are also making the journey toward Jerusalem, where Jesus was put to death. The preparation for the Eucharist reminds the assembly that they, too, are called to share in Christ's sacrifice through their service to one another.

What role does the cross have in your life?

What ways do you share in Christ's sacrifice by living on behalf of others?

Catechist Prayer

Help me, Holy Spirit, to take up the cross of Jesus Christ with courage. May the power of his sacrifice guide me in serving others. Amen.

Lesson Planner

		OBJECTIVES	LESSON PROCESS	ACTIVITIES	MATERIALS
CELEBRATE	15 minutes — Pages 128–129	**Ritual Focus** *Honoring the Cross* To experience a celebration of the word, including Honoring the Cross	Celebrate the opening prayer.		**PROGRAM RESOURCES** *Songs of Celebration* CD, track 11 *And With Your Spirit* CD, track 11
	Pages 130–131	To explore the meaning of the ritual action To teach the meaning of sacrifice	Complete the activity. ✝ Read about and discuss the meaning of the cross or crucifix. Discuss sacrifice. ✝ Read about and discuss the altar.	☀ Reflect Young people reflect on the experience of the celebration and the meaning of Honoring the Cross	**OTHER MATERIALS** Bible, prayer table, candle, large glass bowl filled with water
REMEMBER	30 minutes — Pages 132–133	**Faith Focus** *What does Jesus tell us about serving others?* To explain that Jesus wants us to serve others	Discuss how and why we serve others. 📖 Proclaim the Gospel story. *John 13:4–16* Complete the activity.	☀ Share Young people write a story about a sacrifice. ◗ Faith at Home Suggested activities for the home	**OTHER MATERIALS** Writing materials **PROGRAM RESOURCES** Copies of Activity Master 11, p. CE11
	Pages 134–135	**Faith Focus** *What gifts do we bring to the altar?* To explain why we present gifts at Mass	Explain that the Preparation of the Gifts is part of the Liturgy of the Eucharist. ✝ Read about the bread and wine used as food for body and souls.	◗ Faith at Home Suggested activities for the home	
LIVE	15 minutes — Page 136	To encourage young people to serve others and praise God	Introduce the activity. Pray the Closing Blessing. Read aloud the People of Faith story about Saint Maximilian Kolbe.	☀ Respond Young people make a poster calendar.	**PROGRAM RESOURCES** *Songs of Celebration* CD, track 11 **OTHER MATERIALS** Magazines, newspapers, poster board
FAITH AT HOME	Page 137	◗ Faith at Home To introduce the different parts of the Faith at Home page	Review the Faith at Home page. Encourage young people to share this page at home.	☀ Act Suggested activities for the home	**PROGRAM RESOURCES** Eucharist Family Guide, pp. 24–25

CELEBRATE

Objective

To experience a celebration of the word, including a ritual of Honoring the Cross

Preparation

Familiarize yourself with the movements of the ritual focus for Honoring the Cross on page 128.

Prepare the prayer space ahead of time. You will need:

- a Bible
- a cross or crucifix
- a table covered with a white cloth
- a candle and a large glass bowl filled with water on the prayer table

Prepare young people ahead of time for the ritual of Honoring the Cross. Explain that they may touch the cross or bow before it at the appropriate time.

🎼 Use the *Songs of Celebration* CD, track 11, to rehearse the suggested song, "We Praise You," or one of the optional music suggestions on page 129.

Select young people to carry the cross and the Bible in procession.

We Gather

Invite young people to assemble with their books for a procession.

- Direct them to follow you and the young people who are carrying the Bible and the Cross.

- 🎼 As you process, lead young people in singing using the *Songs of Celebration* CD, track 11.

- When all are assembled in the prayer space, light the prayer candle.

- Begin prayer, and lead young people in the Sign of the Cross.

Follow the order of prayer on pages 128–129.

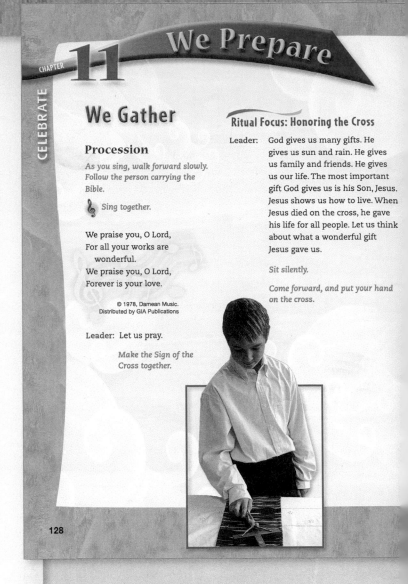

CELEBRATE

We Gather

Procession

As you sing, walk forward slowly. Follow the person carrying the Bible.

🎼 *Sing together.*

We praise you, O Lord,
For all your works are wonderful.
We praise you, O Lord,
Forever is your love.

© 1978, Damean Music.
Distributed by GIA Publications

Leader: Let us pray.

Make the Sign of the Cross together.

Ritual Focus: Honoring the Cross

Leader: God gives us many gifts. He gives us sun and rain. He gives us family and friends. He gives us our life. The most important gift God gives us is his Son, Jesus. Jesus shows us how to live. When Jesus died on the cross, he gave his life for all people. Let us think about what a wonderful gift Jesus gave us.

Sit silently.

Come forward, and put your hand on the cross.

128

Liturgical Background

The cross   The practice of venerating, or honoring, the cross during the liturgy of Good Friday comes from the fourth century in Jerusalem, where people venerated a relic of the true cross.

- Today we use a representation of the cross for veneration. It must be made of wood, to recall the actual material used in the crucifixion.

- There is no veneration of the cross at Sunday Mass, but the gesture might be used in a penitential service, for example, to increase awareness of Christ's sacrifice for our sins.

- A depiction of Christ crucified is present in every Catholic church. Spiritual devotion to the suffering Messiah has long been a strong element of Catholic piety.

We Listen

Leader: Gracious God, open our hearts to hear your word. We ask this through Jesus Christ our Lord.

All: Amen.

Leader: A reading from the holy Gospel according to John.

All: Glory to you, O Lord.

Trace the Sign of the Cross on your forehead, lips, and heart.

Leader: *Read John 13:4–16.*

The Gospel of the Lord.

All: Praise to you, Lord Jesus Christ.

Sit silently.

Leader: Lord God, send us the Holy Spirit to show us how to live for others. We ask this in the name of Jesus, your Son.

All: Amen.

Leader: Let us pray as Jesus taught us:

Pray the Lord's Prayer together.

Let us offer each other the Sign of Peace.

Offer one another a sign of Christ's peace.

Say: The peace of the Lord be with you.

Answer: And with your spirit.

We Go Forth

Leader: Loving God, send us out to share our lives with others. We ask this through Jesus Christ our Lord.

All: Amen.

🎼 *Sing the opening song together.*

129

Ritual Background

Gospel proclamation In the liturgy of the word, the reading of the Gospel is set apart by several actions that proclaim its great dignity and importance.

• The Gospel is read from a special book called the Book of the Gospels.

• The Book of the Gospels is usually carried from the altar to the ambo in procession. This procession may include candles and incense.

• Everyone gathered stands and sings an acclamation before the Gospel is proclaimed.

• The deacon or priest says, "The Lord be with you."

No other reading is surrounded with so many signs of honor. By its actions, the liturgy teaches that the Gospels are "the heart of all the Scriptures" (*CCC* 125, 127).

Ritual Focus: Honoring the Cross

• Direct young people to come forward one by one.

• You may wish to play the *Songs of Celebration* CD, track 11, as background music during the ritual.

We Listen

For the proclamation of the Gospel, you may use a Bible or the adapted reading in the *Candidate's Book* on pages 132–133.

• Invite young people to stand for the Lord's Prayer and the Sign of Peace. You may want to refer young people to page 182 of their books for the words to the Lord's Prayer.

We Go Forth

• Lead the closing prayer.

 As the group processes back to their seats, have them sing *Songs of Celebration* CD, track 11, "We Praise You," or one of the optional music suggestions.

Optional Music Suggestions

"Demos gracias al Señor,"
© Al Valverde. Published by OCP

"Give Thanks and Remember,"
© Jack Miffleton, ©1975 WLP

CELEBRATE

Objective

To explore the meaning of the ritual action of Honoring the Cross

To teach the meaning of sacrifice

Liturgical Catechesis

The purpose of this section is to help young people reflect on their experiences of the signs, rituals, prayers, and gestures of the celebration and to lead them to express their own meaning of the experiences. Allow young people to share their experiences without commenting on them.

The Cross

- On the board or on chart paper, write the following questions: What did you see? What did you hear? What did you do?
- Guide young people to reflect on the celebration by reviewing what happened in the prayer.
- Invite young people to share their responses to the questions.

Reflect

- Explain activity directions to the group.
- Have young people write their responses in the *Candidate's Book*; you may wish to play quiet background music during this activity.
- Invite volunteers to share their responses.

The Cross

- Invite young people to look at and touch the cross or crucifix used in the celebration.
- Read the text aloud.

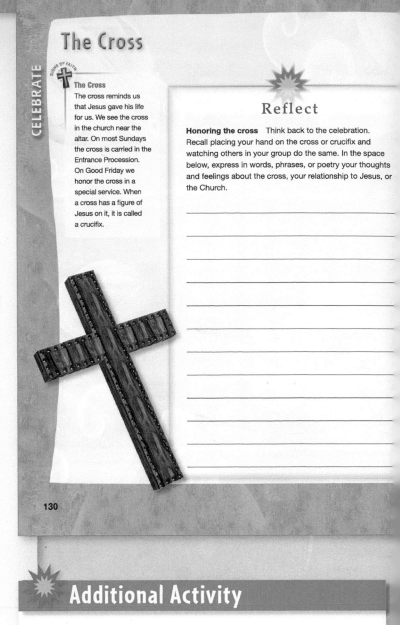

The Cross

The Cross
The cross reminds us that Jesus gave his life for us. We see the cross in the church near the altar. On most Sundays the cross is carried in the Entrance Procession. On Good Friday we honor the cross in a special service. When a cross has a figure of Jesus on it, it is called a crucifix.

Reflect

Honoring the cross   Think back to the celebration. Recall placing your hand on the cross or crucifix and watching others in your group do the same. In the space below, express in words, phrases, or poetry your thoughts and feelings about the cross, your relationship to Jesus, or the Church.

130

Additional Activity

Learn about crosses   Young people may be interested to know that there are many different styles of crosses that the Church recognizes.

Provide references, such as *The Catholic Source Book* (Our Sunday Visitor Curriculum Division, 2000), and have young people look at the various types of crosses and research the significance of the different designs.

You may want to distribute paper and drawing materials and have young people copy their favorite cross, or one that has significance for their heritage.

Young people might also enjoy looking up legends about the cross in books or on the Internet and retelling them to the group.

Sacrifice

The cross reminds us that Jesus died for us. He died for our sins. He gave up his life as a sacrifice for all people. *Sacrifice* means "giving up something out of love for someone else." What a wonderful gift Jesus gave us—his life.

We sacrifice when we share with others or when we give up something valuable such as time, possessions, or money to help another person. Usually we make sacrifices for those we love and care for.

When the Church gathers for Mass, we remember the sacrifice of Jesus on the cross. He gave up his life to save us. The Mass is our sacrifice, too. At Mass we also remember what we have done for God and others. We offer God the gift of our lives.

The Altar
The **altar** is the central table in the front of the church. It is a sign of Jesus' presence with us. It is also a sign that the Mass is a sacrifice and a meal. From ancient times altars were the place where sacrifices were offered. In the Christian tradition, another name for the altar is "the Table of the Lord."

131

Sacrifice

- Write the word *sacrifice* on the board or on chart paper.

- Have young people read the first two paragraphs silently to find the meaning of the word *sacrifice*.

- Ask volunteers to describe *sacrifice* in their own words.

- Discuss the sacrifices young people make in their families and with their friends.

- Summarize the last paragraph and relate it to the previous discussion.

The Altar

- Invite young people to read the text silently and find one thing the altar is a sign of. Jesus' presence. Mass is a sacrifice and a meal.

- Have young people look at the picture of the altar on page 168 of the Words of Faith glossary.

Teaching Tip

Altar   One of the meanings of the word *altar* is "place of sacrifice." In Hebrew the root of that word means, "to slaughter and cut up for the purpose of sacrifice."

Altars actually go back to early biblical times, when people slaughtered animals as a sacrifice to the gods and then placed the animals on the altar, either to be left there or to be burned.

Sacrifice has always been part of human worship.

- We believe Jesus' death on the cross was the ultimate sacrifice.

- The sacrifice of Christ and the sacrifice of the Eucharist are one single sacrifice. Thus, the Mass is the ultimate sacrifice of the Church.

- We participate in that sacrifice as we bring the gift of our lives to the altar.

Objective

To explain that Jesus wants us to serve others

Faith Focus

What does Jesus tell us about serving others?
List young people's responses on the board or on chart paper.

We Serve Others

- Discuss with the group what it means to serve others.

- Summarize the text, emphasizing reasons for serving others.

 Scripture   JOHN 13:4–16

The Washing of the Feet

- Gather the group in a story circle or in the prayer space. Remind them that they will be hearing the Gospel story from John again.

- Ask what they remember from hearing the Gospel during the celebration.

- Reread the story aloud.

- As you read, have two young people pantomime in the roles of Jesus and Peter.

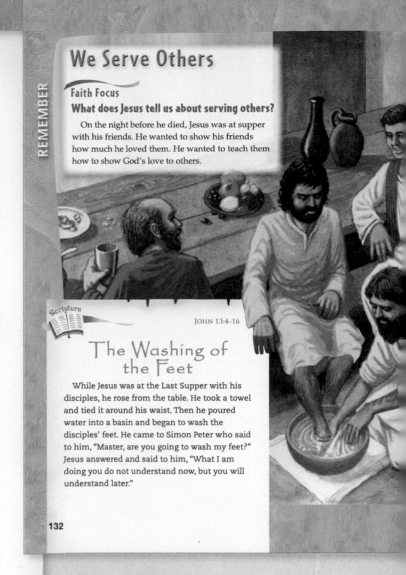

REMEMBER

We Serve Others

Faith Focus

What does Jesus tell us about serving others?

On the night before he died, Jesus was at supper with his friends. He wanted to show his friends how much he loved them. He wanted to teach them how to show God's love to others.

JOHN 13:4–16

The Washing of the Feet

While Jesus was at the Last Supper with his disciples, he rose from the table. He took a towel and tied it around his waist. Then he poured water into a basin and began to wash the disciples' feet. He came to Simon Peter who said to him, "Master, are you going to wash my feet?" Jesus answered and said to him, "What I am doing you do not understand now, but you will understand later."

132

Scripture Background

The Gospel of John   John's Gospel has a long account of the Last Supper but does not describe the institution of the Eucharist. Instead, this gospel describes Jesus' arising from supper and taking a basin and towel to wash the feet of his disciples. Afterward, Jesus interprets this action, explaining, "For I have set you an example, that you also should do as I have done to you" (John 13:15).

The washing of feet stresses the service dimension of following Jesus. It presents Jesus, the Master, performing an act usually done either by the lowest servant in the household or by the host himself as a symbol of respect for his guests. The Gospel of John emphasizes that all those who are "washed clean" are one with him. Disciples are recognized by their imitation of Jesus.

Peter said to him, "You will never wash my feet." Jesus answered him, "Unless I wash you, you will have no inheritance with me." Simon Peter said to him, "Master, then not only my feet but my hands and head as well." Then Jesus washed the feet of all the disciples.

When he was finished, Jesus said, "Do you understand what I just did? You call me 'Teacher' and 'Master.' And you are right, I am. If I have washed your feet, then you should wash one another's feet. I have given you a model to follow. What I do for you, you should do for others."

BASED ON JOHN 13:4–16

Faith at Home

Read the Scripture story with family members. Discuss your responses to both questions. Ask family members to share times they have seen others give up or do something out of love for others.

❓ Why do you think Jesus washed the disciples' feet?

❓ What does Jesus want you to do for others?

Share

Write a story On a separate sheet of paper, write a story about a young person about your age who lives in your town, who makes a sacrifice for a friend. Be sure to describe how and why the young person decided to make that choice.

133

❓ Tell young people that there is more than one answer to the question. Divide them into small groups to think of the answers. Possible responses: their feet were dirty; he wanted to show he loved them; he wanted to serve them.

❓ Challenge the groups to answer the second question. Possible responses: be kind, share, serve others, make sacrifices for others.

Share

- Distribute paper and pencils or pens.
- Have young people read the directions.
- Point out that the story may be real or made up.
- Clarify the amount of time that the young people will have for writing.
- Offer to help young people as they work.
- Have volunteers read their stories to the group.

Activity Master

You may wish to use Activity Master 11 on page CE11 to further integrate the meaning of the Gospel story.

▲ Activity Master 11

Review

- Jesus taught that we should show God's love to others.
- We show love for others by serving them.

Cultural Background

Travel in Jesus' time Travel was very difficult in the first century. Roads were not paved. People went about barefoot or in sandals. Some homes were equipped with a small but welcoming place for people to wash and refresh their feet. In this place there was a stationary tub with still or "running" water as in a fountain. In a modest home, foot washing might be accomplished using a basin and towels. Often travelers washed their own feet upon arrival. However, if there were servants in the household, they would perform the task for invited guests. When a guest was to be honored on a special occasion, the host himself might offer this service as a sign of respect.

Objective

To explain why we present gifts at Mass

Faith Focus

What gifts do we bring to the altar?
List young people's responses on the board or on chart paper.

The Sacrifice of the Mass

- Write the terms *Liturgy of the Eucharist*, *Preparation of the Gifts*, and *sacrifice* on the board or on chart paper. Explain the terms as you work through the text.

- Recall the meaning of the washing of the feet as you summarize the first paragraph.

- Have young people work in pairs to read the next three paragraphs.

- Direct them to make a list of three important points in the reading.

- Have several pairs share their list.

- Emphasize that Jesus is a model for us of sacrificing for others.

Bread and Wine

- Ask a volunteer to read the text aloud.

- Emphasize to young people that the bread and wine are everyday foods that are transformed into Jesus' Body and Blood.

- Point out that this transformation makes bread and wine spiritual food, too.

- If possible, have altar bread and wine in the classroom for young people to look at. Point out that this bread and wine are unconsecrated. Invite them to compare these elements with their everyday bread and drink.

REMEMBER

The Sacrifice of the Mass

SIGNS OF FAITH

Bread and Wine
Bread and wine are foods that people use for special meals. At Mass we use bread that is made without yeast. The wine comes from grapes. By the power of the Holy Spirit and the words and action of the priest, the bread and wine become the Body and Blood of Jesus. They become our spiritual food.

Faith Focus

What gifts do we bring to the altar?

When Jesus washed the feet of the disciples, he showed us a model of how we are called to give our lives for others in service. Jesus gave his life for us on the cross. He saved us from our sins by his life, death, and Resurrection.

The Liturgy of the Eucharist is the second main part of the Mass. *Eucharist* means "thanksgiving." During the Liturgy of the Eucharist we recall and make present Jesus' sacrifice. Through the power of the Holy Spirit and the action of the priest, Jesus offers again the gift of himself to his Father.

During the Liturgy of the Eucharist, we thank God the Father for Jesus' sacrifice on the cross and we bring our own lives and our sacrifices to the altar.

The sacrifices we make during the week are our gifts to God. They prepare us to join in Jesus' sacrifice.

134

Catechist Background

The gifts   As early as the second century, the people began to bring material gifts to the Eucharist for the needs of the Church or for the poor. The offering of these gifts was gradually included in the celebration of the Mass.

Often the gifts included the bread and wine for the celebration. The people brought the gifts to the altar, and the priest received them as an offering.

In the Roman liturgy of the seventh century, the gifts—mostly bread and wine—were not brought directly to the altar by the people but were collected by the celebrant and his assistants after the Gospel reading. When more was collected than was necessary for the Mass, only what was needed for Mass was placed on the altar. The rest was put on special tables and later given to the clergy and the poor.

Preparation of the Gifts

The Liturgy of the Eucharist begins with the Preparation of the Gifts. Members of the assembly bring the bread and wine to the priest, and they are placed on the altar.

We also offer gifts of money or other gifts for the poor and needy. This offering is called a **collection**. These offerings help the parish do its work and take care of those in need. The money offering is also a sign of our sacrifice.

The priest prepares the bread and wine and gives God thanks for his goodness.

We answer, "Blessed be God for ever."

Then the priest prays that our sacrifice will be acceptable to God.

We answer, "May the Lord accept the sacrifice at your hands for the praise and glory of his name, for our good, and the good of all his holy Church."

Faith at Home

Talk with family members about what gifts each of you brings to Mass. Discuss ways you can contribute your time, talent, or money as a gift to God. Use this page to review the responses for the Presentation and Preparation of the Gifts.

 What gifts do you bring to Mass?

135

Preparation of the Gifts

Ask whether any young people have participated in carrying gifts to the altar. Have them report on the experience.

- Write the word *collection* on the board or on chart paper. Invite young people to speculate on how the money is used. Then have them read the second paragraph silently to check their ideas. You may want someone from the parish to come in and discuss with the group how collected money is used by the parish and diocese.

- After young people have read the third paragraph, practice the responses with them.

❓ Discuss the question and response. Emphasize that their presence and contribution to Mass are important. Possible responses: money, my sacrifices, my prayers, my actions.

Review

- The Liturgy of the Eucharist is the second main part of the Mass.
- During the Preparation of the Gifts, we offer ourselves and our gifts to help others.

✴ Additional Activity

Reflecting on sacrifice Expand on the concept of sacrifice by asking the young people to name ways their parents have sacrificed for them. You may have to give them a few examples to start them thinking. Attach a big paper heart to the board or to a wall, and use a marker to write the sacrifices named inside the heart. Then ask them to share some ways they have sacrificed for a friend. Write those in the heart, too.

Explain that love requires sacrifice. Because of God's love for us, he sent his Son to sacrifice his life for us.

Take a large paper cross and tape it over the heart. Explain how during Mass we thank God for his sacrifice of love. Play the song "Savior of the World" (track 11) from the *And With Your Spirit* music CD.

Objective

To encourage young people to serve others and praise God

I Serve Others

Respond

- Explain the activity to young people.

- Distribute magazines, newspapers, poster board, and markers.

- Tell young people how long they will have to work on the poster.

- Brainstorm ways to serve others during the week.

- Place posters around the room and permit young people to view their classmates' work.

- Be sure young people take their poster calendars home to complete the project.

Closing Blessing

- Gather the group in a prayer circle with their books.

- Begin with the Sign of the Cross.

- Read aloud the People of Faith story about Saint Maximilian Kolbe.

- Pray the prayer.

 End with *Songs of Celebration* CD, track 11, "We Praise You" or one of the optional music suggestions on page 129.

I Serve Others

Respond

Make a poster calendar Using magazines and newspapers, select pictures and stories that show people serving others and making sacrifices. Paste them onto a poster board. At the bottom of the poster, design a seven-day calendar with seven writing spaces. Every day this week, record one service or sacrifice you were able to make for others.

Closing Blessing

Gather and begin with the Sign of the Cross.

Leader:	God, our Father, we praise and thank you for the gift of your Son, Jesus.
All:	Amen.
Leader:	Jesus, our Savior, we praise and thank you for giving up your life for us.
All:	Amen.
Leader:	Holy Spirit, giver of God's gifts, we praise and thank you for being with us. Show us how to care about others.
All:	Amen.

Sing together.

We praise you, O Lord,
For all your works are
   wonderful.
We praise you, O Lord,
Forever is your love.

© 1978, Damean Music.
Distributed by GIA Publications

136

People of Faith: A Story

Saint Maximilian Kolbe Maximilian Kolbe was born in Poland. He was considered a "wild young boy." He was very smart and loved science and mathematics. Some people thought he would become a scientist, but he became a Franciscan priest. During World War II, Maximilian was a prisoner in a Nazi concentration camp. One of his fellow prisoners was condemned to die. The man begged the Nazis for his life. He wanted to be able to take care of his family after the war. Maximilian offered to take his place. When Pope John Paul II made Maximilian a saint, the man whose life he had saved was at the ceremony.

1894–1941

Faith at Home

aith Focus

Jesus sacrificed his life for us when he died on the cross.

The Mass is a sacrifice.

At Mass through the power of the Holy Spirit and the words and actions of the priest, Jesus offers again the gift of himself to his Father and to us.

itual Focus
onoring the Cross

he celebration focused on onoring the Cross. You onored the cross during the elebration. Obtain a cross crucifix, and place it where ou will be reminded of Jesus' ft of his life for us. When you e it, pray a prayer of thanks.

mily Prayer

racious God, thank you for the ft of each other and especially r the gift of Jesus. Help us main in your love and teach us share it with others. Amen.

Act

Share Together Read John 13:4–16. With your family members, talk about what Jesus meant when he said, "What I do for you, you should do for others." Together make a list of people who serve your family, such as sanitation workers, street crossing guards, doctors, and dentists. Discuss ways your family can thank these people for sharing their gifts. Choose one of them and act on it.

Do Together With your family members, name some neighbors, family members, or friends who are in need of help or companionship, such as someone who is sick, lives alone, or needs to be tutored. Make a list of actions your family can take to serve these people sometime in the next month. Decide who will do what, and then mark it on the calendar.

GO online **www.osvcurriculum.com**
Visit our website for weekly Scripture readings and questions, family resources, and more activities.

137

Faith at Home

Review the five parts of the Faith at Home page with young people.

Encourage them:

- to ask family members to review the Faith Focus statements with them
- to share the **Ritual Focus: Honoring the Cross** with family members
- to do at least one of the Act activities with family members
- to pray the **Family Prayer** with their family at times when the family is together
- to encourage their family members to go to **www.osvcurriculum.com** with them and do the activities for this chapter sometime during the week

Looking Ahead

For Chapter 12, you will need:

- a Bible
- a prayer table
- a candle
- a large glass bowl filled with water
- the *Songs of Celebration* CD
- copies of Activity Master 12 on p. CE12 for each young person

Teaching Tip

Bring yourselves Young people at this age can be particularly sensitive to what they perceive is expected of them and their families. They are becoming aware of differences in families' circumstances, and the opinions of their contemporaries may be coloring their judgments. Assure young people that the collection is only one way of sharing our gifts with our parish family. Contributing to the collection is not a requirement for attending Mass. Point out that other gifts, such as helping with passing out bulletins or occasionally helping with decorating or cleaning the church also contribute to parish life. This should help those young people who are feeling anxious about attending Mass when they or their families are not able to contribute very much financially to the parish.

General Instruction of the Roman Missal

"Now the center and summit of the entire celebration begins: namely, the Eucharistic Prayer, that is, the prayer of thanksgiving and sanctification.... The meaning of the Prayer is that the entire congregation of the faithful should join itself with Christ in confessing the great deeds of God and in the offering of Sacrifice. The Eucharistic Prayer demands that all listen to it with reverence and in silence" (*no.78*).

Catechism Connection

To deepen your own background and reflection on the Eucharist as a memorial, refer to the *Catechism of the Catholic Church, 1362–1366.*

Catechist Resources

 This Sacred Meal: The Eucharist in Our Lives
(21 min)
Twenty-Third Publications

Explores the Eucharist from an adult perspective

 The Truth About the Eucharist

Father John Dowling
Liguori Publications
Explains the doctrine of the Real Presence of Christ in the Eucharist

Young People's Resources

 Just Like Jesus
Max Lucado for Teens
Tommy Nelson

Retells Biblical stories with explanations of how to imitate Jesus in everyday life

 **Our Faith Comic Book
Jesus, the Ultimate Hero**

David Fielding
Liguori Publications
Retells the events of Palm Sunday to Pentecost in a comic-book format

Catechist Formation

"They... ate their food with glad and generous hearts, praising God and having the goodwill of all the people."

Acts of the Apostles 2:46–4[

Remembering and Presence

Often when we recall people who have died or who live far away, we have a sense of their presence. During the Eucharist we do more than remember or recall the person of Jesus or the events of salvation history. In the Eucharistic Prayer we have more than a sense of the presence of the Risen Lord. He is there as the eternal high priest, offering the Eucharistic sacrifice through the ministry of the priests and under the appearances of bread and wine.

During the Eucharistic prayer of the Mass, the assembly hears and participates in the story of God's presence throughout all of human history, especially through the death and Resurrection of Christ and recognizes God's continuing presence. "In the sense of Sacred Scripture the *memorial* is not merely the recollection of pa[events but the proclamation of the mighty works wrought by God for men. In the liturgical celebration of these events, they become in a certain way present and real" (*Catechism of the Catholic Churc[* 1363).

Joined with All Creation

Through prayer and song, the community is joined with all creation, both living and dead, because the death and Resurrection of Christ has created an unbreakable bond between heaven and earth. The Eucharistic Prayer opens by recounting God's creation and the ways in which God's faithfulness has bee[revealed throughout salvation history. The center point of the Eucharistic Prayer is the institution narrative and the consecratio[It concludes by remembering all people, including those who have died. The Amen that the community proclaims at the end o[the prayer is a sign of its communion in giving glory, honor, and thanksgiving to God for what he has done.

Which part of the Eucharistic Prayer seems to draw your attention each week?

When you say or sing the Amen, what images does it bring to mind?

Catechist Prayer

Blessed are you, O God of all creation. May my life reflect the glory of your love in all that I say and do. Amen.

Lesson Planner

GO online www.osvcurriculum.com
Visit our website for additional resources and information.

		OBJECTIVES	LESSON PROCESS	ACTIVITIES	MATERIALS
CELEBRATE	15 minutes Pages 138–139	Ritual Focus *Mystery of Faith* To experience a celebration of the word, including the gesture of kneeling and the Mystery of Faith	Celebrate the opening prayer.		PROGRAM RESOURCES *Songs of Celebration* CD, track 12 *And With Your Spirit* CD, track 9
	Pages 140–141	To explore the meaning of the ritual action To explain the meaning of the Eucharistic Prayer	Complete the activity. ✝ Read about and discuss kneeling. Explore the mystery of the Eucharist Prayer. ✝ Read about and discuss the role of the priest.	Reflect Young people reflect on the experience of the celebration and the meaning of the Mystery of Faith.	OTHER MATERIALS Bible, prayer table, candle, large glass bowl filled with water
REMEMBER	30 minutes Pages 142–143	Faith Focus *What does Jesus tell his friends?* To explain the significance of the Last Supper	Discuss the importance of the Last Supper. 📖 Proclaim the Gospel story. *Matthew 26:26–28; Luke 22:14–20* Complete the activity.	Share Young people create a parish bulletin announcement. Faith at Home Suggested activities for the home	OTHER MATERIALS Pencils PROGRAM RESOURCES Copies of Activity Master 12, p. CE12
	Pages 144–145	Faith Focus *What do we remember and give thanks for during the Eucharistic Prayer?* To describe the Consecration, Mystery of Faith, and Great Amen	Relate the Consecration, Mystery of Faith, and Great Amen to the Last Supper. ✝ Read about and discuss why the Blessed Sacrament and tabernacle are important.	Faith at Home Suggested activities for the home	
LIVE	15 minutes Page 146	To help young people remember and give thanks for gifts from God	Introduce the activity. Pray the Closing Blessing. Read aloud the People of Faith story about Saint Paschal Baylon.	Respond Young people write an Amen list.	PROGRAM RESOURCES *Songs of Celebration* CD, track 12
FAITH AT HOME	Page 147	Faith at Home To introduce the different parts of the Faith at Home page	Review the Faith at Home page. Encourage young people to share this page at home.	Act Suggested activities for the home	PROGRAM RESOURCES Eucharist Family Guide, pp. 26–27

CELEBRATE

Objective

To experience a celebration of the word, including the gesture of kneeling and the Mystery of Faith

Preparation

Familiarize yourself with the movements of the ritual focus for Mystery of Faith on page 139.

Prepare the prayer space ahead of time. You will need:

- a Bible
- a table covered with a white cloth
- a candle and a large glass bowl filled with water
- Use the *Songs of Celebration* CD, track 12, to rehearse the suggested song, "Te alabaré, Señor," or one of the optional music suggestions on page 139.

Select a young person to carry the Bible in procession.

We Gather

Invite young people to assemble with their books for a procession.

- Direct them to follow you and the young person carrying the Bible.
- As you process, lead young people in singing using the *Songs of Celebration* CD, track 12.
- When all are assembled in the prayer space, light the prayer candle.
- Begin prayer, and lead young people in the Sign of the Cross.

We Listen

For the proclamation of the Gospel, you may use a Bible or the adapted reading in the *Candidate's Book* on pages 142–143.

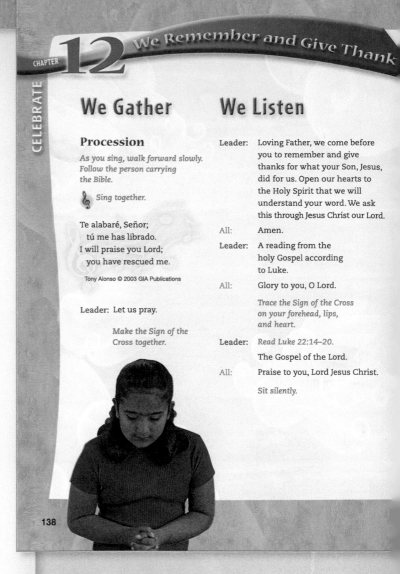

CELEBRATE

We Gather

Procession

As you sing, walk forward slowly. Follow the person carrying the Bible.

♪ *Sing together.*

Te alabaré, Señor;
 tú me has librado.
I will praise you Lord;
 you have rescued me.

Tony Alonso © 2003 GIA Publications

Leader: Let us pray.

Make the Sign of the Cross together.

138

We Listen

Leader: Loving Father, we come before you to remember and give thanks for what your Son, Jesus, did for us. Open our hearts to the Holy Spirit that we will understand your word. We ask this through Jesus Christ our Lord.

All: Amen.

Leader: A reading from the holy Gospel according to Luke.

All: Glory to you, O Lord.

Trace the Sign of the Cross on your forehead, lips, and heart.

Leader: Read Luke 22:14–20.

The Gospel of the Lord.

All: Praise to you, Lord Jesus Christ.

Sit silently.

✦ Liturgical Background

Kneeling   Kneeling can be a sign of penitence, humility, and submission. It is also a posture of prayer, adoration, and reverence. When we kneel during the Eucharistic Prayer at Mass, we express reverence.

Throughout the worldwide Church, kneeling to show reverence for the presence of Christ in the Sacrament of his Body and Blood, is the posture recommended at the consecration. In the dioceses of the United States, however, people kneel during the whole Eucharistic Prayer, unless some good reason prevents them. Those who do not kneel make a profound bow when the priest genuflects after the consecration (*GIRM* 43).

Leader: Every time we gather together at the Eucharist, we know Jesus comes again to be with us. We are happy. We give God the Father thanks and praise for the mystery of Jesus' presence. We pray.

Kneel.

The mystery of faith:

All: We proclaim your Death, O Lord, and profess your Resurrection until you come again.

Stand.

Leader: Let us pray as Jesus taught us:

Pray the Lord's Prayer together.

Leader: Let us offer each other the Sign of Peace.

Offer one another a sign of Christ's peace.

Say: The peace of the Lord be with you.

Answer: And with your spirit.

We Go Forth

Leader: Loving Father, send us forth to bring Jesus' presence to one another. Help us to remember him. We ask this through Jesus Christ our Lord.

All: Amen.

 Sing together.

139

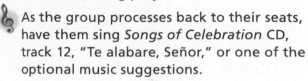

Ritual Focus: Mystery of Faith

- Direct young people to kneel and stand at appropriate times.

- You may wish to sing the Mystery of Faith. If so, use a tune that is often sung in your parish.

- You may want to refer young people to page 182 in their books for the words of the Lord's Prayer.

- If young people can say the Lord's Prayer without their books, invite them to extend their arms outward with their palms up in a gesture of praise (orans position) to pray the Lord's Prayer.

We Go Forth

- Lead the closing prayer.

- As the group processes back to their seats, have them sing *Songs of Celebration* CD, track 12, "Te alabare, Señor," or one of the optional music suggestions.

Optional Music Suggestions

"Holy Lord God of Hosts,"
© 2011 John Burland

"We Remember,"
Marty Haugen, © GIA Publications

"One Bread, One Body,"
© New Dawn, John Foley. Published by OCP

Ritual Background

Mystery of Faith Memory is important to liturgy. When we remember the death and Resurrection of Jesus in the liturgy, we do more than just acknowledge something that happened long ago. We affirm that this sacred event is present to us right now through the words and actions of the priest and the working of the Holy Spirit.

When the liturgy was reformed after the Second Vatican Council, an acclamation of faith was inserted after the consecration. Initially called the Memorial Acclamation, it became known as the Mystery of Faith after the Third Edition of the *Roman Missal* revisions implemented in 2011. This acclamation begins with the priest's words; "The Mystery of Faith," reflecting the ancient Latin expression *Mysterium fidei*, which means "mystery of faith."

The Mystery of Faith is located in the heart of the Eucharistic Prayer, the whole of which recalls the death and Resurrection of Jesus. The Mystery of Faith expresses the assembly's faith in the Paschal mystery.

CELEBRATE

Objective

To explore the meaning of the ritual action of kneeling and the words of the Mystery of Faith

To explain the meaning of the Eucharistic Prayer

Liturgical Catechesis

The purpose of this section is to help young people reflect on how their experiences of the signs, rituals, prayers, and gestures of the celebration and to lead them to express their own meaning of the experiences. Allow young people to share their experiences without commenting on them.

We Remember

- On the board or on chart paper, write the following questions: What did you see? What did you hear? What did you do?

- Guide young people to reflect on the celebration by reviewing what happened in the prayer.

- Invite young people to share their responses to the questions.

Reflect

- Explain the activity to young people.

- Point out there are two parts to the activity.

- Invite volunteers to share their paragraphs.

Kneeling

- Ask young people to talk about their experience of kneeling.

- Invite a volunteer to read the first three sentences.

- Ask young people whether there are other ways we use our bodies in prayer. Possible responses: We fold our hands; we close our eyes; we stand; we process.

- Invite young people to read the rest of the text silently to find when we kneel during the Mass.

We Remember

Kneeling

We kneel as a sign that we are God's children. When we kneel, we show we depend on God. Kneeling is one of the many ways we use our bodies to pray. Sometimes we kneel when we want to ask God for something. Other times we kneel when we seek God's forgiveness. At Mass we kneel after the Holy, Holy, Holy (Preface Acclamation) through the Great Amen. We also kneel during the Lamb of God (*Agnus Dei*) before Holy Communion.

Reflect

Mystery of Faith Think and write about the celebration.

When I heard the story of the Last Supper

_____

_____

_____

When I knelt down

_____

_____

_____

Write a short paragraph and explain why the words, "We proclaim your Death, O Lord, and profess your Resurrection until you come again." are important for you.

_____

_____

_____

_____

_____

_____

_____

140

Additional Activity

Investigate prayer postures The change in posture from standing to kneeling during the opening ceremony may catch young people's attention. Help them understand the implications of the various prayer postures.

- Provide references, such as *The Catholic Source Book* (Our Sunday Visitor Curriculum Division; available at **www.osvcurriculum.com**), and have young people look up the various types of prayer postures and gestures.

- You may wish to assign specific postures and gestures to pairs or groups of young people, or you can have them choose their own from a list that could include bowing, genuflecting, standing, folding hands, and so on.

- Have groups report their findings to the class. Experiment with different prayer postures during prayer services.

The Eucharistic Prayer

The Eucharistic Prayer is the Church's great prayer of praise and thanksgiving to God. The priest begins this prayer, and then we sing with all the angels and saints, "Holy, Holy, Holy." Then we kneel as the prayer continues.

The priest prays the epiclesis, a prayer that God will send the Holy Spirit to make our gifts holy so they become the Body and Blood of Jesus. He retells the story of the Last Supper and we remember what Jesus did for us on the night before he died.

We proclaim the mystery of faith. A **mystery** of faith is something we believe but we do not understand. We believe that Jesus is with us now and we believe that all people who love God will live with him in Heaven when they die. We believe because Jesus promised us that this is true. We want to say, "thank you" for this wonderful mystery.

SIGNS OF FAITH

The Priest

In the Eucharistic Prayer, we join our voices with all Catholics around the world. Jesus acts through the ministry of the priest. Only an ordained **priest** can lead the celebration of the Eucharist. This is the most important thing a priest does. Priests do many other things, too. They teach, preach, take care of the sick, and lead the parish.

141

The Eucharistic Prayer

- Read aloud the first paragraph.

- Discuss the word *holy* with young people.

- Ask whether anyone remembers how to sing the Holy, Holy, Holy from hearing it during the Mass. If so, sing it together.

- Summarize the last two paragraphs.

- Use the Teaching Tip at the bottom of the page to guide your discussion.

- Emphasize that the Eucharistic Prayer tells the story of God's love for humans and that it is a prayer of thanksgiving.

- Encourage young people to listen carefully to the story of the Last Supper as the priest tells it during the Mass next Sunday.

The Priest

- Invite young people to read the text silently to find out what is the most important thing a priest does. leads the celebration of the Eucharist

- Be sure young people know the name of the parish pastor or other priest. If possible, invite one of the priests to visit your session.

Teaching Tip

A mystery is a mystery   This chapter touches on the mystery of the Real Presence of Jesus in the Eucharist. Young people of this age are moving from concrete to abstract thinking. It is not helpful to dwell on the concrete question of how bread and wine are transformed. In fact, if that is the emphasis, young people are likely to be skeptical.

It is more important at this age for young people to hear about your belief in the presence of Jesus in the Eucharist and to be led to reverence for the belief that Jesus is present just as he was at the Last Supper when he told his Apostles, "This is my body" and "This is my blood."

Objective

To explain the significance of the Last Supper

Faith Focus

What does Jesus tell his friends?
List young people's responses on the board or on chart paper.

Jesus Gives Thanks

Have young people interpret what is happening in the illustration.

- Recall the Washing of the Feet Gospel story from the last session. Point out that the Washing of the Feet took place at the Last Supper.

- As you read the paragraph, explain that Passover was part of Jesus' Jewish heritage. Catholics share in this heritage, too.

 Scripture MATTHEW 26:26–28, LUKE 22:14–20

The Last Supper

- Gather the group in a story circle or in the prayer space. Remind them that they will be hearing the Gospel story from Matthew and Luke again.

- Ask what they remember from hearing the Gospel during the celebration.

- Read the story aloud, pausing to emphasize Jesus' words over the bread and wine.

- Ask young people where they have heard Jesus' words before. at Mass, during the Consecration

- Discuss what Jesus meant when he said, "Remember me."

REMEMBER

Jesus Gives Thanks

Faith Focus

What does Jesus tell his friends?

Long ago, God led the people of Israel out of the land of Egypt where they had been slaves. He saved the people and set them free. Every year at the Passover meal, Jewish people remember and give thanks for God's saving love. They remember God's promises.

Scripture   MATTHEW 26:26–28 AND LUKE 22:14–20

The Last Supper

On the night before he died, Jesus shared a special meal with his Apostles. They gathered to celebrate the Passover, a great Jewish holiday of thanksgiving.

We call this meal the Last Supper. During the meal, Jesus told his followers how to remember the mystery of our faith.

When it was time to begin, Jesus told his disciples that he had looked forward to eating the Passover meal with them. He said, "I have eagerly desired to eat this Passover with you before I suffer."

142

Scripture Background

The Last Supper   Passover is a great Jewish feast. It commemorates the liberation of the Jewish people from slavery in Egypt. The Jewish people continue to celebrate it today as a remembrance of God's liberating presence in history.

It was during the course of a Passover meal that Jesus took the elements of bread and wine. He said, "This is my body" over the bread. Then he took the cup, saying over it, "This is my blood" (*Matthew 26:26–28, Luke 22:14–20*).

Through this action Jesus initiated something new, namely, a new covenant "for the forgiveness of sins." By partaking of the Body and Blood of Jesus, Catholics share the blessings of this covenant, receiving forgiveness, and liberation from sin. They are empowered to continue to spread the Gospel of salvation and reconciliation.

Jesus then used the bread and wine of the Passover in a new way. While they were eating, Jesus took bread, said the blessing, and broke it. He gave it to his disciples and said, "Take and eat, this is my body."

Then Jesus took a cup of wine, gave thanks, and gave it to them, saying "Drink from it all of you, for this is the blood of the covenant, which will be shed for many for the forgiveness of sins. Do this in memory of me."

BASED ON MATTHEW 26:26–28 AND LUKE 22:14–20

? **What did Jesus and his disciples remember at the Passover?**

? **How do you remember Jesus?**

Share

Create a parish bulletin announcement With a partner, create a four- or five-line parish bulletin announcement on a separate piece of paper. Title the announcement, "Do this in memory of me."

143

? Discuss the question. Jesus and his followers remembered that God saved his people and set them free in Egypt.

? Read the second question aloud. As a class, brainstorm ways to remember Jesus. Write answers on the board or on chart paper. Possible responses: by helping others, by loving others, by serving God, by going to Mass.

Share

- Distribute paper and writing materials.
- Discuss what Jesus would want you to include in the announcement.
- Offer suggestions and answer questions as young people work.
- Have volunteers share their announcements with the group.

Review

- Jesus and his friends celebrated Passover at the Last Supper.
- Jesus asked us to remember him at the Last Supper.

Cultural Background

Meals For the Jewish people, to eat with another was to make a commitment of common ground and friendship with those present at the table. It meant to share "life" with one another. Because a meal was an intimate vehicle of exchange, people tended only to eat with those they trusted or with whom they enjoyed a close relationship. For the most part, people ate only with others of the same social status. These observations make it all the more poignant that Jesus identifies his betrayer as "one who is with me at the table" (*Luke 22:21*).

Objective

To describe the Consecration, Mystery of Faith, and Great Amen

Faith Focus

What do we remember and give thanks for during the Eucharistic Prayer?
List young people's responses on the board or on chart paper.

We Remember and Give Thanks

- As you summarize the first paragraph, elicit reasons from young people about why "The Lord's Supper" is an appropriate name for the Eucharist.

- Recall from the last lesson that the Liturgy of the Eucharist is one of the main parts of the Mass.

- Read the second and third paragraphs aloud. Highlight our reasons for giving thanks and our reasons for praying.

✝ Blessed Sacrament

- Write the word *tabernacle* on the board or on chart paper.

- Recall with young people where the tabernacle is in your church building. If possible, make a short visit to the church to pray in front of it.

- Discuss why it is a special gift for parish members to receive the Blessed Sacrament when they cannot attend Mass in person.

We Remember and Give Thanks

REMEMBER

SIGNS OF FAITH ✝ Blessed Sacrament

The consecrated Bread and Wine are the Body and Blood of Jesus. They are called the Blessed Sacrament. After Mass the remaining Hosts are put in a special place called a **tabernacle**. The tabernacle is usually in a chapel or at a side altar in the church. We keep the Blessed Sacrament there so it can be brought to parish members who are ill and cannot be present. We can also spend time before the tabernacle praying to Jesus in the Blessed Sacrament.

Faith Focus

What do we remember and give thanks for during the Eucharistic Prayer?

Another name for the Eucharist is "The Lord's Supper." At the Last Supper Jesus and the disciples remembered the Passover. As they remembered the story, they said special prayers of thanks. At Mass we remember the Last Supper and Jesus' death on the cross; we too, say special prayers of thanks.

During the Eucharistic Prayer, the priest joins all of our prayers into one. He prays in our name and the name of the Church. We take part in the prayer, too. During the prayer we remember all the ways that God has saved us. We offer ourselves to God with Jesus. We share in Jesus' death and Resurrection through the power of the Holy Spirit. We remember and we say "thank you" for:

- all of God's gifts
- the gift of Jesus, God's Son
- Jesus' death, his Resurrection, and his Ascension
- Jesus' promise

The priest asks God to accept our sacrifice. We pray that God will make us holy like the saints in Heaven with him. We pray for one another. We offer the Mass for the people who have died.

144

✦ Liturgical Background

Revised Roman Missal   On November 27, 2011, the First Sunday of Advent, we began to use a revised translation of the text of the Mass. Throughout the history of the Church, there have been only a few times when *official* changes in the text of the Mass prayers have occurred, and it is important to remember that the key elements of Catholic worship have remained constant since the time of the early Church. None of the changes, including the Third Edition of the *Roman Missal*, ever changes the original ritual and essence of Jesus' actions at the Last Supper. By the power of the Holy Spirit, the Church, from apostolic time to the present, preserves the fundamental structure of the Mass everywhere in the Church. The Mass is the center of the Church's life.

Consecration

An important part of the Eucharistic Prayer is the **consecration**. The priest says the words Jesus did at the Last Supper. The gifts of bread and wine become the Body and Blood of Christ. Through the power of the Holy Spirit and the words and actions of the priest, Jesus becomes really, truly, present in the bread and wine.

Only an ordained priest can consecrate the gifts of bread and wine. After the consecration we remember that Jesus gave his life for us. The priest says or sings: "The mystery of faith." We answer with a special response: "We proclaim your Death, O Lord, and profess your Resurrection until you come again." This response is called the **mystery of faith**.

The Great Amen

At the end of the Eucharistic Prayer, the priest prays the prayer that begins,

"Through him, and with him, and in him. . ."

We answer, "Amen."

This is the Great Amen. When we pray the Great Amen, we say "yes" to God's promises. We praise him for his gifts and saving actions.

? How is the Eucharist like the Last Supper?

Faith at Home

Explain your response to the question with your family members. If you have friends who are Jewish, ask if you can invite them to your home to share a meal and talk about what Passover means to them.

145

Sacrament Background

Doxology The Eucharistic Prayer ends with a prayer often called the Great Amen. However, "Amen" is an immediate response to a doxology, which is a prayer expressing glory to the triune God, the Trinity—Father, Son, and Holy Spirit.

It has been customary from earliest times that all public prayer closes with praise of God. Historically consistent, the doxology reminds us of the essential purpose of all prayer: we bow before our Creator.

No matter what form the Eucharistic Prayer has taken through the ages, the doxology has always been its conclusion and the wording of the doxology has always been emphatic. Here around this altar and table, God does receive honor and praise.

Consecration

As you work through the text, point out that the photo shows one of the priest's gestures during the consecration.

- Write the terms *consecration*, *Mystery of Faith*, and *Great Amen* on the board or on chart paper. Invite young people to write a short explanation under each term as you work through the text.

- After the second paragraph, recall any particular Mystery of Faith that your parish uses. Discuss its meaning.

The Great Amen

- Invite young people to tell you what "Amen" means. If they do not know, challenge them to find the meaning in a dictionary.

- Explain that since ancient times, this has been a term that shows agreement.

- Read the text aloud to show what the Great Amen agrees to.

? Have young people work in pairs or small groups to draw parallels between the Mass and the Last Supper. Possible responses: It is a gathering of people who love Jesus; it is a meal; it is a remembrance of Jesus' love for us; it is a prayer.

Activity Master

You may wish to use Activity Master 12 on page CE12 to guide young people in naming what they want to thank God for and for whom they want to pray.

▲ Activity Master 12

Review

- We recall the Last Supper at the Eucharist.
- The consecration, the Mystery of Faith, and the Great Amen are part of the Eucharistic Prayer.

Objective

To help young people remember and give thanks for gifts from God

Say "Yes"

Respond

- Explain the activity.
- Distribute pencils or pens.
- Set a time limit for young people to complete their lists.
- Invite young people to share one or two items from their list with the class.

Closing Blessing

- Gather the group in a prayer circle with their books.
- Begin with the Sign of the Cross.
- Read aloud the People of Faith story about Saint Paschal Baylon.
- Pray the prayer.

 End with *Songs of Celebration* CD, track 12, "Te alabaré, Senor."

Say "Yes"

Respond

Create an amen list When we say "Amen" at the end of the Eucharistic Prayer, we are saying "yes" to God's promises—not just at Mass, but also in our daily life. In the space below, make a list of ways that you show your belief in Jesus and say "Amen" every day.

"My Amen List"

Closing Blessing

Gather and begin with the Sign of the Cross.

Leader: God, our Father, we remember and give thanks for all your good gifts.

All: Amen.

Leader: Jesus, our Savior, we remember and give thanks for your death and Resurrection.

All: Amen.

Leader: Holy Spirit, we remember and give thanks that you are with us.

All: Amen.

Sing together.

Te alabaré, Señor;
  tú me has librado.
I will praise you Lord;
  you have rescued me.

Tony Alonso © 2003 GIA Publications

146

People of Faith: A Story

Saint Paschal Baylon   Paschal was born in Aragon, part of the Spanish kingdom, on Pentecost Sunday. His family named him Paschal because he was born during the Easter season. Another name for the Easter season is the Paschal season. As a boy Paschal helped his father on the family farm. He took care of the sheep. Paschal taught himself to read. He loved to pray to Jesus in the Blessed Sacrament. He became a Franciscan lay brother, often serving as a cook or doorkeeper. As an adult he kept his great love of the Eucharist and helped other people believe that Jesus is present in the Eucharist.

Faith Focus

• The Eucharistic Prayer is a prayer of thanksgiving, remembering, and consecration.

• Through the power of the Holy Spirit and the words and actions of the priest, the bread and wine become the Body and Blood of Jesus.

• At the Great Amen, the assembly says "yes" to all of God's saving actions and promises.

Ritual Focus
Mystery of Faith

The celebration focused on the Mystery of Faith. You prayed an Acclamation. During the week, use the Family Prayer as a prayer before or after meals.

Family Prayer

Giving God, we give you thanks for all the gifts you give us: for the gifts of creation, for family and friends, and especially for the gift of your Son, Jesus. Help us to always remember that you are here with us. Amen.

Act

Share Together Talk about ways your family remembers people who have moved away or died. Use examples of pictures or stories to get the sharing started. Make a list of the examples that family members share. Use the list to talk about ways your family can remember Jesus during the week.

Do Together Invite family members to plan a time to make a visit to the Blessed Sacrament together. Your parish church may have a Blessed Sacrament chapel in the church, or the tabernacle may be in another special place. Go near the place where the tabernacle is located. Spend some quiet time in conversation with Jesus in the Blessed Sacrament.

GO online **www.osvcurriculum.com**
Visit our website for weekly Scripture readings and questions, family resources, and more activities.

147

Faith at Home

Review the five parts of the Faith at Home page with young people.

Encourage them:

• to ask family members to review the **Faith Focus** statements with them

• to share the **Ritual Focus: Mystery of Faith** with family members

• to do at least one of the ☀ **Act** activities with family members

• to pray the **Family Prayer** with their family at times when the family is together

• to encourage their family members to go to **www.osvcurriculum.com** with them and do the activities for this chapter sometime during the week

Looking Ahead

For Chapter 13, you will need:

• a Bible

• a prayer table

• a candle

 the *Songs of Celebration* CD

• healthy refreshments, such as juice, bread, and fruit, for the celebration

• copies of Activity Master 13 on p. CE13 for each young person

General Instruction of the Roman Missal

"Since the Eucharistic Celebration is the Paschal Banquet, it is desirable that in keeping with the Lord's command, his Body and Blood should be received by the faithful who are properly disposed as spiritual food... (*no.80*)."

Catechism Connection

To deepen your own background and reflection on the Eucharist as a meal, refer to the *Catechism of the Catholic Church, 1382–1398.*

Catechist Resources

Children Discover the Mass: Lessons, Crafts, Cutouts, and More

Mary Doerfler Dall
Ave Maria Press

Contains many hands-on projects relating to the Mass

The Welcome Table: Planning Masses with Children

Elizabeth McMahon Jeep et al.
Liturgy Training Publications

Help for teaching young people about liturgy as you plan Mass together

Young People's Resources

We Go to Church: A Child's Guide to the Mass
Ken Meitz, JLP International, and Paulist Press
Paulist Press

This interactive CD-ROM includes an exploration of the Mass

What Do We Do at Mass? (17 minutes)

Liturgy Training Publications

Teaches about the Mass and includes the thoughts of young people ages 7–13

The Tortilla Factory (17 minutes)

Gary Paulsen
Voyager Books

Traces the cycle of life from seed to plant to tortilla

Catechist Formation

"The glory that you have given me I have given them, so that they may be one, as we are one."

John 17:22

Meals and Communion

The times when families gather together for a meal are treasured moments. Sharing a meal provides a time for families to bond. Time together around the table provides nourishment for both body and spirit.

The Sunday gathering for Eucharist enables members of the Church family to realize their oneness with Christ and with one another. The celebration of the Eucharist as both meal and sacrifice centers on the union of the assembly with Christ through Communion. Before approaching the Table of the Lord to receive Holy Communion, those gathered pray the Lord's Prayer and share the Sign of Peace with one another to acknowledge the importance of being one.

Meals and Faith

With the reception of Holy Communion, the Amen of the communicants acknowledges that they believe Christ is present under the appearances of Bread and Wine. They believe that through sharing in Holy Communion, Christ is transforming them and the whole Church into the Body of Christ. Communion is a sign of the intimate link that Christ has with every believer. It is also a sign that the Church stands together to witness to the world as a community of Christ's love for all.

What signs remind you that you are growing in a deeper union with Christ?

What unique gifts do you bring to the Body of Christ, the Church?

Catechist Prayer

Heavenly Father, thank you for the gift of your Son in the Eucharist. Deepen my oneness with him. Help me follow his example. Amen.

Lesson Planner

www.osvcurriculum.com
Visit our website for additional resources and information.

		OBJECTIVES	LESSON PROCESS	ACTIVITIES	MATERIALS
CELEBRATE	15 minutes Pages 148–149	Ritual Focus *Sharing a Meal* — To experience a celebration of the word, including the Sharing a Meal	Celebrate the opening prayer.		PROGRAM RESOURCES *Songs of Celebration* CD, track 13 — *And With Your Spirit* CD, track 12
	Pages 150–151	To explore the meaning of the ritual action — To explain that the Eucharist is the Church's special meal	Discuss the Sign of Peace. — Describe the Eucharist as the Church's meal. — Read about and discuss the paten, chalice, and ciborium.	Reflect Young people reflect on the experience of the celebration and the meaning of sharing a meal by completing a questionnaire.	OTHER MATERIALS Bible, cross, prayer table, candle, large glass bowl filled with water, simple healthy refreshments, table and chairs for the meal, eating utensils
REMEMBER	30 minutes Pages 152–153	Faith Focus *What does Jesus tell us about himself?* — To explain the connection between the Eucharist and eternal life	Recall the significance of Biblical meals. — Proclaim the Gospel story. *John 6:30–58* — Complete the activity.	Share Young people design a billboard. — Faith at Home Suggested activities for the home	OTHER MATERIALS Drawing materials — PROGRAM RESOURCES Copies of Activity Master 13, p. CE13
	Pages 154–155	Faith Focus *What happens at the Communion Rite?* — To describe what happens during the Communion Rite	Discuss the meaning of Holy Communion. — Read about and discuss the Lamb of God (*Agnus Dei*) prayer. — Examine the correct procedure for receiving Holy Communion.	Faith at Home Suggested activities for the home	
LIVE	15 minutes Page 156	To reflect on the meaning of Holy Communion	Introduce the activity. — Pray the Closing Blessing. — Read aloud the People of Faith story about Venerable Maria Teresa Quevedo.	Respond Young people write a prayer.	PROGRAM RESOURCES *Songs of Celebration* CD, track 13
FAITH AT HOME	Page 157	Faith at Home To introduce the different parts of the Faith at Home page	Review the Faith at Home page. — Encourage young people to share this page at home.	Act Suggested activities for the home	PROGRAM RESOURCES Eucharist Family Guide, pp. 28–29

CELEBRATE

Objective

To experience a celebration of the word, including Sharing a Meal

Preparation

Familiarize yourself with the movements of the ritual focus for Sharing a Meal on page 149. You will need:

- a Bible
- a cross
- a table covered with a white cloth
- a candle and a large glass bowl filled with water on the prayer table
- simple healthy refreshments, such as bread, grape juice, fruit
- a table and chairs for the meal
- eating utensils
- Use the *Songs of Celebration* CD, track 13, to rehearse the suggested song, "Come to the Table," or one of the optional music suggestions on page 149.

Select a young person to carry the Bible in procession.

We Gather

Invite young people to assemble with their books for a procession.

- Direct them to follow you and the young person who is carrying the Bible.
- As you process, lead young people in singing using the *Songs of Celebration* CD, track 13.
- When all are assembled in the prayer space, light the prayer candle.
- Begin prayer, and lead young people in the Sign of the Cross.

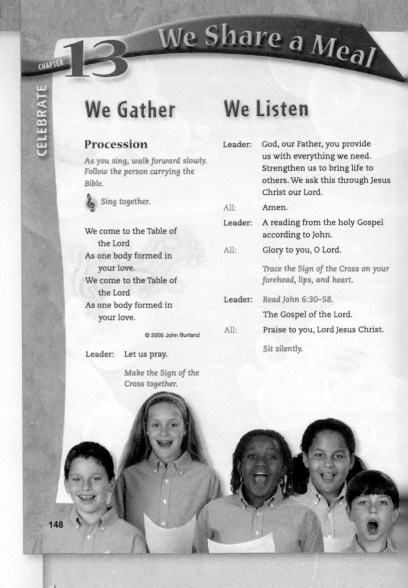

We Gather

Procession

As you sing, walk forward slowly. Follow the person carrying the Bible.

♪ *Sing together.*

We come to the Table of
   the Lord
As one body formed in
   your love.
We come to the Table of
   the Lord
As one body formed in
   your love.

© 2005 John Burland

Leader: Let us pray.

Make the Sign of the Cross together.

We Listen

Leader: God, our Father, you provide us with everything we need. Strengthen us to bring life to others. We ask this through Jesus Christ our Lord.

All: Amen.

Leader: A reading from the holy Gospel according to John.

All: Glory to you, O Lord.

Trace the Sign of the Cross on your forehead, lips, and heart.

Leader: Read John 6:30–58.

The Gospel of the Lord.

All: Praise to you, Lord Jesus Christ.

Sit silently.

148

✳ Ritual Background

Sharing food   Eating and drinking are ritual-laden human activities. The way we eat and drink reflects the customs of our culture and society. Sharing food can also have religious significance, as it does, for example, in the Jewish Passover meal or in the breaking of the Muslim fast during the month of Ramadan.

The Eucharist is a sacrifice and the sacred meal of our salvation. As a meal, the Eucharist taps into a deep reservoir of human experience concerning the sharing of food. We participate with care and respect for our brothers and sisters.

When Saint Paul chastised the community at Corinth, he pointed to their selfish behavior at table as a sign that they did not fully understand the Eucharist (*1 Corinthians 11:17–22*).

Ritual Focus: Sharing a Meal

Be seated around the table.

Leader: Blessed are you,
almighty Father,

who gives us our
daily bread.

Blessed is your only
begotten Son,

who continually feeds us
with the word of life.

Blessed is the Holy Spirit,

who brings us together at
this table of love.

Blessed be God now and
for ever.

All: Amen.

BOOK OF BLESSINGS, 1069

Share the food at the table.

Leader: We give you thanks for
all your gifts, almighty
God, living and reigning
now and for ever.

All: Amen.

BOOK OF BLESSINGS, 1070

We Go Forth

Leader: Loving God, we thank you for
food, for families, for friends,
and for the gift of your Son,
Jesus. Help us to share the gifts
of life with others. We ask this in
the name of your Son, Jesus.

All: Amen.

 Sing the opening song together.

149

Liturgical Background

Sign of Peace   In the ancient Church the Sign of Peace was a kiss. More than simply a gesture of Christian affection, the kiss indicated a mutual sharing of the Spirit of Christ. This gesture was common to the early Christian community. It was used at the conclusion of prayer and at the conclusion of initiation and ordination rites to affirm everything that went before it.

Today, the kiss of peace is modified out of respect for modern sensibilities about touch. Usually the gesture is a hand clasp, a hug, or something similar, rather than a kiss. We share the Sign of Peace in a way that includes those around us equally, because it is an acknowledgment of the peace Christ gives to all. The Sign of Peace does not "come from the altar" as it did in the late Middle Ages, but it is exchanged immediately within the congregation, once the invitation is given. It is a sign of solidarity and commitment with one another before coming to the table.

We Listen

For the proclamation of the Gospel, you may use a Bible or the adapted reading in the *Candidate's Book* on pages 152–153.

Ritual Focus: Sharing a Meal

- Direct young people to gather around the table and be seated.
- Pray the Blessing Prayer.
- Share the meal.
- At the end of the meal, gather young people around the prayer table.
- Invite young people to exchange the Sign of Peace.

We Go Forth

- Lead the closing prayer.
- As the group processes back to their seats, have them sing *Songs of Celebration* CD, track 13, "Come to the Table," or one of the optional music suggestions.

Optional Music Suggestions

"Canción del cuerpo de Cristo,"
Donna Pena ©1989 GIA

"Let Us Break Bread Together,"
African-American Traditional

CELEBRATE

Objective

To explore the meaning of the ritual action of Sharing a Meal

To explain that the Eucharist is the Church's special meal

Liturgical Catechesis

The purpose of this section is to help young people reflect on their experiences of the signs, rituals, prayers, and gestures of the celebration and to lead them to express their own meaning of the experiences. Allow young people to share their experiences without commenting on them.

Special Meals

- On the board or on chart paper, write the following questions: What did you see? What did you hear? What did you do?

- Guide young people to reflect on the celebration by reviewing what happened in the prayer and as they shared food.

- Invite young people to share their responses to the questions.

Reflect

- Invite young people to fill in the questionnaire.

- In small groups have young people share their responses.

- Summarize the sharing, noting similarities and differences.

Sign of Peace

- Ask young people to read the text silently and have them tell what giving the Sign of Peace means. We are united with one another at the Table of the Lord.

- Practice the Sign of Peace with young people.

Special Meals

Sign of Peace

During Mass we offer one another the **Sign of Peace** before Holy Communion. The Sign of Peace is an action prayer. We reach out our hands to people around us. We wish them God's peace. Giving the Sign of Peace to others is a sign that we are united with one another at the Table of the Lord.

150

Reflect

Sharing a meal   Fill out the following questionnaire about sharing a meal.

1. What is your favorite meal?

   _____

2. What do you like best about eating with other people?

   _____

3. What do you like least about eating with other people?

   _____

4. In your family, what is the difference between an ordina[ry] meal and a special meal?

   _____

5. What are your family rules about mealtime?

   _____

6. Who blesses the meal when you are together?

Additional Activity

Lamb of God   Play the song "The Supper of the Lamb" (track 12) from the *And With Your Spirit* music CD. Emphasize that Jesus is the Lamb of God, so at Mass we are invited to his supper that is a sacrifice of love. Tell the young people:

- Because God gave us life, all the wonders of the Earth, and the ability to know him, we want to thank him by giving our best.

- People long ago offered God the best animal they had on a stone altar. Something offered to God is called a *sacrifice*. A lamb represents the most perfect sacrifice.

- Saint Paul said that the sacrifice of love that Jesus made when he died for us was greater than any perfect lamb offered to God. We call Jesus the Lamb of God because he is the greatest sacrifice of love.

The Eucharist as a Meal

Sharing a meal brings people closer together. A special meal, sometimes called a banquet or feast, is a time to celebrate. It is a time to share stories, sing songs, and eat special food. When families and friends gather for special meals, they grow in love.

The Eucharist is the Church's special meal. The Holy Spirit gathers us with our parish family and with Catholics all over the world. We gather at the Eucharist as the Body of Christ to celebrate God's love for us. We also share Jesus' own Body and Blood in Holy Communion. Jesus is truly present in both the consecrated Bread and the Wine.

Jesus is the Bread of Life. In the meal of the Eucharist, we share in the life of the Risen Christ.

Paten, Ciborium, and Chalice
The food for our Eucharistic meal is placed on special dishes. The **paten** holds the hosts. A **ciborium** may be used as well. The wine is poured into a **chalice**.

151

Teaching Tip

Guidelines for receiving Communion Remind young people about these guidelines for receiving Communion:

1. If we have committed a serious sin, we must celebrate the Sacrament of Reconciliation before receiving Communion.

2. We do not eat or drink anything except water for one hour before receiving Communion.

3. How we act and the way we dress for Mass should show respect for Jesus' presence in the Eucharist.

4. We are encouraged to receive Holy Communion at every Eucharist we attend, unless we have committed a serious sin.

The Eucharist as a Meal

- Read the first paragraph aloud.

- Ask young people what special meals their families share.

- Invite volunteers to tell why the meal they chose is special.

- Read aloud the second paragraph.

- Point out that Catholics all over the world share in the meal of the Eucharist.

- Invite young people to silently reread the paragraph to find two reasons the Eucharist is a special meal.

- Invite volunteers to share their reasons. Possible responses: The Holy Spirit gathers us; we celebrate God's love; we share Jesus' own body and blood.

- Read the final paragraph aloud.

Paten, Ciborium, and Chalice

- Refer to pages 169–172 in the Words of Faith glossary.

- Invite young people to read the text silently to find out what the difference is between the chalice and the ciborium. The chalice holds the Blood of Christ, and the paten and ciborium hold his Body.

- Show young people the paten which the priest uses during Mass and the ciborium which may be used for distribution of hosts during Mass and for storing hosts in the tabernacle.

Objective

To explain the connection between the Eucharist and eternal life

Faith Focus

What does Jesus tell us about himself?
List young people's responses on the board or on chart paper.

We Share the Bread of Life

- Prepare young people for the Gospel story by having a young person read the paragraph.

- Point out that providing food for people is a sign of loving and caring.

Scripture   JOHN 6:30–58

I Am the Bread of Life

- Gather the group in a story circle or in the prayer space. Remind them that they will be hearing the Gospel story from John again.

- Ask what they remember from hearing the Gospel during the celebration.

- As you read the story aloud, discuss what is happening in the illustration.

- Discuss why the people in the story are confused by Jesus words. Jesus has not yet instituted the Eucharist, so they do not know what he means.

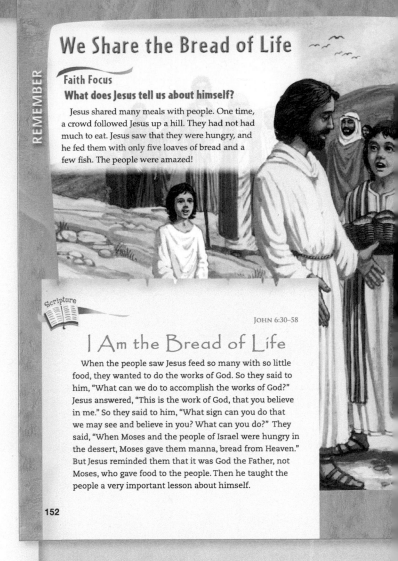

We Share the Bread of Life

Faith Focus

What does Jesus tell us about himself?

Jesus shared many meals with people. One time, a crowd followed Jesus up a hill. They had not had much to eat. Jesus saw that they were hungry, and he fed them with only five loaves of bread and a few fish. The people were amazed!

Scripture

JOHN 6:30–58

I Am the Bread of Life

When the people saw Jesus feed so many with so little food, they wanted to do the works of God. So they said to him, "What can we do to accomplish the works of God?" Jesus answered, "This is the work of God, that you believe in me." So they said to him, "What sign can you do that we may see and believe in you? What can you do?" They said, "When Moses and the people of Israel were hungry in the dessert, Moses gave them manna, bread from Heaven." But Jesus reminded them that it was God the Father, not Moses, who gave food to the people. Then he taught the people a very important lesson about himself.

152

Scripture Background

Signs of Divinity Jesus' listeners understood the "I am" phrase in the light of the revelation of God's own name to Moses in the burning bush (*Exodus 3:14*). When Moses wondered by what authority he was sent to the Egyptian pharaoh, God answered that Moses should tell the pharaoh that "I am" sent him. Because of this understanding, some of those who heard him accused Jesus of blasphemy.

An example of this claim is then used throughout the Gospel according to John where Jesus also performs signs so that people will recognize his identity. The sign of the multiplication of the loaves and fish points to the reality that Jesus himself is manna to feed the people. What the people did not understand at that time was that Jesus and the Father were one.

"My Father sent me to bring you life that lasts forever. I myself am the Bread of Life; whoever comes to me will never be hungry. No one who believes in me will ever be thirsty."

Jesus continued, "I am the Bread from Heaven. The people who ate manna in the desert eventually died, as all humans die. But if you share my own flesh and blood, I will always be with you. You will live forever with God."

"What is he talking about?" some people asked. Jesus answered them, "I am the Bread of Life. Whoever eats it will live forever. Just as the Father sent me and I have life because of him, so too will the one who eats the Bread of Life live forever."

BASED ON JOHN 6:30–58

 What do you think Jesus means when he says he is the Bread of Life?

 How can you share in Jesus' life?

Faith at Home

Read the Scripture story with your family. Talk about the connections between the effects of food for our physical bodies and Jesus as the food for our spirit. Together, decide on one activity you can do this week to remember that Jesus is the Bread of Life.

Share

Sketch a design In small groups or with a partner, sketch a billboard design on a separate piece of paper that shows members of your group inviting other people to share in Jesus' life. Give your design an interesting title.

153

❓ Allow time for personal reflection before calling on volunteers to answer the first question. He is our food. He will nourish us.

❓ Discuss the second question. We share Jesus' life by going to Holy Communion.

Share

- Have young people work in pairs or small groups on the activity.

- Allow time for young people to brainstorm their design.

- Assist with brainstorming titles for the designs.

- Post designs around the room and have young people walk around to enjoy them.

Review

- Jesus is the Bread of Life.

- God gives us life that will last forever.

Cultural Background

Bread In Jesus' time, bread was usually made from either wheat or barley. Bread made from barley was the bread for those who were poor. However, bread might also be made by mixing grains such as lentils, beans, and millet. The best bread was made from wheat in which only the grain was ground and the bran was not used. Bread was baked either on hot stones, on an iron griddle, or in an oven heated with twigs or grass.

Bread is always included in the major Jewish religious feasts. In the Gospel of John, this Bread of Life discourse takes place around the time of the feast of Passover.

Objective

To describe what happens at the Communion Rite

Faith Focus

What happens during the Communion Rite? List young people's responses on the board or on chart paper.

The Communion Rite

- As you read bulleted information, pause after each statement. Have volunteers restate or interpret the statement.

- Ask young people how they prepare for meals at home. Have them read the last paragraph of text to discover how we prepare to receive Communion.

Lamb of God

- Point out that there are many names for Jesus and for Holy Communion.

- Ask young people where they have heard the term "Lamb of God." Point out that it is one name for Jesus and also the name of a prayer.

- After reading the text, have volunteers recite the prayer, or have young people find it on page 183.

REMEMBER

The Communion Rite

SIGNS OF FAITH

***Agnus Dei* (Lamb of God)** The ***Agnus Dei* (Lamb of God)** is a title for Jesus. This title reminds us that Jesus gave his life for our sins. When we pray or sing this prayer before Holy Communion, we remember that through Jesus' death and Resurrection, our sins are forgiven and we have peace.

Faith Focus

What happens during the Communion Rite?

We receive Jesus, the Bread of Life, in Holy Communion. What does this mean?

- We are united with Jesus.
- Our friendship with Jesus grows stronger.
- God forgives our less serious sins if we are sorry and gives us strength to avoid serious sin.
- We are united with the whole Church, the Body of Christ.
- We share in God's promise that we will live in Heaven with Jesus, Mary, and all the saints.

We prepare ourselves to receive Holy Communion. Together we stand and pray the Lord's Prayer. We remember we are one family with God. As a sign of unity, we share the Sign of Peace with each other.

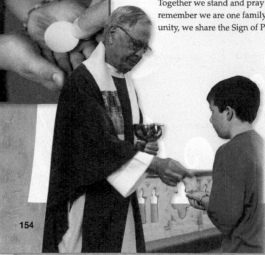

154

Catechist Background

Real presence After the consecration, Jesus' Body and Blood are truly and fully present. Once the bread and wine are consecrated, they are no longer the bread and wine but the Body and Blood of Christ. His presence—Body and Blood, soul and divinity—remains after the celebration of the Eucharist is over. This is one reason why we reserve the Blessed Sacrament in the tabernacle after Mass. The doctrine of Real Presence is a doctrine of faith. As Saint Thomas Aquinas said, it "cannot be apprehended by the senses but only by faith" (*Summa Theologica IIIa, 9.75, a.1*).

- One of the primary criteria to discern young people's readiness to receive Holy Communion for the first time is that they know the difference between the consecrated Bread we share at Eucharist and ordinary bread.

Holy Communion

When the time comes for Holy Communion, the priest invites us to the table. He reminds us of Jesus' sacrifice and presence in the Eucharist. He holds up the large Host and says, "Behold the Lamb of God, behold him who takes away the sins of the world. Blessed are those called to the supper of the Lamb." We come forward in a procession. Sometimes we sing a song.

When it is our turn to receive Jesus, we cup our hands with one hand on top of the other. The priest, deacon, or extraordinary minister of Holy Communion says, "The Body of Christ." We answer, "Amen."

We often receive from the cup. After we swallow the Host, we go to the deacon or extraordinary minister of Holy Communion, who offers the cup. We hear, "The Blood of Christ." We answer, "Amen." We return to our places. We pray or sing a prayer of thanksgiving.

We should receive Holy Communion every time we participate in the Mass. We must do so at least once a year.

Faith at Home

Ask family members to share their responses to the question. Talk about what happens when we receive Holy Communion by referring to the list on page 154. Together look at the pictures on pages 154 and 155, and review how to go to Holy Communion.

? Why are we blessed to share in the Lord's Supper?

155

Sacrament Background

Communion under both species   In the very early Church, receiving Communion under both species was normal. The fact that the Eucharist had its beginnings in the Passover meal, and in other fraternal meals that included rituals around bread and wine, shaped this custom.

When the practice of fully initiating infants became the norm, the practice developed in many churches of giving infants a small piece of the consecrated Bread and a sip of consecrated Wine. When an infant could not swallow the consecrated Bread, the child was given Communion with a sip of consecrated Wine.

Over time the practice of Communion under both species fell into disuse. However, the practice was restored in the liturgical renewal after the Second Vatican Council and continues today under the direction of local bishops (*GIRM 283*).

Holy Communion

Write the words *Host*, *deacon*, and *extraordinary minister* on the board or on chart paper. Have students define these words as the group shares the information on the page.

- Call attention to the various photos as you work through the text.
- Select volunteers to read the text aloud.
- Have young people practice holding their hands in the proper position for receiving Communion.
- Ask why we pray a prayer of thanksgiving after receiving Communion. because we are blessed to have received Jesus; because we want to thank Jesus for all the gifts he gives us

? Read and discuss the question. Accept all reasonable responses.

Activity Master

You may wish to use Activity Master 13 on page CE13 to further integrate the steps for receiving Communion.

▲ Activity Master 13

Review

- We receive Jesus in Holy Communion during the Communion Rite.
- Priests, deacons, and extraordinary ministers of Holy Communion distribute Communion to us.

Objective

To reflect on the meaning of Holy Communion

Receive Jesus

Respond

- Explain the activity.
- Distribute writing materials.
- Set a time limit.
- Walk among young people praising their work.
- Ask volunteers to share their work.

Closing Blessing

- Gather the group in a prayer circle with their books.
- Begin with the Sign of the Cross.
- Read aloud the People of Faith story about Venerable Maria Teresa Quevedo.
- Pray the prayer.
- End with *Songs of Celebration* CD, track 13, "Come to the Table," or one of the optional music suggestions from page 149.

Receive Jesus

Respond

Write a prayer In the space below, write a prayer. Share your thoughts and feelings about participating fully in the Mass by receiving Jesus in Holy Communion.

_____

_____

_____

_____

_____

_____

_____

_____

Closing Blessing

Gather and begin with the Sign of the Cross.

Leader: God, our Father, we praise and thank you for the gift of life.

All: Amen.

Leader: Jesus, our Savior, we praise and thank you for giving yourself to us in Holy Communion.

All: Amen.

Leader: Holy Spirit, giver of God's gifts, we praise and thank you for helping us live as members of the Body of Christ.

All: Amen.

Sing together.

We come to the Table of the Lord
As one body formed in your love.
We come to the Table of the Lord
As one body formed in your love.

© 2005 John Burlan

✦ People of Faith: A Story

Venerable Maria Teresa Quevedo Maria Teresa was born in Spain. When she was three, Maria Teresa's mother said: "She is a bundle of happiness. Everyone loves her. She is pretty as a picture but terribly self-willed. She cannot be crossed." Maria Teresa was a picky eater. Sometimes she was rude to others and would not say she was sorry when she hurt them. After her First Communion, her parents noticed that she changed. She began to be kind and loving toward others. As she grew up, Maria Teresa kept her happy spirit and made many friends. When she was eleven years old, she wrote in her notebook, "I have decided to become a saint." She lived a short life, but she used the time to become close to Jesus.

aith Focus

The Mass is a meal of thanksgiving.

Jesus is the Bread of Life.

In Holy Communion we are united to Jesus and the Church. We share in the promise of life forever with God.

itual Focus
haring a Meal

he celebration focused on haring a meal. You prayed blessing prayer and shared od. During the week, use e Blessing Prayer on page 49 as the prayer before your ain meal.

mily Prayer

rd, thank you for all the gifts u have given us. Thank you r family and friends. Help grow strong in love for one ther and for you. Send us e Holy Spirit to show us how share your life and love with hers. Amen.

Act

Share Together Plan a special meal of remembering and celebration with your family members. Decide whether it will be at home or at a restaurant. If it is at home, share in the preparation of the food. Ask each family member to bring pictures, symbols, or souvenirs of their favorite time as a family. Share the memories during the meal, and pray the blessings on page 149 before and after your meal.

Do Together As a family, prepare a meal for an elderly couple, or a family in which a parent is sick or a new baby has arrived. Plan the meal, contact the family to choose a convenient time, prepare the meal, and deliver it. As an alternative, volunteer to serve meals at a soup kitchen or Catholic Worker house.

GO online **www.osvcurriculum.com**
Visit our website for weekly Scripture readings and questions, family resources, and more activities.

157

Faith at Home

Review the five parts of the Faith at Home page with young people.

Encourage them:

- to ask family members to review the **Faith Focus** statements with them
- to share the **Ritual Focus: Sharing a Meal** with family members
- to do at least one of the  **Act** activities with family members
- to pray the **Family Prayer** with their family at times when the family is together
- to encourage their family members to go to **www.osvcurriculum.com** with them and do the activities for this chapter sometime during the week

Looking Ahead

For Chapter 14, you will need:

- a Bible
- a prayer table
- a candle
- a large glass bowl filled with water
- the *Songs of Celebration* CD
- a large cross or crucifix
- copies of Activity Master 14 on p. CE14 for each young person

General Instruction of the Roman Missal

The Concluding Rites include "the dismissal of the people by the deacon or the priest so that each may go out to do good works, praising and blessing God... (no. 90)."

Catechism Connection

To deepen your own background and reflection on the fruits of Holy Communion, refer to the *Catechism of the Catholic Church, 1391–1397.*

Catechist Resources

 Introducing Catholic Social Teaching to Children with Stories and Activities

Anne E. Neuberger
Twenty-Third Publications

Uses stories to foster awareness of justice

 This Sacred People: Living the Mystery of Faith *(21 min)*

Daniel Connors
Twenty-Third Publications

Discusses how to live the Eucharist in daily life

Young People's Resources

 The Catholic Kid's Guide to Stewardship

Elizabeth M. Johnson
Twenty-Third Publications

Uses the corporal works of mercy to suggest ways that even young people can serve others

 The Angel's First Communion Lesson *(13 min)*

Twenty-Third Publications

Angels tell of Jesus' presence at the Mass

Catechist Formation

> "Go therefore and make disciples of all nations . . ."
>
> Matthew 28:19

Going Forth

Usually when people receive an assignment or task to carry out, some words of encouragement help to instill confidence as they move forward with the assigned project. The duty to carry out a task does not have to be seen as a burden; it can be seen as recognition that the person who receives the task has the gifts and ability to carry out a certain responsibility.

This kind of thinking underlies the Concluding Rites of the Mass when people are blessed and sent into the world as disciples of Christ. Even though Mass comes to a conclusion, its impact and meaning continue as those who have shared in the Eucharist serve as a blessing for others in their lives and in the world. Those gathered for the Eucharist do not only receive Christ for their own sake. They take the Body and Blood of Christ into their hearts and are transformed so that they can be witnesses of Christ to others in the world through their words and actions.

Apostolic Witness

In this way, they carry on the mission of the Apostles whom Christ sent out to all the nations to proclaim the good news (*Matthew 28:19*). Catholics are sent out from Mass in the same way, with a blessing that instills courage and confidence, and with a responsibility that assures God's message of salvation will continue to be visible in the world. This responsibility includes deepening their union with Christ, a commitment to the poor, and working for the unity of Christians.

How does your participation in Sunday Mass affect your life?

In what ways do you see the Church reaching out to others in the world?

Catechist Prayer

Almighty God, deepen in me a spirit of discipleship. May the Sacrament of the Eucharist help me to live the values of the Gospel in every word and action. Amen.

Lesson Planner

www.osvcurriculum.com
Visit our website for additional resources and information.

	OBJECTIVES	LESSON PROCESS	ACTIVITIES	MATERIALS
CELEBRATE — 15 minutes — Pages 158–159	Ritual Focus *Blessing for Mission* To experience a celebration of the word, including a blessing for mission	Celebrate the opening prayer.		PROGRAM RESOURCES *Songs of Celebration* CD, track 14 *And With Your Spirit* CD, track 8
Pages 160–161	To explore the meaning of the ritual action To teach that we are sent forth from Mass to carry God's love to others	Complete the activity. ✝ Read about and discuss blessing. Describe our mission as followers of Jesus. ✝ Read about and discuss the call to be a witness.	☀ Reflect Young people reflect on the experience of the celebration and the meaning of being blessed for mission.	OTHER MATERIALS Bible, prayer table, candle, large glass bowl filled with water
REMEMBER — 30 minutes — Pages 162–163	Faith Focus *What happens when we receive the Holy Spirit?* To explain that the Holy Spirit is in our lives today	Discuss why and how the Holy Spirit helps us today. 📖 Proclaim the Scripture/Bible story of Pentecost. *Acts 2:1–41* Complete the activity.	☀ Share Young people write a poem. Faith at Home Suggested activities for the home	OTHER MATERIALS Writing materials PROGRAM RESOURCES copies of Activity Master 14, p. CE14
Pages 164–165	Faith Focus *How do we love and serve Jesus?* To explain why we are sent forth from Mass	Identify tasks that the Holy Spirit helps us with. ✝ Read about and discuss the role of deacons. Discuss how and why we are sent forth from Mass.	Faith at Home Suggested activities for the home	
LIVE — 15 minutes — Page 166	To reinforce the concept of service	Introduce the activity. Pray the Closing Blessing. Read aloud the People of Faith story about Saint Thérèse of Lisieux.	☀ Respond Young people create a slide presentation.	PROGRAM RESOURCES *Songs of Celebration* CD, track 14
FAITH AT HOME — Page 167	Faith at Home To introduce the different parts of the Faith at Home page	Review the Faith at Home page. Encourage young people to share this page at home.	☀ Act Suggested activities for the home	PROGRAM RESOURCES Eucharist Family Guide, pp. 30–31

CELEBRATE

Objective

To experience a celebration of the word, including a Blessing for Mission

Preparation

Familiarize yourself with the movements of the ritual focus for the Blessing for Mission on page 159. You will need:

• a Bible

• a table covered with a white cloth

• a candle and a large glass bowl filled with water on the prayer table

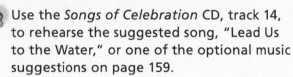 Use the *Songs of Celebration* CD, track 14, to rehearse the suggested song, "Lead Us to the Water," or one of the optional music suggestions on page 159.

Select a young person to carry the Bible in procession.

We Gather

Invite young people to assemble with their books for a procession.

• Direct them to follow you and the young person who is carrying the Bible.

• As you process, lead young people in singing using the *Songs of Celebration* CD, track 14.

• When all are assembled in the prayer space, light the prayer candle.

• Begin prayer, and lead young people in the Sign of the Cross.

Follow the order of prayer on pages 158–159.

We Listen

For the proclamation of the Scripture, you may use a Bible or the adapted reading in the *Candidate's Book* on pages 162–163.

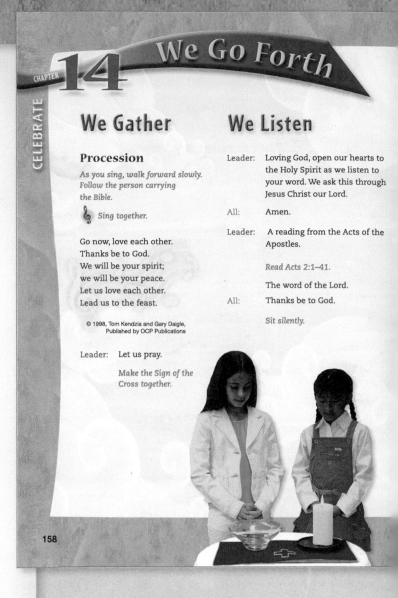

CHAPTER **14** We Go Forth

CELEBRATE

We Gather

Procession

As you sing, walk forward slowly. Follow the person carrying the Bible.

♪ *Sing together.*

Go now, love each other.
Thanks be to God.
We will be your spirit;
we will be your peace.
Let us love each other.
Lead us to the feast.

© 1998, Tom Kendzia and Gary Daigle, Published by OCP Publications

Leader: Let us pray.

Make the Sign of the Cross together.

We Listen

Leader: Loving God, open our hearts to the Holy Spirit as we listen to your word. We ask this through Jesus Christ our Lord.

All: Amen.

Leader: A reading from the Acts of the Apostles.

Read Acts 2:1–41.

The word of the Lord.

All: Thanks be to God.

Sit silently.

158

Liturgical Background

Rite of Dismissal   The word Mass is taken from some of the last words of the liturgy in Latin: *Ite, missa est.* In English these words for the dismissal of the assembly are translated: "Go forth, the Mass is ended." The word *missa*, from which the English word Mass comes, means "sent."

Another option when dismissed is, "Go in peace." When people hear these words, they may think this means only that the celebration has ended. In fact, these simple words remind us that being Catholic means not only being called, but also being sent. Nourished by the Eucharist, we go forth to praise and serve God in the circumstances of our daily lives.

Ritual Focus: Blessing for Mission

Come forward and gather around the holy water.

Sprinkle candidates with water.

Leader: Just as the disciples were filled with the Holy Spirit and told the good news in word and action, so are we. Let us pray for God's blessing.

Lord, you came on Earth to serve others. May your example strengthen us.

All: Amen.

Leader: Through your dying and rising, you made a new world where we are all neighbors called to love one another. May we live our lives according to your Gospel.

All: Amen.

Leader: Let us pray that God, who is love, will light our hearts with the fire of the Holy Spirit and give us a love for others.

Bow your heads and pray for God's blessing.

Blessed are you God of mercy. Through your Son, Jesus, you gave us an example of love.

Send down your blessing on these your children. Help them to generously serve others when they see their need. Let them serve you in their neighbor.

All: Amen.

ADAPTED FROM THE BOOK OF BLESSINGS, 587

We Go Forth

Make the Sign of the Cross with the water.

Leader: Go and announce the Gospel of the Lord.

All: Thanks be to God.

 Sing the opening song together.

159

Ritual Focus: Blessing for Mission

- Invite young people to stand and gather around the holy water.
- Raise your right hand as you pray the blessing.

We Go Forth

- Invite young people to come forward individually and bless themselves.
- When all have blessed themselves, lead the closing prayer.
- As the group processes back to their seats, have them sing *Songs of Celebration* CD, track 14, "Lead Us to the Water," or one of the optional music suggestions.

Optional Music Suggestions

"Id y enseñad/Go and Teach,"
© Gabarain. Published by OCP

"Eat This Bread,"
Les Presses de Taize. © GIA Publications

✳ Ritual Background

Blessing   A blessing has two aspects: the calling down of God's gifts and thanksgiving returned to God. When we bow to receive a blessing, we express an attitude of humility before God. But there is also a spirit of gratitude that rises up within us in response to God's blessing. Thus, with the psalmist we can say:

"Bless the LORD, O my soul, and all that is within me, bless his holy name!" (*Psalm 103:1*)

The *Catechism* teaches that every baptized person is called to be a blessing and to bless (*CCC 1669*). So, parents may bless their children, lay catechists may bless catechumens, and so on. At Mass, however, it is only the priest who blesses the assembly. The blessing may be a simple invocation of the Trinity. On some occasions, a more solemn blessing may be used. To each of the invocations, the people respond, "Amen."

CELEBRATE

Objective

To explore the meaning of the ritual action of Blessing for Mission

To teach that we are sent forth from Mass to carry God's love to others

Liturgical Catechesis

The purpose of this section is to help young people reflect on their experiences of the signs, rituals, prayers, and gestures of the celebration and to lead them to express their own meaning of the experiences. Allow young people to share their experiences without commenting on them.

Being Blessed

- On the board or on chart paper, write the following questions: What did you see? What did you hear? What did you do?

- Guide young people to reflect on the celebration by reviewing what happened in the prayer.

- Invite young people to share their responses to the questions.

Reflect

- Invite young people to complete the phrases with their own thoughts and feelings.

- In pairs have young people share their responses.

Blessing

- Read aloud the text.

- Discuss the different kinds of blessing.

Being Blessed

Blessing

A **blessing** is an action using words and gestures to ask God to show his kindness to us. There are many kinds of blessings. The Church blesses people and objects. Parents are blessed when their children are baptized. Animals are blessed on the feast of Saint Francis. Parents bless children at night or when they wake in the morning. The priest blesses special objects such as rosaries. At Mass the priest blesses the assembly.

Reflect

Blessing for a mission Think and write about the celebration. Go back and read the Blessing Prayer on page 159. Then write a few sentences to complete the journal entries below.

Today I was blessed. I felt really

_____

_____

_____

_____

I am being blessed to go out and serve others. I think that means

_____

_____

_____

_____

_____

160

Additional Activity

Seek doable possibilities   Many young people may feel that they must do impressive projects in order to have an impact on the world. Try to avoid their possible discouragement with these suggestions.

- Point out that what seems like a small contribution may be significant.

- Encourage young people to take part in group efforts, such as community clean-up days, school carnivals, and other projects.

- Have young people assess their talents and use them in new ways. For example, singers, dancers, and musicians can offer to perform at local retirement communities.

- Have them design their own service project and report back on its implementation at a later date. Be sure parents are aware of their children's projects.

Sent on Mission

Have you ever been sent to do a special job? Being sent means you are trusted. You represent someone else. You are responsible. Someone is counting on you. Without you, the job will not get done.

At the end of Mass, we are sent to carry the message of God's love to others. We are sent to help carry out the work of Jesus in the world. The word *Mass* comes from a word that means "to be sent on a mission." Receiving Jesus in Holy Communion strengthens us to love and serve others. We go out from Mass with God's blessing.

SIGNS OF FAITH

Witness

At the end of Mass, we are sent forth to be witnesses of faith in Jesus' presence in the world today. A witness is somebody who sees or hears something and tells others about it. We are witnesses to Jesus' presence when we tell others about him in our words and in our actions.

161

Sent on a Mission

- Summarize the first paragraph, and have young people share their experiences of being sent to do a special job.

- Have five volunteers each read aloud a sentence in the second paragraph.

- Pause for discussion after each sentence is read.

- Encourage young people to share their ideas about how they can carry God's love to others.

Witness

- Summarize the text for young people.

- Share one or two examples of people who are everyday witnesses of faith to you.

- Invite young people to think of their own examples and share them.

Teaching Tip

Use ordinary experiences When relating experiences or stories of people who are witnesses of faith or when giving examples of possibilities for mission, use experiences and examples young people can relate to and possibly imitate. Otherwise, they may feel that acting for mission is not possible for them.

At the same time, be sure to use some examples that challenge young people to think beyond the communities of family and school. You may be able to find these kinds of examples in newspaper stories of individual young people or groups of young people who have reached out to others.

If possible, invite a representative from a parish organization or committee that is involved in outreach or social concerns activities. Ask him or her to present some ideas to the group that would be possible activities for young people or families to be involved in.

Objective

To explain that the Holy Spirit is in our lives today

Faith Focus

What happens when we receive the Holy Spirit? List young people's responses on the board or on chart paper.

The Holy Spirit

- Recall that the Trinity is three Persons in one God—God the Father, God the Son, and God the Holy Spirit.

- Use the text to explain that Jesus sent the Holy Spirit to guide us throughout our lives, not just when we are in church.

Scripture   ACTS 2:1–41

Pentecost

- Gather the group in a story circle or in the prayer space. Remind them that they will be hearing the story from Acts again.

- Ask what they remember from hearing the story during the celebration.

- If possible, darken the room for the first paragraph to simulate the darkness the disciples felt.

- Turn on the lights for the remainder of the reading.

- Emphasize Peter's words, proclaiming them as he would have to a large crowd.

REMEMBER

The Holy Spirit

Faith Focus

What happens when we receive the Holy Spirit?

Before Jesus returned to his Father in Heaven, he gave his disciples a mission. He wanted them to teach others about his message. Jesus promised the disciples he would send the Holy Spirit to help them with their mission. Fifty days after Jesus' Resurrection, his promise came true.

Scripture   ACTS 2:1–41

Pentecost

During the feast of Pentecost, the disciples were all in one place together. Suddenly, there came from the sky a noise like a strong driving wind, and it filled the entire house in which they were sitting. Then there appeared tongues as of fire, which parted and came to rest on each one of them. And they were all filled with the Holy Spirit and began to speak in different languages.

They went out into the street and began to tell the crowd about Jesus and his message. The people who listened were surprised because the disciples were speaking in different languages. They wondered what had happened.

162

 ## Scripture Background

Beginnings Prior to the Christian Pentecost, the Jewish disciples of Jesus were quite small in number. The Acts of the Apostles tells us that they numbered only 120 (See *Acts 1:15*). When the Holy Spirit descended upon the followers of Jesus on Pentecost, they were transformed. They realized their mission was to preach the message of Jesus.

Although the Jewish people who had assembled for the Jewish feast of Pentecost were from different places and spoke different languages and dialects, they understood what the disciples were saying as they began to preach.

After Peter spoke to the large crowd, 3,000 people were added to the number of believers (See *Acts 2:41*). Empowered by this event, the Church spread to the Gentile world and grew rapidly.

Peter raised his voice and said, "What has happened is the work of the Holy Spirit. Jesus of Nazareth has sent the Holy Spirit as he promised." Then Peter said, "This Jesus whom you crucified has been raised from the dead. He is the Messiah." When the people heard this they asked Peter and the other Apostles, "What are we to do my brothers?" Peter told them, "Repent and be baptized, every one of you, in the name of Jesus Christ for the forgiveness of your sins; and you will receive the gift of the holy Spirit." Those who accepted his message were baptized, and about three thousand persons were added that day.

BASED ON ACTS 2:1–41

? What did the Holy Spirit do for the disciples?

? How does the Holy Spirit help you?

Faith at Home

Read the Scripture story with your family members. Discuss everyone's responses to the questions. Ask family members to share times when they called on the Holy Spirit for help. Review the prayer Come, Holy Spirit on page 191. Choose an appropriate time each day to pray the prayer.

Share

Write a poem On a separate sheet of paper, create your own poem about the Holy Spirit. Use at least five of the words below.

Holy Spirit	wind	wide	gift
in	be	guide	soar
today	pray	fire	fill

163

? Discuss the first question as a group. Possible responses: gave them power, courage to go out into the crowd, people who spoke foreign languages could understand them

? Allow time for personal reflection on the second question. Accept all reasonable responses.

Share

- Distribute paper and pens or pencils.
- Tell young people how much time they will have for the exercise.
- Direct candidates as they work; circulate among them to provide assistance.
- Consider having young people decorate their papers and display them in the room.

Review

- Jesus sent the Holy Spirit to help us teach about God the Father.
- The Holy Spirit came to the disciples on Pentecost.

Cultural Background

Pentecost Pentecost is a Greek word meaning "fifty." Sometimes referred to as the Feast of Weeks, this Jewish Feast of Pentecost (*Exodus 34:22*) is celebrated at the end of the seven weeks of the cereal harvest. It was a major feast for which the Jewish people would travel from their homes to Jerusalem to make offerings at the Temple. This is probably why there were so many people of diverse languages and dialects in Jerusalem when Peter preached.

The descent of the Holy Spirit at the time of the Jewish Feast of Pentecost gave the feast new meaning for the Christians. The Jewish Feast of Pentecost provided a ready-made opportunity for the early Church to celebrate the descent of the Holy Spirit upon the first Christian community.

REMEMBER

Objective
To explain why we are sent forth from Mass

Faith Focus

How do we love and serve Jesus?
List young people's responses on the board or on chart paper.

We Are Sent

- Help young people recall that in the opening ceremony, they were blessed for their mission. Jesus also sent his disciples on a mission.

- Point out that we share the mission of the disciples. Whenever we leave Mass, we are sent on that mission.

- Work through the bulleted list and have young people give examples of ways that they can fulfill their mission.

✝ Deacon

- Write the term *deacon* on the board or on chart paper.

- As you read through the duties of a deacon, invite young people to summarize them on the board or chart paper.

- If your parish has a deacon, consider having him speak to the group about his role in the Church.

We Are Sent

SIGNS OF FAITH ✝ Deacon

A **deacon** is a man ordained by the bishop to do works of charity and to have a special role in worship. Some deacons become priests. Other deacons do not, but they help the bishop and care for people who need it. All deacons can baptize and witness a marriage. At Mass deacons may carry the Book of the Gospels, read the Gospel, and preach. They can also send us forth for mission at the end of Mass.

Faith Focus

How do we love and serve Jesus?

Like Peter and the disciples, Jesus promises us the Holy Spirit. The Holy Spirit is with us always. The Holy Spirit helps us:

- tell others about his love
- do the work of a disciple
- forgive others
- care about people who need help, especially those who are poor

✦ Additional Activity

Acting justly Explain to the young people at the beginning of the Liturgy of the Eucharist we respond to the priest that to love and serve the Lord is right and just. Reinforce this point with the song "It is Right and Just" (track 8) from the *And With Your Spirit* music CD. Replay the song so that they become familiar with the definitions of the words *right* and *just* in the chorus. Then:

- Post a map of the world on the board or on chart paper.

- Ask the young people to name ways that they can act "right and just" in the world. If they need help to get started, remind them to reflect on the verses of the song and include both actions bring justice to our neighbors and also things that put God first in our lives, such as prayer, sacraments, and fasting.

- Print their responses on white mailing labels.

- When you have a number of suggestions that is equal to the number of learners, give each young person a sticker. Have them come to the front of the room to attach their stickers to the map.

Go Forth

At the end of Mass, we are sent forth to serve others. The priest or deacon says, "The Mass has ended." We respond, "Thanks be to God." We go forth to announce the joyful good news that Jesus is alive. We share the good news by what we say and what we do.

When we leave the church after Mass, we are different from when we came in. Participating in the Eucharist changes us. It brings us closer to God the Father, Son, and Holy Spirit. It also brings us closer to one another. Just as many grains of wheat make one loaf of bread, in the Eucharist we become one body. We are filled with God's grace and love. We go forth in peace to give glory to God. We go forth to help those who need our help. We love and serve Jesus when we love and serve one another.

❓ **How will you ask the Holy Spirit to help you look at your life?**

165

Go Forth

- Point out to the young people that Jesus expects us to always serve others.
- Practice the dismissal response with the young people. Ask why we are thankful at the end of Mass. for our gifts from God, for one another, for the Church
- Point out that not everyone feels different after Mass. Make an analogy between spiritual and physical growth: even though the young people are growing, they don't always feel it, but over time, they can tell a difference in their height and weight. Spiritual growth is the same; it is not always readily apparent.
- Read the last paragraph aloud, clarifying the mission of all to serve others.

❓ Invite volunteers to answer the question. Possible answers: helping at home, collecting money for a charity

Activity Master

You may wish to use Activity Master 14 on page CE14 to clarify the roles of bishops, priests, deacons, and extraordinary ministers.

▲ Activity Master 14

Review

- The Holy Spirit helps us serve others.
- When Mass ends, we are sent forth in peace to share the good news.

Sacrament Background

Deacons According to the oldest practices of the Catholic Church, the ministry of deacons as we know it today originated in the story found in *Acts 6:1–6*. The diaconate arose out of an expressed need articulated by the community of the Hellenistic Jews, who complained to the Apostles that their widows were being neglected.

The Apostles discerned that they could not leave their own service of the word and instead established the ministry of the diaconate for service to the widows. Stephen, who was also the first martyr, was one of the first deacons.

LIVE

Objective

To reinforce the concept of service

Sent to Serve

Respond

- Explain the activity to young people. Point out that people who plan movies and commercials use frames like these to organize their work.

- Distribute crayons and pencils.

- Set a time limit.

- Invite volunteers to present their ideas to the group.

Closing Blessing

- Gather the group in a prayer circle with their books.

- Begin with the Sign of the Cross.

- Read aloud the People of Faith story about Saint Thérèse of Lisieux.

- Pray the prayer.

 End with *Songs of Celebration* CD, track 14, "Lead Us to the Water," or one of the optional music suggestions on page 159.

Sent to Serve

Respond

Draw a slide presentation In the frames provided, draw a slide presentation that shows how you will live out your mission as part of the Body of Christ.

Closing Blessing

Gather and begin with the Sign of the Cross.

Leader: God, our Father, send us forth to tell the world about your love.

All: Amen.

Leader: Jesus, our Savior, send us forth to serve others

All: Amen.

Leader: Holy Spirit, guide us to see the places where we are called to love and serve.

All: Amen.

 Sing together.

Go now, love each other.
Thanks be to God.
We will be your spirit.
We will be your peace.
Let us love each other.
Lead us to the feast.

© 1998, Tom Kendzia and Gary Daigle, Published by OCP Publications

166

People of Faith: A Story

Saint Thérèse of Lisieux Thérèse was the youngest of five daughters. She lived in France. She loved Jesus very much and wanted to serve God as a missionary, but she was not strong enough. At fifteen, Thérèse became a Carmelite sister. She decided that the best thing she could do for others was to do the ordinary everyday things very well. She became known for her goodness. She wrote a book about her friendship with God. She only lived twenty-four years, but millions of people have read the book she wrote. Many of them learned to serve God by following Thérèse's example. After she died, the pope named her patroness of the missions.

1873–1897

Faith at Home

Faith Focus

- The Eucharist changes us.

- The Holy Spirit helps us to live out our mission.

- At Mass we are sent forth in peace to announce the good news.

Ritual Focus
Blessing for Mission

The celebration focused on being sent forth for mission. You were blessed by your catechist and sent forth. Talk with family members about doing a family ritual of blessing each other with the Sign of the Cross on the forehead when you leave the house in the morning or at other times you decide would be appropriate.

Family Prayer

Come Holy Spirit, show us the way and give us the strength to love and serve others. Amen.

Act

Share Together Make a list of ways members of your family show love and care for each other. Then brainstorm together other ways the family might continue to show love and care. Suggest a family "love and serve" week. Write the names of family members on a slip of paper. Have each member draw a name. Invite family members to do some "love and serve" actions for that person.

Do Together Obtain copies of the parish bulletin or newsletter. With your family, go through it and locate parish activities of service and outreach. Choose one that the whole family can get involved in, and call the parish to volunteer. After volunteering, hold a family discussion about the experience and how it felt to love and serve others.

Love and Serve Week

GO online www.osvcurriculum.com
Visit our website for weekly Scripture readings and questions, family resources, and more activities.

Faith at Home

Review the five parts of the Faith at Home page with young people.

Encourage them:

- to ask family members to review the Faith Focus statements with them

- to share the **Ritual Focus: Blessing for Mission** with family members

- to do at least one of the ☀ Act activities with family members

- to pray the **Family Prayer** with their family at times when the family is together

- to encourage their family members to go to **www.osvcurriculum.com** with them and do the activities for this chapter sometime during the week

Words of Faith

Words of Faith

A

Agnus Dei (Lamb of God) A title for Jesus that reminds us that he offered his life through suffering and death to take away our sins.

altar The table of the Eucharist. The Liturgy of the Eucharist is celebrated at the altar.

altar server A person who helps the priest and deacon at Mass.

ambo The reading stand from which the Scriptures are proclaimed. It is sometimes called the lectern.

assembly The baptized community gathered to celebrate the Eucharist, the Sacraments, or other liturgy.

B

Baptism One of the three Sacraments of Initiation. Baptism gives us new life in God and makes us members of the Church.

baptismal font A bowl-shaped container or pool of water used for Baptism. The word *font* means "fountain."

Bible God's word written in human words. The Bible is the holy book of the Church.

Blessed Sacrament Another name for the Body and Blood of Jesus.

blessing An action using words and gestures which asks God to show his kindness to us.

Body of Christ A name for the Church. It tells us that Christ is the head and the baptized are the members of the body.

Book of the Gospels A decorated book containing the readings from the four Gospels used during the Liturgy of the Word.

C

cantor The leader of song during the Mass and other Church celebrations.

chalice The special silver or gold cup used at Mass to hold the wine that becomes the Blood of Christ.

chrism The oil blessed by the bishop used in the Sacraments of Baptism, Confirmation, and Holy Orders.

Christian The name given to people who are baptized and follow Jesus.

Church The community of all baptized people who believe in God and follow Jesus.

ciborium The special silver or gold container used at Mass to hold the smaller consecrated Hosts for communion. A covered ciborium also holds the Blessed Sacrament in the tabernacle.

collection The gifts of money collected from members of the assembly and presented during the time of the Presentation and Preparation of the Gifts.

Confirmation One of the three Sacraments of Initiation. It is the Sacrament that strengthens the life of God we received at Baptism and seals us with the gift of the Holy Spirit.

Confiteor A prayer of sorrow for sin. In it each person tells God and the Church family, "I am sorry." We ask for forgiveness.

168   169

Illustrated Words of Faith

This section gives young people a visual reference for the people, places, and things associated with the Eucharistic celebration. It contains some of the important words of faith used by the Church to help us understand the mystery of the Eucharist. Learning these words and their meanings will help young people develop a Catholic vocabulary.

▶ Have young people refer to pages 168–173 as the highlighted words of faith appear in each lesson. Have volunteers read the definitions aloud and then use each word in a sentence.

consecation The part of the Eucharistic Prayer when, through the prayers and actions of the priest and the power of the Holy Spirit, the gifts of bread and wine become the Body and Blood of Jesus.

 cruets Small pitchers or containers that hold the water and wine used at Mass.

 deacon A man who is ordained to serve the Church. Deacons may baptize, proclaim the Gospel, preach, assist the priest at Mass, witness marriages, and do works of charity.

 Eucharist One of the three Sacraments of Initiation. It is the Sacrament of the Body and Blood of Christ. Jesus is truly and really present in the Eucharist. The word *Eucharist* means "thanksgiving."

G

grace A sharing in God's own life.

H

Holy Communion The Body and Blood of Christ that we receive in the Eucharist.

Holy Trinity The three Persons in one God: God the Father, God the Son, and God the Holy Spirit.

host A round piece of unleavened bread used at Mass. When the host is consecrated at Mass, it becomes the Body and Blood of Christ.

I

 incense Oils and spices that are burned in liturgical celebrations to show honor for holy things. It is also used as a sign of our prayers rising to God.

L

Lamb of God (*Agnes Dei*) A title for Jesus that reminds us that he offered his life through suffering and death to take away our sins.

 lectionary The book of Scripture readings used at Mass.

lector A person who proclaims God's word at Mass or other liturgical celebrations. The word *lector* means "reader."

Liturgy of the Eucharist The second main part of the Mass. It is the time when we call on the Holy Spirit and the priest consecrates the bread and wine. We remember and give thanks for all of God's gifts, especially Jesus' life, death, and Resurrection.

Liturgy of the Word The first main part of the Mass. It is the time when we listen to God's word in the Scriptures.

M

Mass Another name for the Eucharist.

memorial Another word for remembering. In the Mass, it means to remember and proclaim God's works.

mission A job or duty someone is sent to do and takes responsibility for. The Church's mission is to announce the good news of God's Kingdom.

mystery Something we believe about God and his actions, but we do not understand how it happens.

Mystery of Faith This is the part of the Eucharistic Prayer that reflects upon the death, Resurrection, and Second Coming of Christ.

O

Original Sin The first sin committed by the first humans.

As these words come up in the lessons, wave young people make their own set of Words of Faith vocabulary cards. Use index cards. Have young people write the word on one side and the definition on the other side. They could also use these cards for a vocabulary word game, either in the session, while they are waiting for the session to begin, or at home with family members.

▶ Refer to these pages throughout the sessions to help young people associate liturgical names with the objects, rituals, and people they describe.

▶ Invite young people to draw their own illustrations for each of the terms.

Paschal candle Another name for the Easter Candle that is lit at the Easter Vigil.

paten The silver or gold plate or dish used at Mass to hold the large Host.

Pentecost The feast that celebrates the coming of the Holy Spirit on the Apostles and disciples fifty days after Easter. We celebrate this day as the beginning of the Church.

People of God A name for the Church which tells us that we are sent by Christ to preach God's love to all people.

prayer Talking and listening to God. It is raising our minds and hearts to God.

preparation of the altar and gifts The part of the Mass when the altar is prepared and members of the assembly bring the bread and wine, which will become the Body and Blood of Jesus, to the priest at the altar.

priest A man who is ordained to serve God and lead the Church by celebrating the Sacraments, preaching and presiding at Mass, and performing other spiritual works.

procession A group of people moving forward as part of a celebration.

Roman Missal The book containing the Order of the Mass, special celebrations during the year, and various prayers used by the priest at Mass.

Sacrament A holy sign that comes from Jesus, which gives us a share in God's life.

Sacraments of Initiation The three Sacraments of Baptism, Confirmation, and Holy Eucharist that together make us full members of the Church. They are signs that we belong to God and to the Catholic Church.

sanctuary The part of the church where the altar and ambo are located. The word *sanctuary* means "holy place."

Sign of Peace The Sign of Peace is an action prayer that we exchange before Communion as a sign to wish God's peace on those who receive it. It shows that we are one in Christ's love.

tabernacle The container in which the Blessed Sacrament is kept. It may be located in the sanctuary or a special chapel in the church. A lamp or candle is kept burning near the tabernacle as a sign that Jesus is present. The word *tabernacle* means "meeting place."

unity A word that means to be one with others.

usher A person of hospitality who welcomes members of the assembly to Mass and helps direct processions and collections.

vestments The special clothing worn by the priest and some others for Mass and other liturgical celebrations.

▶ If possible, take young people on a tour of the church. Ask the sacristan or a parish minister to show young people some of the sacred vessels and vestments used by your parish community. Have young people note how what they see in the parish church is the same or different from the pictures in the book.

▶ At the end of the last eight sessions (Chapters 7–14), go through the Words of Faith glossary word by word and ask young people to tell what each word means.

Order of Mass

Every Sunday we gather together united as one with all the members of the Church to give praise and thanks to God.

Introductory Rites

During the Introductory Rites, we prepare to listen to God's word and prepare to celebrate the Eucharist.

Entrance Chant

The priest, deacon, and other ministers begin the procession to the altar. We stand and sing. The Greeting and our response shows that we are gathered together as the Church.

Greeting

When the procession reaches the altar, the priest, deacon, and other ministers make a profound bow. The priest and deacon also kiss the altar as a sign of reverence. At special times the priest will burn incense at the cross and altar. The priest goes to his chair and leads us in the Sign of the Cross and Greeting.

Priest: In the name of the Father, and of the Son, and of the Holy Spirit.
People: Amen.
Priest: The grace of our Lord Jesus Christ, and the love of God, and the communion of the Holy Spirit be with you all.
People: And with your spirit.

Rite for the Blessing and Sprinkling of Water

On some Sundays, the priest does a Rite of Sprinkling in place of the Penitential Act. We are blessed with holy water to remind us of our Baptism.

Penitential Act

The priest invites the assembly to confess our sins together.

Confiteor

I confess to almighty God
and to you, my brothers and sisters,
that I have greatly sinned,
in my thoughts and in my words,
in what I have done and in what I
have failed to do,

Gently strike your chest with a closed fist.

through my fault, through my
fault,
through my most grievous fault;

Continue:

therefore I ask blessed Mary ever-Virgin,
all the Angels and Saints,
and you, my brothers and sisters,
to pray for me to the Lord our God.

Kyrie

Kyrie, eleison (Lord, have mercy)

Priest: You were sent to heal the contrite of heart:
Lord, have mercy. Or: Kyrie, eleison.
People: Lord, have mercy. Or: Kyrie, eleison.
Priest: You came to call sinners:
Christ, have mercy. Or: Christe, eleison.
People: Christ, have mercy. Or: Christe, eleison.
Priest: You are seated at the right hand of the Father to intercede for us:
Lord, have mercy. Or: Kyrie, eleison.
People: Lord, have mercy. Or: Kyrie, eleison

Gloria

On some Sundays, we praise God the Father, the Son, and the Holy Spirit.

Glory to God in the highest,
and on earth peace to people of good will.
We praise you,
we bless you,
we adore you,
we glorify you,
we give you thanks for your great glory,
Lord God, heavenly King,
O God, almighty Father.

Lord Jesus Christ, Only Begotten Son,
Lord God, Lamb of God, Son of the Father,
you take away the sins of the world,
    have mercy on us;
you take away the sins of the world,
    receive our prayer;
you are seated at the right hand of the
    Father,
    have mercy on us.

For you alone are the Holy One,
you alone are the Lord,
you alone are the Most High,
Jesus Christ,
with the Holy Spirit,
in the glory of God the Father.
Amen.

174

175

...se the Order of Mass on pages 174–185 ...f the *Candidate's Book* to help young people ...arn the parts of the Mass. The Order of Mass ...cludes the prayers and responses used during ...e Mass.

...ere are some suggested uses ...or these pages:

At the end of Chapter 7, invite young people to turn to these pages. Explain that over the next seven chapters they will be learning different parts of the Mass. Do a general review of the Order of Mass with them. Use the headings and pictures to review. This will also help you know what young people already know about the Mass.

▶ Direct the young people's attention to these pages and encourage them to go through the pages with family members at home.

▶ Refer to the appropriate sections of the Order of Mass as you teach each lesson:

Chapter 8   Introductory Rites and Gloria

Chapter 9   Penitential Act

Chapter 10   Liturgy of the Word

Chapter 11   Liturgy of the Eucharist: Preparation of the Gifts

Chapter 12   Liturgy of the Eucharist: Eucharistic Prayer

Chapter 13   Liturgy of the Eucharist: Communion Rite

Chapter 14   Concluding Rites: Dismissal

Collect

The priest invites us to pray. We are silent for a moment and remember we are in God's presence. We think about what we want to pray for.

Priest: Let us pray...
People: Amen.

Liturgy of the Word

The Liturgy of the Word is celebrated at every Mass. We listen to God's word in the Readings and Homily, and we respond to God's word in the Creed and Prayer of the Faithful. The lectors and the priest or deacon read the readings from the ambo.

First Reading

We sit and listen to God's word from the Old Testament or the Acts of the Apostles. At the end of the reading, we respond:

Reader: The word of the Lord.
People: Thanks be to God.

Responsorial Psalm

At the end of the first reading, the cantor, or song leader, leads us in singing a psalm from the Old Testament.

People: Sing or say the refrain.

Second Reading

We listen to God's word from the New Testament books that are not Gospels. At the end of the reading, we respond:

Reader: The word of the Lord.
People: Thanks be to God.

Gospel Acclamation

We stand and welcome the Lord, who speaks to us in the Gospel reading. We sing an Alleluia or another acclamation to profess our faith in God's presence.

People: Sing or say the Alleluia or Gospel Acclamation.

Gospel Dialogue

Priest or deacon: The Lord be with you.
People: And with your spirit.
Priest or deacon: A reading from the Holy Gospel according to...
People: Glory to you, O Lord.

The priest and people make the Sign of the Cross on the forehead, lips, and heart.

Gospel Reading

At the end of the Gospel, we respond:

Priest or deacon: The Gospel of the Lord.
People: Praise to you, Lord Jesus Christ.

Homily

We sit and listen. The priest or deacon helps us understand the word of God. He shows us how we can live as Jesus' disciples.

Profession of Faith

We stand and respond to the readings by saying the Creed. We profess our faith in God the Father, God the Son, and God the Holy Spirit. We pray the Nicene Creed or the Apostles' Creed. *(For Nicene Creed, see page 178. For Apostles' Creed, see page 188.)*

Here are some suggested uses for these pages:

▶ Review the parts of the Liturgy of the Word Go over the different postures during this part of the Mass. Be sure young people know when to sit and when to stand.

▶ Read the Nicene Creed on page 178 with young people. Point out where the Persons of the Blessed Trinity are mentioned. Have young people read the Creed aloud.

▶ Have young people look at the Apostles' Creed on page 188. Point out that the Apostles' Creed is shorter than the Nicene Creed but also contains statements about what we believe.

Nicene Creed

People: I believe in one God,
    the Father almighty,
    maker of heaven and earth,
    of all things visible and invisible.
I believe in one Lord Jesus Christ,
    the Only Begotten Son of God,
    born of the Father before all ages.
    God from God, Light from Light,
    true God from true God,
    begotten, not made,
      consubstantial with the Father;
    through him all things
      were made.
For us men and for our salvation
    he came down from heaven,

*At the words that follow up to and including
and became man, all bow.*

    and by the Holy Spirit was incarnate
    of the Virgin Mary,
    and became man.
For our sake he was crucified
    under Pontius Pilate,
he suffered death and was buried,

and rose again on the third day
    in accordance with the Scriptures.
He ascended into heaven and is
    seated at the right hand of
    the Father.
He will come again in glory
    to judge the living and the dead
and his kingdom will have no end.
I believe in the Holy Spirit,
    the Lord, the giver of life,
who proceeds from the Father
    and the Son,
who with the Father and the Son is
    adored and glorified,
who has spoken through the
    prophets.
I believe in one, holy, catholic and
    apostolic Church.
I confess one Baptism for the
    forgiveness of sins
and I look forward to the
    resurrection of the dead
    and the life of the world to come.
Amen.

Prayer of the Faithful

We stand and the priest, deacon, or a layperson leads us in praying for the needs of the Church, the world, those who need our prayers, and our local community. We say or sing the response that the leader tells us to say or sing.

Liturgy of the Eucharist

During the Liturgy of the Eucharist, we bring our gifts of bread and wine to the altar. We give thanks to God the Father for all the ways he has saved us. Our gifts of bread and wine become the Body and Blood of Christ. We all receive the Lord's Body and the Lord's Blood in communion.

Preparation of the Gifts

We sit as the gifts of bread and wine are brought to the altar. The altar is prepared as the collection is taken up. Sometimes we sing a song during the preparation.

The priest lifts up the bread and prays:

Priest: Blessed are you, Lord God of
    all creation,
    for through your goodness we
    have received the bread we offer
    you:
    fruit of the earth and work of
    human hands, it will become for
    us the bread of life.

People: Blessed be God for ever.

The priest lifts up the chalice of wine and prays:

Priest: Blessed are you, Lord God of
    all creation, for through your
    goodness we have received the
    wine we offer you:
    fruit of the vine and work of
    human hands it will become our
    spiritual drink.

People: Blessed be God for ever.

Invitation to Prayer

The priest calls us to pray:

Priest: Pray, brethren (brothers and
    sisters), that my sacrifice and
    yours may be acceptable to God,
    the almighty Father.

The people rise and reply:

People: May the Lord accept the sacrifice
    at your hands for the praise
    and glory of his name, for our
    good and the good of all his holy
    Church.

▶ Explain the different groups we pray for in the Prayer of the Faithful (also known as the Universal Prayer or Bidding Prayers; before the *Roman Missal* changes in 2011, this prayer was known as the general intercessions). If you have time during the session, organize young people into four groups and have each group write a prayer.

▶ Review the responses your parish usually prays in the Prayer of the Faithful.

Prayer over the Offerings
We stand and pray with the priest. We prepare for the Eucharistic Prayer.

People: Amen.

Eucharistic Prayer
This is the central prayer of the Eucharist. It is a prayer of thanksgiving and making holy.

Preface Dialogue
The priest invites us to pray. We say or sing the preface.

Priest: The Lord be with you.
People: And with your spirit.
Priest: Lift up your hearts.
People: We lift them up to the Lord.
Priest: Let us give thanks to the Lord our God.
People: It is right and just.

Preface
The priest, with hands extended, continues the preface.

Preface Acclamation
Together with the priest, we say or sing:

Holy, holy, holy Lord God of hosts,
Heaven and earth are full of your glory.
Hosanna in the highest.
Blessed is he who comes in the name of the Lord.
Hosanna in the highest.

The priest continues to pray the Eucharistic prayer. During the Eucharistic prayer the priest tells the story of all of God's saving actions.

Consecration
The priest takes the bread and says the words of Jesus:

TAKE THIS, ALL OF YOU, AND EAT OF IT,
FOR THIS IS MY BODY,
WHICH WILL BE GIVEN UP FOR YOU.

The priest holds up the consecrated bread, the Host, which is now the Body of Christ.

Then the priest takes the chalice, the cup of wine, and says the words of Jesus:

TAKE THIS, ALL OF YOU, AND DRINK FROM IT,
FOR THIS IS THE CHALICE OF MY BLOOD,
THE BLOOD OF THE NEW AND ETERNAL COVENANT,
WHICH WILL BE POURED OUT FOR YOU AND FOR MANY
FOR THE FORGIVENESS OF SINS.
DO THIS IN MEMORY OF ME.

The bread and wine become the Body and Blood of Jesus through the power of the Holy Spirit and the words and actions of the priest. Jesus is truly present under the appearances of bread and wine. We proclaim our faith in Jesus.

Mystery of Faith
Priest: The mystery of faith.
People: We proclaim your Death, O Lord, and profess your Resurrection until you come again.

Concluding Doxology
The priest continues the Eucharistic Prayer. He prays for the whole Church, those who are living and those who are dead. He ends the prayer by singing or saying aloud:

Priest: Through him, and with him, and in him, O God, almighty Father in the unity of the Holy Spirit, all glory and honor is yours, for ever and ever.
People: Amen.

180

181

▶ If possible, obtain permission to take young people to the church. Have them bring their books. Have some young people gather around the altar and others in the pews. Go through the actions of each part of the Mass from the presider's part and the assembly's responses.

▶ Have young people note what is the same and what is different when comparing the photos in the book to their church.

▶ Point out that although there are differences in the building, vestments, or vessels used in their parish, the prayers, responses, and actions of the priest and the assembly during Mass are the same.

▶ Using these pages, go over all the acclamations and responses in this section with young people. Role-play them with young people taking turns being the presider.

▶ Practice the sung parts of the Eucharistic Prayer with young people. If you are not musically inclined, invite one of the parish musicians to sing with them.

Communion Rite

We stand for the Lord's Prayer. We pray for our daily bread. We pray our sins will be forgiven.

The Lord's Prayer

People: Our Father, who art in heaven,
hallowed be thy name;
thy kingdom come;
thy will be done on earth as it is
in heaven.
Give us this day our daily bread;
and forgive us our trespasses,
as we forgive those who trespass
against us;
and lead us not into temptation,
But deliver us from evil.

Priest: Deliver us, Lord, we pray from
every evil...

People: For the kingdom, the power
and the glory are yours,
now and for ever.

Sign of Peace

The priest or deacon invites us to share a Sign of Peace with those around us. We pray for peace and that the Church and the world will be united as one.

Priest: The peace of the Lord be with you always.

People: And with your spirit.

We offer one another a sign of peace.

Lamb of God or Fraction of the Bread

Just as Jesus broke bread at the Last Supper and gave it to his disciples, the priest breaks the consecrated bread and puts a piece of it into the chalice to show the unity of Jesus' Body and Blood. During the breaking of the bread, we say or sing the Lamb of God (Agnes Dei):

People: Lamb of God, you take away the
sins of the world:
have mercy on us.
Lamb of God, you take away the
sins of the world:
have mercy on us.
Lamb of God, you take away the
sins of the world:
grant us peace.

Invitation to Communion

The priest shows us the consecrated bread. He holds the Host up and invites us to the banquet of the Lord. We respond:

People: Lord, I am not worthy that you
should enter under my roof, but
only say the word and my soul
shall be healed.

Communion

The priest receives Holy Communion. We sing the Communion hymn. When it is time, we walk in procession to receive Holy Communion. The minister offers us the consecrated bread, the Body of Christ. We bow our heads as a sign of reverence before receiving the Body of Christ.

Priest or extraordinary minister: The Body of Christ.

People: Amen.

▶ As a final preparation for the celebration of First Holy Communion, use the Order of Mass to review all the prayers and responses.

▶ Teach young people a sung *Agnus Dei* (Lamb of God) that is part of the parish repertoire. If you are not musically inclined, invite one of the parish musicians to sing with them.

▶ Show young people how to pray the Lord's Prayer with arms and hands in the orans position. The orans position is one where the forearms are extended with palms of the hands facing up.

We receive the Body of Christ in our hand or on our tongue. We reverently chew and swallow the consecrated bread.

If we are receiving the consecrated wine, the Blood of Christ, the minister offers us the cup. We bow our head as a sign of reverence before receiving the Blood of Christ.

Priest or extraordinary minister: The Blood of Christ.
People: Amen.

We return to our seats and give thanks for the wonderful gift of Jesus we have received in Communion.

When the distribution of Communion is finished, the priest and people pray privately. A song may be sung at this time.

Prayer After Communion

We stand. The priest invites us to pray with him as he asks God to help us live as God's People, the Body of Christ.

Priest: Let us pray…
People: Amen.

Concluding Rites

We stand for the Concluding Rites. The priest greets us, blesses us in the name of the Holy Trinity, and sends us forth to live as Jesus' disciples.

Greeting

Priest: The Lord be with you.
People: And with your spirit.

Blessing

Priest: May Almighty God bless you in the name of the Father, the Son, and the Holy Spirit.
People: Amen.

Dismissal

Priest: Go forth, the Mass is ended.
People: Thanks be to God.

We sing a hymn of praise. The priest kisses the altar as a sign of reverence. He and the other ministers leave in procession.

▶ Talk with young people about the period of silence after Communion. Suggest that they use that time for prayer and reflection.

▶ Discuss why the priest reverences the altar by kissing it.

Holy Communion

Rules for Receiving Holy Communion

- Only baptized Catholics may receive Communion.

- To receive Holy Communion, we must be in the state of grace, free from mortal sin. If we have sinned mortally, we must first go to the Sacrament of Reconciliation and receive absolution before receiving Holy Communion. When we are sorry for our venial sins, receiving Holy Communion frees us from them.

- To honor the Lord, we fast for one hour before the time we receive Communion. This means we go without food or drink, except water or medicine.

- Catholics are required to receive Holy Communion at least once a year during Easter time. But we are encouraged to receive Communion every time we participate in the Mass.

How to Receive Communion

When we receive Jesus in Holy Communion, we welcome him by showing reverence. These steps can help you.

- Fold your hands, and join in the singing as you wait in line.

- When it is your turn, you can receive the Body of Christ in your hand or on your tongue.

- When you are shown the Eucharist, bow in reverence.

- To receive the Body of Christ in your hand, hold your hands out with the palms up. Place one hand underneath the other, and cup your hands slightly.

- To receive the Host on your tongue, fold your hands, open your mouth, and put your tongue out.

- The person who offers you Communion will say, "The Body of Christ." You say, "Amen." The priest, deacon, or extraordinary minister of Holy Communion places the Host in your hand or on your tongue. Step aside, and chew and swallow the Host.

- You may choose to drink from the cup. When the cup is offered to you, the person will say, "The Blood of Christ." You say, "Amen." Take a small sip.

- Return to your place in church. Pray quietly in your own words. Thank Jesus for being with you.

186 · 187

Rules for Receiving Holy Communion

- Review these rules and regulations with young people and encourage them to go over them with their parents.

- The rules for receiving Holy Communion are based on Canon Law, the official law of the Church. Be sure to point that the Church emphasizes the importance of receiving Holy Communion frequently.

- Explain to young people that not all Christians share our belief in the real Presence of Jesus in the Eucharist. That is why only Roman Catholics may receive Holy Communion at Mass.

- Review the definitions of mortal and venial sin. Remind young people that through reception of Holy Communion venial sins are forgiven.

How to Receive Communion

▶ Review the directions for receiving Communion as the time for the celebration draws near. Role-play receiving the Body and Blood of Jesus so young people are comfortable and at ease. If possible, invite parish extraordinary ministers of Holy Communion to practice with young people. If appropriate, use unconsecrated hosts and wine. Emphasize the importance of reverence in receiving Communion. Be sure to practice the bowing gesture.

▶ Provide any additional information about how Holy Communion is distributed in your parish, such as directions for coming forward and returning to one's place, standing and kneeling, and receiving Holy Communion in the hand or on the tongue.

186–187

Catholic Prayers

The Lord's Prayer

Our Father, who art in heaven,
hallowed be thy name;
thy kingdom come;
thy will be done on earth as it is
 in heaven.
Give us this day our daily bread;
and forgive us our trespasses,
as we forgive those who trespass
 against us;
and lead us not into temptation,
but deliver us from evil.
Amen.

Apostles' Creed

I believe in God,
the Father almighty,
Creator of heaven and earth,
and in Jesus Christ, his only Son, our Lord,

*At the words that follow, up to and including the
Virgin Mary, all bow.*

who was conceived by the Holy Spirit,
born of the Virgin Mary,
suffered under Pontius Pilate,
was crucified, died and was buried;
he descended into hell;
on the third day he rose again from the
 dead;
he ascended into heaven,
and is seated at the right hand of God
 the Father almighty;
from there he will come to judge the living
 and the dead.
I believe in the Holy Spirit,
the holy catholic Church,
the communion of saints,
the forgiveness of sins,
the resurrection of the body,
and life everlasting. Amen.

Nicene Creed

I believe in one God,
 the Father almighty,
 maker of heaven and earth,
 of all things visible and invisible.
I believe in one Lord Jesus Christ,
 the Only Begotten Son of God,
 born of the Father before all ages.
 God from God, Light from Light,
 true God from true God,
 begotten, not made,
  consubstantial with the Father;
 through him all things were made.
For us men and for our salvation
 he came down from heaven,

*At the words that follow up to and including
and became man, all bow.*

and by the Holy Spirit was incarnate
 of the Virgin Mary,
 and became man.
For our sake he was crucified under
 Pontius Pilate,
 he suffered death and was buried,
and rose again on the third day

in accordance with the Scriptures.
He ascended into heaven
 and is seated at the right hand of
 the Father.
He will come again in glory
 to judge the living and the dead
and his kingdom will have
 no end.
I believe in the Holy Spirit, the
 Lord, the giver of life,
 who proceeds from the Father
 and the Son.
who with the Father and the Son is
 adored and glorified.
who has spoken through the
 prophets.
I believe in one, holy,
 catholic and apostolic Church.
I confess one Baptism for
 the forgiveness of sins.
and I look forward to the resurrection of
 the dead, and the life of the world
 to come.
Amen.

The Lord's Prayer

▶ Teach young people a musical version of the Lord's Prayer. Choose a selection where the phrases of the prayer are echoed.

▶ Show young people the orans posture used when the Lord's Prayer is prayed during the Eucharist. Remind them to join in praying or singing the Lord's Prayer during the Eucharist.

Apostles' Creed

▶ Tell young people that the Apostles' Creed contains the truths taught by the Apostles.

▶ Point out that the Creed outlines Christian doctrine and our Catholic faith.

▶ The Apostles' Creed, Nicene Creed, and Confiteor changed when the revised *Roman Missal* was introduced in November 2011.

188–189

Nicene Creed

▶ Have young people compare the Nicene Creed to the Apostles' Creed. Ask: What are the differences? What is the same?

Confiteor

▶ Explain to young people that *Confiteor* means "I confess."

▶ Remind young people that this prayer on page 190 is sometimes used as part of the Penitential Act at Mass.

▶ Go through each of the phrases of the Confiteor with young people. Point out:

• that the confession is to God and the community;

• that sin includes commission and omission

• that we ask help from Mary, the angels and saints, and one another not to sin again.

Confiteor

I confess to almighty God
and to you, my brothers and sisters,
that I have greatly sinned,
in my thoughts and in my words,
in what I have done and
in what I have failed to do,

Gently strike your chest with a closed fist.

through my fault, through my fault,
through my most grievous fault;

Continue:

therefore I ask blessed Mary ever-Virgin,
all the Angels and Saints,
and you, my brothers and sisters,
to pray for me to the Lord our God.

Gloria

Glory to God in the highest,
and on earth peace to people of good
   will.
We praise you,
we bless you,
we adore you,
we glorify you,
we give you thanks for your great glory,
Lord God, heavenly King,
O God, almighty Father.

Lord Jesus Christ, Only Begotten Son,
Lord God, Lamb of God, Son of the Father,
you take away the sins of the world,
   have mercy on us;
you take away the sins of the world,
   receive our prayer;
you are seated at the right hand of the
   Father,
   have mercy on us.

For you alone are the Holy One,
you alone are the Lord,
you alone are the Most High,
Jesus Christ,
with the Holy Spirit,
in the glory of God the Father.
Amen.

Hail Mary

Hail, Mary, full of grace!
The Lord is with you!
Blessed are you among women,
and blessed is the fruit of your
   womb, Jesus.
Holy Mary, Mother of God,
pray for us sinners,
now and at the hour of our death.
Amen.

Come, Holy Spirit

Come, Holy Spirit, fill the hearts of your
   faithful
And kindle in them the fire of your love.
Send forth your Spirit and they shall be
   created.
And you shall renew the face of the
   earth.

Grace Before Meals

Bless us, O Lord, and these your gifts,
which we are about to receive
from your goodness.
Through Christ our Lord.
Amen.

Grace After Meals

We give you thanks for all your gifts,
almighty God,
living and reigning now and forever.
Amen.

Explain to young people that the Confiteor is an expression of sorrow for our sins during the Penitential Act.

Have young people make prayer cards with the words of the Confiteor to use as a reminder when they celebrate Mass.

Gloria

Point out that the Gloria can be said or sung at Mass.

Tell young people that the Gloria is sometimes called the "Angelic Hymn" because it is similar to the song the angels sang at Bethlehem in Luke 2:14. You may wish to read this passage aloud so young people can hear the similarity.

Note that the words of the Gloria changed slightly when the revised Roman Missal was introduced in November 2011. The changed text more closely matches the wording of the Third Edition of the *Roman Missal* in Latin.

Hail Mary

► Explain to young people that the Hail Mary combines elements of the angel Gabriel's greeting (Luke 1:28) and Elizabeth's greeting (Luke 1:42) to Mary. You may wish to read these passages aloud so they can hear the similarity to the words of the Hail Mary.

Come, Holy Spirit

► Encourage young people to learn this prayer and to say it any time they want to call upon the Holy Spirit for help but especially before examining their consciences.

Grace Before and After Meals

► Encourage young people to share these prayers with their families at mealtime.

Boldfaced numbers refer to pages on which the terms are defined in the *Candidate's Book*.

A–D

absolution, **55**
Act of Contrition, 39, **45**, 55, 75
Agnus Dei (Lamb of God), **154**
Alleluia, **124**
altar, **131**
ambo, **124**
Apostles' Creed, **188**
assembly, **100**

Baptism, **11**, 15, 20, 60, 88, 89, 90, **91**, 97, 120
baptismal name, **10**
baptismal promises, 18
Beatitudes, the, 31, 76
Bible, **31**, **41**, **47**, **121**, **127**
Bidding Prayers, 125
bishops, **64**
Blessed Sacrament, **144**
blessing, **160**
Body and Blood of Jesus/Christ, 95, **134**, 141, **144**, 145, 147, 179
Body of Christ, 91, **107**, **187**
Book of the Gospels, **124**
bowing, **30**
bread and wine/Bread and Wine, **134**, 135, **144**, 155
Bread of Life, 151, 154, 157

candles, **21**
Celebration of the Word of God, 35, 74
chalice, **151**
chrism, **95**
Christ
    light of, 91
    new life in, 94
Christian(s), **91**, 102–103, 107
Church, **15**, 64, **91**, **107**
ciborium, **151**
collection, **135**
Come, Holy Spirit, **191**
communal celebration(s), **25**, 74
Communion Rite, 154, 182
community of faith, **102**, 104, 107
confession, **44**, 74
confessor, **45**
Confirmation, 15, **95**, 97
Confiteor, 108, 110, **115**, 117, 175, **190**
conscience, **34**
consecration, **145**, 180
contrition, **41**
conversion, **61**
Creed, 125, 177
cross, 128, **130**, 131, 137
crucifix, **130**

deacon, **164**
disciples, **91**, 92, 120, 134, 142

E–M

Easter, 91
Eucharist, 15, **95**, 97, **107**, 114, **117**, **134**, **151**, 165, 167
Eucharistic Prayer, **141**, 144, 145, **147**, 180
examination of conscience, **34**, 39, 74

forgiveness, **55**
free will, **24**

Gloria, 98, 107, 175, **190**
God, 121
God's saving actions and promises, 147
God's word/word of God, 125, 127
good news, 121, 122, 124, 125, 165
Gospel(s), **122**, 124, 177
grace, **11**, 15
Grace After Meals, **191**
Grace Before Meals, **191**
Great Amen, **145**, 147
Great Commandment, 32, **33**, 76

Hail Mary, **191**
Holy Communion, 95, 151, 154, 155, 157, 161, 186
holy oil of chrism, 95
Holy Spirit, 31, 41, 51, 61, 65, 91, 94, 121, 134, 137, 141, 147, 151, 164, 167
    gift of the, 95
Holy Trinity, **14**, **94**, 100
holy water, **20**, 60, 114
homily, **125**, 177
Honoring the Cross, 128, 137
Host(s), **144**, 155

individual celebration(s), **25**, 75
Introductory Rites, **105**, **107**, 124, 174

Jesus, 14, 22-23, 32-33, 41, 42-43, 52-53, 62-63, 92–93, 105, 121, 122–123, 134, 141, 142–143, 144, 157, 161
    new life with, 91
    sacrifice of, 131, 137

kneeling, **40**, **140**
Kyrie, eleison (Lord Have Mercy), **110**, 175

Lamb of God (*Agnus Dei*), **154**, 155
Last Supper, 141, **142**, 144, 145
laying on of hands, **50**
lectionary, **124**
Liturgy of the Eucharist, **124**, 132, 134, 135, 179
Liturgy of the Word, **124**, 125, 127, 176
Lord Have Mercy (*Kyrie, eleison*), **110**, 175
Lord's Prayer, 154, **187**

Mass, 95, 114, 121, 124, 131, 134, 137, **157**, 161, 165, 167
mission, 161, 167
mortal sin, **24**
mystery, **141**
mystery of faith/Mystery of Faith, 139, **145**, 147, 181

N–R

New Testament, **121**, 124
Nicene Creed, **178**, **189**

Old Testament, **121**, 124
Original Sin, 11, **14**, 95

Paschal candle, **21**, **95**
Passover, 142–143
paten, **151**
Penance/penance, 25, **44**, 45
penitent, **44**
Penitential Act, 60, **108**, 110, 114, 115, 117, 174
People of God, **107**, 117
Prayer of the Faithful, **125**
prayer, **101**, 190
Precepts of the Church, **34**, 78
Preparation of the Gifts, **135**, 179
priest(s), 20, 45, 55, 60, **64**, **105**, **141**, **147**
procession, 98, **101**, 107
psalm, **124**

readings, 124
reconciliation, **51**, 64
Reconciliation room, **24**
renewal of baptismal promises, 88, 97

S–W

Sacrament(s), **15**, **94**, **97**
Sacrament of Penance, **24**, 51
Sacrament of Reconciliation, 24, 31, 35, 54, 55, 61, 65, 74, 75
Sacraments of Initiation, 15, **94**, **97**
sacrifice(s), **131**, 134, 135, 137, 144
Scripture(s), **31**, 35, **121**
Sign of Peace, 59, **61**, **109**, 129, **150**, 154, 182
Sign of the Cross, **11**, 14, 20, 25, **120**, 127
silence, 101, **111**
sin(s), 11, 41, 65, 117
singing, **104**
sower, the, 122–123
sprinkling with holy water, **60**, **114**, 174
stole, **54**

tabernacle, **144**
Table of the Lord, 150
Ten Commandments, 31, **33**, 77

Universal Prayer, 125

venial sin, **24**
vine and the branches, 92–93

water, **90**
witness, **161**
Works of Mercy, 78

CALL to CELEBRATE

Activity Masters

Name _____

We Are Called

The symbols in the left column represent one of the Sacraments of Initiation. Write the name of the sacrament underneath the symbol. In the box next to the symbol describe what happens in each of the sacraments.

Name _____

We Are Welcomed

After reading about Zacchaeus and Jesus, read the portions of the story below. They are out of order. In the space next to the words, rewrite the phrases in the correct order.

Zacchaeus promised to help the people he had cheated.	1 _____ _____ _____
Jesus looked up and told Zacchaeus he wanted to eat at his house.	2 _____ _____ _____
Zacchaeus climbed a tree to see Jesus passing by.	3 _____ _____ _____
Jesus told Zacchaeus that God had forgiven him.	4 _____ _____ _____

Name _____

We Reflect

Here are three bookmarks that will remind you about the Great Commandment to love God. Decorate them, and cut them out. Use them in books where you will see them often.

I

You shall have no other gods besides me.

II

You shall not take the name of the Lord, your God, in vain.

III

Remember to keep holy the sabbath day.

CE3

Name _____

Ways I Show Sorrow

The woman who was sorry washed and anointed Jesus' feet. In the space below, draw or write a description of how you show sorrow to God, others, or yourself.

God

Others

Me

Name _____

We Are Forgiven

Here are the parts of a communal Reconciliation celebration. Put them in order from beginning to end. Number them from 1–8 in the blank spaces.

___ We pray an opening prayer.　　　　___ We hear a homily.

___ We say or do our penance.　　　　___ We receive a penance.

___ We receive absolution.　　　　___ We hear a Scripture reading.

___ We examine our conscience.　　　　___ We confess our sins.

We Go Forth

Peace poles have been set up in many places throughout the world. A peace pole is a wooden pole with four sides. Each side has the prayer "May peace prevail on Earth" written on it in several languages. Peace poles are put where many people will see them. They remind us to work for peace every day. Here is a peace pole for you to make. Decorate it, and then cut it out. Fold it on the dotted lines. Tape or glue the flap to join the ends. Put the pole where you will see it often. It will remind you to thank God for the gift of peace in Reconciliation.

Panel 1:
peace
vrede
paz
اسلام
(salaam)

Panel 2:
paix
عمان
(aman)
béke
damai

Panel 3:
frid
pace
МИр
(mir)
平和
(heiwa)

Panel 4:
평화
(pyeong-hwa)
friede
ཞི་བདེ་
(zhi-bde-ne)
ειρήνη
(iríni)

Name _____

The Vine and the Branches

Finish the branches on this vine. Next to each branch, write a time that shows you belong to God. Draw a picture that illustrates that occasion in the oval nearest to the time.

Name _____

The Early Christians

Decorate these wristbands, and cut them out. Wear one yourself.
Give the others to members of your faith community.

We share.

We help one another.

We eat together.

We pray together.

We follow Jesus together.

We teach one another about God.

We love one another.

Name _____

All Are Welcome!

To show your understanding of the Gospel story, The Call of Matthew, use the answers to the questions below to fill in the crossword puzzle.

Across:

1. The Pharisees were Jewish leaders and _____.

3. Jesus did NOT come to call the _____.

5. Matthew was a _____.

Down:

2. I desire mercy, not _____.

4. Tax collectors and _____ sat with Jesus and his disciples.

6. What did Jesus say to Matthew?

Name _____

The Sower

Jesus told a story about a sower who sowed seeds. The seeds are like people who hear God's word. When you sow a seed in good soil, it grows in different stages. Read the words in the boxes. Then number the boxes from 1 to 6 to show how the seeds grow.

The farmer harvests the crop.

The farmer weeds the ground between the plants.

The stalks grow strong and tall.

The tall stalks produce many grains.

Rain and sun help the seeds to grow.

The sower sows the seeds.

Name _____

We Prepare

Interview three people who do service activities and ask them what kinds of sacrifices they have to make and why they do it. Write the most important thing you learned from your interview.

Interview 1

Name: _____   I learned _____

_____

_____.

Interview 2

Name: _____   I learned _____

_____

_____.

Interview 3

Name: _____   I learned _____

_____

_____.

Name ____________________

ACTIVITY MASTER 12

Prayerful Remembrances

On the top half of this sheet, write what you are thankful for. On the bottom half, write the names of people you want to pray for.

I want to thank God for...

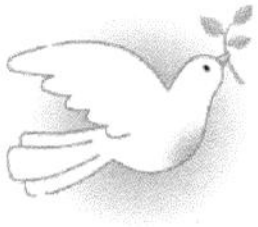

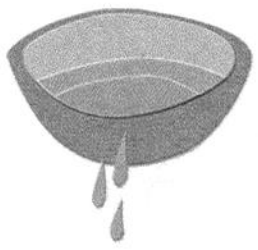

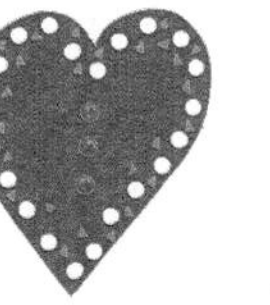

I want to pray for...

Name _____

Receiving Communion

Below are all the steps for receiving Holy Communion. Using numbers 1 through 9 put them in order from beginning to end. Insert the numbers in the blank spaces provided in each box.

___ Pray the Lamb of God.

___ Answer "Amen" to "The Blood of Christ."

___ Bow before you receive the Host.

___ Say a prayer of thanksgiving.

___ Return to your place.

___ Answer "Amen" to "The Body of Christ."

___ Hold your hands open or open your mouth to receive the Host.

___ Walk in procession to the altar.

___ Bow before you receive the Cup.

Name _____

Receiving Communion

Interview a Priest, Deacon, or Extraordinary minister at your parish.
Use the following questions as a guide for the interview:

1. Why did you become a _____?

    _____

    _____

2. What do you like best about being a _____?

    _____

    _____

3. What advice would you give someone who was thinking about

    becoming a _____?

    _____

    _____

4. How has being a _____ brought you closer to God?

    _____

    _____

Gifts of the Spirit

"Those who have been baptized continue on the path of Christian Initiation through the Sacrament of Confirmation. In this Sacrament, they receive the Holy Spirit whom the Lord sent upon the Apostles on Pentecost" (1).

Catechism Connection

To deepen your own background and reflection on the Sacrament of Confirmation, refer to the *Catechism of the Catholic Church, 1830– 1831.*

Catechist Resources

The Baby in Solomon's Court
Rev. Paul Turner
Paulist Press
An introduction to the history and practice of Confirmation

Confirmed as Children, Affirmed as Teens
James A. Wilde Ed.
Liturgy Training Publications
A collection of articles on the question of Confirmation

Young People's Resources

The Choice *(19 min)*
Franciscan Communications
Young girl preparing for Confirmation is taught a lesson of service.

Spirit With Us Faith Stories Ages 11–14
Judith Dunlap and Mary Cummins Wlodarski,
St. Anthony Messenger Press
Stories that help young people explore the role of the Holy Spirit from New Testament times until today.

Catechist Formation

> "The Spirit of the Lord is upon me…"
> Luke 4:18

The Gift of the Holy Spirit

There are some gifts that do keep on giving. There is the large wrapped box with all kinds of little wrapped boxes inside of it. There is the first gift of flowers or fruit which is followed up every month with a new offering. There is that special gift which brings joy and happy memories each time we look at it. There is the gift which holds a promise for the future, such as, "I will care for your children for four hours on Saturday." We greet these gifts with joy and gratitude and we remember them for a long time.

While it is trite to say the gift of the Holy Spirit is a "gift that keeps on giving," the phrase may help us probe the marvel of God's gift to us. The Holy Spirit is our advocate, one who believes in us and speaks for us—always. He is our sanctifier and makes us holy. He helps us in our weakness and teaches us to pray. From the moment of our Baptism, the Holy Spirit comes to dwell in us. We become temples of the Holy Spirit, and the gift of God's love is poured out in us.

The Sacrament of Confirmation

Confirmation connects us more closely with the Church and gives us a special strength of the Holy Spirit. We receive the fullness of the Holy Spirit in the outpouring of his gifts of Wisdom, Understanding, Right Judgment or Counsel, Courage or Fortitude, Knowledge, Reverence or Piety, and Wonder and Awe or Fear of the Lord. These gifts enable us to build up the Body of Christ.

How would you describe your relationship with the Holy Spirit?
Which gift of the Holy Spirit do you use most often?

Catechist Prayer

Holy Spirit, giver of life and goodness, fill me with your divine love that I may share it with others. Amen.

CELEBRATE

CE17

CE18–19

OBJECTIVE:
▶ To experience the celebration of the word, including a Blessing
▶ To explain that God gives us the gift of his Holy Spirit

LESSON PROCESS:
Begin the prayer service by leading young people in the Sign of the Cross. (You may want to choose a song from the *Songs of Celebration* CD as background music.) Follow the order of prayer on pages CE17–18.

▶ Help young people reflect on the celebration. Ask them: What did you see? What did you hear? What did you do?
▶ Read aloud and discuss the text for the Signs of Faith on page CE18.
▶ Have young people complete the activity on page CE18.
▶ Encourage young people to complete the Faith at Home activity on page CE18.
▶ Summarize the text on page CE19.
▶ Read aloud the text for the Signs of Faith on page CE19.

REMEMBER

CE20

OBJECTIVE:
▶ To proclaim Jesus' words about the Holy Spirit

LESSON PROCESS:
Gather young people in the prayer space, and read aloud the Gospel story.

▶ Discuss young people's responses to the questions.
▶ Allow time for young people to complete their drawings.

CE21   **CE22**

OBJECTIVE:
▶ To teach the meaning of the gifts of the Holy Spirit
▶ To describe part of the Rite of Confirmation

LESSON PROCESS:
▶ Read aloud the opening paragraph.
▶ Discuss each of the Gifts of the Holy Spirit.
▶ Use the Activity Master on page CE25.
▶ Read aloud the prayer of the Rite on page CE22.
▶ Encourage children to complete the Faith at Home activity on page CE22.

LIVE

CE23

OBJECTIVE:
▶ To encourage young people to express their desire for the gifts of the Holy Spirit

LESSON PROCESS:
Explain the activity, and have young people complete it.

▶ Gather young people in the prayer circle.
▶ Pray the Closing Blessing.

FAITH AT HOME

CE24

OBJECTIVE:
▶ To introduce different parts of the Faith at Home page

LESSON PROCESS:
Review the five parts of the Faith at Home page with young people.

▶ Encourage young people to share this page with their family members at home.

Materials:

PROGRAM RESOURCES
Songs of Celebration CD
And With Your Spirit CD

OTHER MATERIALS
Bible, cross or crucifix, prayer table, candle, large bowl filled with water

Before You Begin:

Make copies of pages CE17–25 for each young person, and a reference copy for yourself.

Familiarize yourself with the movements of the ritual on pages CE17–18.

We Gather

Procession

As you sing, walk forward slowly. Follow the young person carrying the Bible.

 Sing together.

Come Lord Jesus, send us your Spirit, renew the face of the earth.

Send Us Your Spirit, David Haas © GIA Publications

Leader: God, our Father, we belong to you. We are your children. Open our hearts to the gift of the Holy Spirit. We ask this through Jesus Christ our Lord.

All: Amen.

We Listen

Leader: A reading from the holy Gospel according to John.

All: Glory to you, O Lord.

Leader: Read John 14:15–26.

The Gospel of the Lord.

All: Praise to you, Lord Jesus Christ.

Sit silently.

Ritual Focus: Blessing

Leader: In Baptism you were given the gift of the Holy Spirit. By water and the Holy Spirit you received the gifts of faith and new life. Let us remember that the Holy Spirit is with us always.

Come forward one by one.

Leader: Extend your hands over the head of each young person.

[Name], remember that the Holy Spirit is with you always.

Young person: Amen.

We Go Forth
The Holy Spirit

Leader: Loving Father, we thank you for the gift of your Spirit. Send us forth to bring your love to others. We ask this through Jesus Christ our Lord.

All: Amen.

Sing the opening song together.

Reflect

Power of the Holy Spirit Write a rhyme about the gift of the Holy Spirit.

The Holy Spirit lives in me.
The Holy Spirit helps me be

_____

_____

_____

_____

Imposition of Hands

One of the signs the Church uses to call upon the power of the Holy Spirit is imposition of hands. The priest extends his hands during the Eucharist and calls on the power of the Holy Spirit to change bread and wine into the Body and Blood of Jesus. When people are sick the priest extends his hands over them and prays that they will be healed by the power of the Holy Spirit. During the Sacrament of Confirmation, the bishop extends his hands over the people being confirmed. The bishop prays that God the Father will send the Holy Spirit upon them.

The Gift of the Holy Spirit

God gives us many gifts. He gives us the gift of creation, the gift of his Son Jesus, and the gift of the Holy Spirit. The Holy Spirit is the third Person of the Holy Trinity. The Trinity is the Church's name for the three Persons in one God.

We receive the gift of the Holy Spirit when we are baptized. He comes to live in our hearts. We cannot see the Holy Spirit, but we can see what he does. He guides the Church. He makes us holy. He is our helper.

Confirmation increases the gifts of the Holy Spirit in us. The gifts of the Holy Spirit at Confirmation help us become stronger followers of Jesus. They help us act as Jesus' disciples and share the good news about Jesus with others.

SIGNS OF FAITH

Chrism

Chrism (cri-zhum) is a mixture of olive oil and balsam. It is blessed by the bishop at a special Mass just before Easter. It is used to anoint people who are celebrating Baptism. During Baptism, chrism is put on the head of the person being baptized. During Confirmation, the bishop or priest anoints the forehead of the person receiving Confirmation. In Holy Orders the hands of the priest are anointed by the Bishop. Chrism is also used to bless new churches and altars. The anointing with chrism is a sign of God's grace and presence.

Jesus Promises the Holy Spirit

Faith Focus

What does Jesus tell us about the Holy Spirit?

Jesus wanted his disciples to keep on sharing the good news with others even after his death and Resurrection. He knew they would need a helper.

 Scripture

JOHN 14:15–17, 26, 27

During the Last Supper Jesus said to his disciples: "If you love me, you will keep my commandments. And I will ask the Father, and he will give you another Advocate, to be with you forever. You know him, because he abides with you and he will be in you….

"But the Advocate, the Holy Spirit whom the Father will send in my name, will teach you everything, and remind you of all that I have said to you. Peace I leave with you; my peace I give to you."

BASED ON JOHN 14:15–17, 26, 27

❓ **Why did the disciples need a helper?**

❓ **How can the Holy Spirit help you?**

Share

Make a list With a partner or in a small group brainstorm the ways you want the Holy Spirit to help you. Then make a "top ten" list.

Faith at Home

Read the scripture story with a family member. Talk about ways that the Holy Spirit helps you. Discuss times and circumstances when you might pray to the Holy Spirit. Together pray the Come, Holy Spirit prayer on page 191 of your *Candidate's Book*.

The Gifts of the Holy Spirit

Faith Focus

What gifts of the Holy Spirit are given at Confirmation?

The Holy Spirit is our helper too. Another name for the Holy Spirit is Advocate. *Advocate* means "helper." An advocate is someone who believes in us and supports us. The Holy Spirit is always with us to help us live as Jesus' followers.

At Confirmation, the Holy Spirit gives us seven special gifts.

SIGNS OF FAITH

Bishop

Bishops are ordained men who work with the pope in teaching and guiding the Church. They are successors of the Apostles. They teach, they help us become holy, and they show us how to tell the good news to others. Before a man is made a bishop, he is a priest. The bishop usually presides at Confirmation. Sometimes he chooses another priest to act in his place.

Wisdom helps us place God first in our life so we can make wise choices.

Understanding helps us know what our faith and life mean in God's plan.

Right Judgment or Counsel helps us make right choices and helps others to do the same.

Courage or Fortitude helps us be strong and to do what is right and avoid what is wrong.

Knowledge helps us know God and the teachings of the Church.

Reverence or Piety helps us worship and give praise to God.

Wonder and Awe or Fear of the Lord helps us know God's power and to trust him.

Confirmation

At Confirmation, the bishop talks to us. He speaks about the first Pentecost. At the first Pentecost, the Holy Spirit came to the disciples just as Jesus promised.

The bishop reminds us that we first received the Holy Spirit at Baptism. He tells us that we are to live in a way that others will see God's goodness in us. In his own words, he says:

"Christ gives different gifts to you. These gifts are given so you can build up the Body of Christ in oneness and love. Be active members of the Church, alive in Jesus Christ. With the help of the Holy Spirit, help others as Jesus did."

BASED ON RITE OF CONFIRMATION, 22

After we renew our baptismal promises, the bishop extends his hands over us. The bishop sings or says this prayer,

"All-powerful God, Father of our Lord Jesus Christ,

by water and the Holy Spirit

you freed your sons and daughters from sin

and gave them new life.

Send your Holy Spirit upon them

to be their Helper and Guide.

Give them the spirit of wisdom and understanding,

the spirit of right judgment and courage,

the spirit of knowledge and reverence.

Fill them with the spirit and wonder and awe in your presence."

RITE OF CONFIRMATION, 25

Faith at Home

Discuss the seven gifts of the Holy Spirit with a family member. Ask them to give examples of how they express these gifts in their life. For example, when we make good choices we use wisdom and right judgment, or when we take time to admire nature or to thank and praise God we use wonder and awe. Talk about which gifts you need the most.

The Holy Spirit Is with Us

Respond

Write a letter to the Holy Spirit   In the space below, write a note to the Holy Spirit. Tell the Holy Spirit which of his gifts you most want to receive and how it will help you show God's love to others.

_____

_____

_____

_____

_____

_____

Closing Blessing

Gather and begin with the Sign of the Cross.

Leader: God, our Father, we praise and thank you for the gift of the Holy Spirit.

All: Amen.

Leader: Jesus, our Savior, we praise and thank you for showing us how to live and love.

All: Amen.

Leader: Holy Spirit, giver of God's gifts, we praise and thank you for being our helper and guide.

All: Amen.

 Sing together.

Come Lord Jesus, send us your Spirit, renew the face of the earth.

Send Us Your Spirit, David Haas © GIA Publications

Faith at Home

Faith Focus

- The Holy Spirit is the third Person of the Holy Trinity.
- The Holy Spirit is our Advocate, our helper.
- We receive the seven gifts of the Holy Spirit at Confirmation.

Ritual Focus

Blessing   You were blessed and prayed over by the catechist. During the week ask a family member to use the text on page CE17 and bless you.

Family Prayer

Spirit of the Living God, be our helper and guide. Give us the gifts we need to live as your children and to serve one another. Amen.

Act

Share Together   Read the Pentecost story (*Acts 2:1–12*), and talk about the signs of the Holy Spirit in the reading. Use concrete and positive examples of how wind and fire affect us in our daily lives. For instance, wind creates a breeze on a hot day; fire keeps us warm. Relate the discussion to what the Holy Spirit does for us in our lives. Talk about how his coming changed the disciples. Have individual members share what they would like to receive from the Holy Spirit. Pray the Come, Holy Spirit prayer on page 191 together.

Do Together   Write the names of family members on a large sheet of paper. Have family members think about what talents or gifts each member has and write them next to their names on the paper. Decide how family members together can use their gifts or talents to be of service to another family member or neighbor.

© Our Sunday Visitor Curriculum Division

 www.osvcurriculum.com
Visit our website for weekly Scripture readings and questions, family resources, and more activities.

Name _____

Gifts of the Holy Spirit

In the space below, write one way the Holy Spirit will be your helper.

Wisdom

Understanding

Right Judgment or Counsel

Courage or Fortitude

Reverence or Piety

Knowledge

Wonder and Awe or Fear of the Lord

Rite of Confirmation

"This giving of the Holy Spirit conforms believers more fully to Christ and strengthens them so that they may bear witness to Christ for the building up of his Body in faith and love..." (2).

Catechism Connection

To deepen your own background and reflection on the effects of the Sacrament of Confirmation, refer to the *Catechism of the Catholic Church, 1302–1305.*

Catechist Resources

The Church Speaks about Sacraments with Children

Mark Searle, commentator
Liturgical Press

A collection of liturgical and catechetical documents that give insight into the meaning of the sacraments

Rethinking the Sacraments

Bill Huebsch
Twenty-Third Publications

Relates the meaning of sacraments to a contemporary spirituality

Young People's Resources

Moving On: Responding in the Spirit
(20 min)

St. Anthony Messenger Press

A family story of moving and being challenged to follow Christ's call

The Wondrous Adventures of Saint Francis of Assisi

Tricia Gray
St. Anthony Messenger Press

Stories of Saint Francis to help young people understand holiness

Catechist Formation

> "[God], who saved us and called us with a holy calling... Guard the good treasure entrusted to you, with the help of the Holy Spirit living in us."
>
> 2 Timothy 1:9,14

Called to Be Holy

When we are called upon to name a holy person, we often think of people who have performed great deeds for God. Blessed Mother Tere Saint Francis of Assisi, Saint Elizabeth Seton, or Saint Vincent de Paul would all be candidates. In them we see people of prayer and action who have done extraordinary things to build up the Body of Christ. Fe of us would think of ourselves in reference to the term "holy." Some of our reluctance to include ourselves in the cast of holy ones may be tha we see too much of our unholy side or it may be that for us holiness is reserved for those who do unusual things. Or "being holy" may conju up a notion of being odd. Whatever the reason that we find ourselves reluctant to be called holy, it is not a good enough reason.

At Baptism we become part of the Body of Christ—members of " chosen race, a holy nation, God's own people" (*1 Peter 2:9*). The H Spirit comes to dwell in us. On the one hand, we are holy. On the other hand, we become holy through the power of the Holy Spirit who acts to make us holy and to guide us to right choices. During the Sacrament of Confirmation, prayers are said that God the Fatl will pour out his Holy Spirit so that we may be more like Christ a that we will give witness to Christ by our lives.

Living Witnesses

The essence of holiness is being close to God. Through the anoint at Confirmation we are sanctified or set apart to be living example of what it means to be holy. We become holy as we deepen our relationship with God in prayer and as we continue to follow the promptings of the Holy Spirit. As we do these things, the sick are healed, the prisoners are freed, and the poor are taken care of. Through us others come to know that the kingdom of God is her

What does the call to holiness mean for you at this point in your life?

Who are the "living witnesses" who are an example for you today?

Catechist Prayer

Holy Spirit, live in me that I may be a living witness of God's lov and mercy to all those with whom I come in contact. Amen.

"We Are Holy" Lesson Outline

CELEBRATE

CE28–29

CE30

OBJECTIVE:

▶ To experience the celebration of the word, including the Blessing

▶ To explain that we are called to bring the light of Christ to others

LESSON PROCESS:

Begin the prayer service by leading young people in a procession. (You may want to choose a song from the *Songs of Celebration* CD as background music.) Follow the order of prayer on pages CE28–29.

▶ Help young people reflect on the celebration. Ask: What did you see? What did you hear? What did you do?

▶ Have young people complete the activity on page CE29.

▶ Read aloud and discuss the text for the Signs of Faith on page CE29.

▶ Summarize the text on page CE30.

▶ Read aloud and discuss the text for the Signs of Faith on page CE30.

REMEMBER

CE31

OBJECTIVE:

▶ To proclaim Jesus' words about the Holy Spirit being upon him

LESSON PROCESS:

Gather young people in the prayer space and read aloud the Gospel story on page CE31.

▶ Discuss young people's responses to the questions.

▶ Allow time for young people to complete their scrolls.

▶ Encourage young people to complete the Faith at Home activity.

CE32–33

OBJECTIVE:

▶ To teach the meaning of holiness

▶ To describe parts of the Rite of Confirmation

LESSON PROCESS:

▶ Discuss the meaning of the words *holy* and *sanctified*.

▶ Explain the role of the Holy Spirit.

▶ Read aloud and discuss the Signs of Faith.

▶ Use the Activity Master on page CE36.

LIVE

CE34

OBJECTIVE:

▶ To encourage young people to express how they will be living witnesses of Jesus

LESSON PROCESS:

Explain the activity and have young people complete it.

▶ Gather the young people in the prayer circle.

▶ Pray the Closing Blessing.

FAITH AT HOME

CE35

OBJECTIVE:

▶ To introduce different parts of the Faith at Home page

LESSON PROCESS:

Review the Faith at Home page.

▶ Encourage young people to share this page at home.

Materials:

PROGRAM RESOURCES
Songs of Celebration CD
And With Your Spirit CD

OTHER MATERIALS
Bible, cross or crucifix, prayer table, candle, large bowl filled with water

Before You Begin:

Make copies of pages CE28–36 for each young person, and a reference copy for yourself.

Familiarize yourself with the movements of the ritual on pages CE28–29.

We Gather

Procession

As you sing, walk forward slowly. Follow the young person carrying the Bible.

 Sing together.

We are marching in the light of God,

We are marching in the light of God.

We are marching, we are marching in the light of God.

We are marching, we are marching in the light of God.

South African Traditional

Leader: Come, Holy Spirit, open our hearts to you and fill us with the flame of your love. We ask this through Jesus Christ our Lord.

All: Amen.

Leader: A reading from the holy Gospel according to Luke.

All: Glory to you, O Lord.

Leader: Read Luke 4:16–30.

The Gospel of the Lord.

All: Praise to you, Lord Jesus Christ.

Sit silently.

Ritual Focus: Blessing

Leader: We are called by the Holy Spirit to do the things that Jesus did. We are called to bring the good news and the light of Christ to others. Let us remember that the Holy Spirit keeps the light of Christ alive in us always.

Come forward one by one.

Leader: Extend hands over the head of each young person.

[Name], may the Holy Spirit dwell in you and help you bring the light of Christ to others.

Young person: Amen.

We Go Forth

Leader: Loving God, we thank you for the gifts of the Holy Spirit. Send us forth to bring your love to others. We ask this through Jesus Christ our Lord.

All: Amen.

🎵 Sing the opening song together.

SIGNS OF FAITH

Fire

On the night before Easter Sunday, the Easter fire is lit and blessed by the priest. He lights the Paschal candle from this fire. The Paschal candle is lit every time there is a Baptism. It is a sign of the light of Christ. It reminds us that Christians are called to keep the light of Christ burning in their hearts. When the Holy Spirit came to the Apostles on Pentecost, tongues of fire were seen over their heads. Fire is also a sign of the Holy Spirit and the warmth of his love.

The Holy Spirit

Reflect

Let your light shine In the space below make a list of the ways you bring good news to others.

The Light of Christ

When we sit around a campfire on a cool evening, we feel warm. If it is dark, the fire lights up the darkness and helps us see. Sometimes when we are very excited about something we want to do, people might say we are all fired up.

The light of Christ is within us. It warms us. It helps us see things better. With the help of God the Holy Spirit, it also fires us up to do Christ's work here on earth. Doing God's work is not always easy. Often we need the gifts of the Holy Spirit, especially wisdom and courage to help us.

When we do God's work, we bring the light of Christ to others. We show others what God is like. We are living examples or witnesses of what it means to be holy.

SIGNS OF FAITH

Miter and Crosier

The headdress that a bishop wears is called a miter (mi-tuhr). The bishop wears a miter at Confirmation. He also wears it at other special sacramental celebrations. The miter is shaped like a shield and ends in a peak. It also has two pieces of cloth attached to it. They hang down over the bishop's shoulders. He always wears a miter when he carries his staff. The bishop's staff is called a crosier (crow-zhur). The crosier is shaped like a shepherd's staff. It reminds us that the bishop is our shepherd.

Jesus Teaches About Holiness

ith Focus

What does Jesus teach about holiness?

During his life on earth, Jesus showed the eople what God was like. He told them how to e witnesses of holiness.

Scripture

LUKE 4:16–30

Jesus went to the synagogue in Nazareth on the Sabbath day. Nazareth was the place where Jesus grew up. He stood up to read and was handed a scroll of the Prophet Isaiah. He read:

"The Spirit of the Lord is upon me, because he has anointed me to bring good news to the poor. He has sent me to proclaim release to the captives and recovery of sight to the blind, to let the oppressed go free, and to proclaim the year of the Lord's favor."

When he was finished everyone was looking at him. He said, "Today this scripture has been fulfilled in your hearing."

At first the people were amazed at him. They saw his power and goodness. But Jesus began to tell them that sometimes they did not do what God wanted them to do. The people became angry with Jesus.

BASED ON LUKE 4:16–30

❓ **What was Jesus telling the people about the Holy Spirit?**

❓ **Why do you need the Holy Spirit to be a witness of holiness?**

Share

Make a scroll With a partner make your own scrolls. On the scroll draw or write two ways you show others that the Holy Spirit is in you.

Faith at Home

Read the scripture story with a family member. Discuss the questions. Talk about ways that people today can be witnesses of Christ. Together pray the Come, Holy Spirit prayer on page 191 of your *Candidate's Book*. Choose one of the ways you have discussed and plan how your family can do that activity.

Holiness

What does it mean to be holy?

The Holy Spirit is upon us too. One of the ways the Holy Spirit helps us is by making us holy. Being *holy* means "being close to God." It means choosing what he wants.

Another word for holy is sanctified. One of the names of the Holy Spirit is Sanctifier. He is an Advocate and a Sanctifier. Being *sanctified* means "to be set aside for a holy purpose."

When the bishop anoints us at Confirmation, we are sanctified by the Holy Spirit. We are set aside for a special purpose. We are meant to be living examples or witnesses of what it means to be holy. We are called to be saints.

SIGNS OF FAITH

Saint
Saints are people of faith who live a good life and bring the light of Christ into the world by their prayers and actions for others.

© Our Sunday Visitor Curriculum Division

Sealed with the Spirit

During Confirmation, the bishop calls each person forward with his or her sponsor. A sponsor is a person who is a good example and witness of faith. The sponsor places his or her hand on the shoulder of the person being confirmed. The bishop dips his right thumb in the chrism and makes the Sign of the Cross on the forehead of the one being confirmed. He seals the person with the Gift of the Holy Spirit.

The bishop prays the final blessing. In the blessing he tells us what we need to do to be holy and living witnesses of Jesus.

- We use the gifts of the Holy Spirit.

- We live the Gospel.

- We want to do God's will.

- We tell others about Jesus.

We know the Holy Spirit will help us do these things.

Faith at Home

Ask family members what they think it means to be holy. Share some examples of people you both know who you think are living witnesses of Jesus or talk about a favorite saint. Discuss some ways that you can be a sign of God's presence in the family and at school.

Being Holy

Respond

Make a List Make a list of at least four ways you can be a living witness of Jesus.

1._____

2._____

3._____

4._____

Choose one of these ways and write how you will act on it this week.

_____

_____

_____

_____

Closing Blessing

Gather and begin with the Sign of the Cross.

Leader: Holy Spirit, guide us to be living witnesses of Jesus. God, our Father, we praise and thank you for the gifts of the Holy Spirit.

All: Hear us we pray.

Leader: Holy Spirit, help us to be your holy children.

All: Hear us we pray.

Leader: Holy Spirit, giver of God's gifts, we praise and thank you for being our helper and guide.

All: Hear us we pray.

Sing together.

We are marching in the light of God,

We are marching in the light of God.

We are marching, we are marching in the light of God.

We are marching, we are marching in the light of God.

South African Traditional

Faith Focus

- The gifts of the Holy Spirit help us do Christ's work.

- The Holy Spirit makes us holy.

- Being *holy* means being close to God and choosing what he wants.

Ritual Focus

Blessing The celebration focused on a blessing, which reminded you that you are blessed with the presence of the Holy Spirit, who is guiding you to bring the light of Christ to others. At an appropriate time during the week, have family members share ways they brought the light of Christ to others or how others brought the light of Christ to them. At the conclusion of the sharing, extend your hands over family members and say, "May the Holy Spirit dwell in you and help you bring the light of Christ to others."

Family Prayer

Spirit of the Living God, live in us so we may be witnesses of Christ's light and life to others. Amen.

Act

Share Together Read the story of Jesus in the synagogue at Nazareth (*Luke 4:16–30*). Discuss the reading. Use these questions:

- When do you feel the Holy Spirit is in or near you?

- Do we know anyone who is sad or sick or poor and needs to have someone bring them a glad or happy message?

- How can we take a happy message to them?

Do Together Discuss the idea of what it means to be a living witness. Have individual family members name people whom they think are living witnesses of faith—people who bring the light of Christ to others. Of the people mentioned, select one or two whom the whole family knows. Together decide on an appropriate way to thank the person for his or her witness. You might make a card or write a note and send it to him or her or do something anonymously that would be of service to him or her.

 www.osvcurriculum.com
Visit our website for weekly Scripture readings and questions, family resources, and more activities.

We Are Holy

The Beatitudes give us eight different ways of being holy. After each Beatitude write one way you can live it.

Blessed are the poor in spirit,

    for theirs is the kingdom of heaven. _____

Blessed are those who mourn,

    for they shall be comforted. _____

Blessed are the meek,

    for they will inherit the earth. _____

Blessed are those who hunger and thirst for righteousness,

    for they will be filled. _____

Blessed are the merciful,

    for they will receive mercy. _____

Blessed are the pure in heart,

    for they will see God. _____

Blessed are the peacemakers,

    for they will be called children of God. _____

Blessed are those who are persecuted for rightouseness' sake,

    for theirs is the kingdom of heaven. _____

Author
Maureen A. Kelly, M.A.

Nihil Obstat
Msgr. Louis R. Piermarini

Imprimatur
✝ Most Rev. Robert J. McManus, S.T.D.
Bishop of Worcester
February 2, 2006

The Imprimatur is an official declaration that a book or pamphlet is free of doctrinal or moral error. No implication is contained therein that anyone who granted the Imprimatur agrees with the contents, opinions, or statements expressed.

Write: **Our Sunday Visitor Curriculum Division**
Our Sunday Visitor, Inc.
200 Noll Plaza, Huntington, Indiana 46750

Call to Celebrate is a registered trademark of Our Sunday Visitor Curriculum Division, Our Sunday Visitor, 200 Noll Plaza, Huntington, Indiana 46750.

Text Credits
For permission to reprint copyrighted material, grateful acknowledgment is made to the following sources:

Michael Balhoff: Lyrics from "Remember Your Love" by Mike Balhoff, Darryl Ducote, and Gary Daigle. Lyrics © 1973, 1978 by Damean Music. Lyrics from "We Praise You" by Mike Balhoff, Darryl Ducote, and Gary Daigle. Lyrics © 1978 by Damean Music.

John Burland: Lyrics from "Come to the Table" by John Burland. Lyrics © 2005 by John Burland. Lyrics from "Coming Back Together" by John Burland. Lyrics © 2000 by John Burland. Lyrics from "Yes Lord I Believe!" by John Burland. Lyrics © 2000 by John Burland. Lyrics from "And With Your Spirit: Songs for Deepening Children's Understanding of the Mass." Our Sunday Visitor Curriculum Division, printed in partnership with Ovation Music Service. Lyrics © 2011 by John Burland

Division of Christian Education of the National Council of the Churches of Christ in the U.S.A.: Scripture quotations from the *New Revised Standard Version Bible: Catholic Edition.* Text © 1993 and 1989 by the Division of Christian Education of the National Council of Churches of Christ in the U.S.A.

GIA Publications, Inc., 7404 S. Mason Ave., Chicago, IL 60638 www.giamusic.com, 800-442-1358. Lyrics from "We Are Called" by David Haas. Lyrics © 1988 by GIA Publications, Inc.

International Committee for English in the Liturgy: Excerpts from the English translation of *Rite of Baptism for Children* © 1969, International Commission on English in the Liturgy Corporation (ICEL); excerpts from the English translation of the *Rite of Penance* © 1974, ICEL; excerpts from the English translation of *Rite of Confirmation (Second Edition)* © 1975, ICEL; excerpts from the English translation of *A Book of Prayers* © 1982, ICEL; excerpts form the English translation of *Book of Blessings* © 1988, ICEL; excerpts from the English translation of *The Roman Missal* © 2010, ICEL. All rights reserved.

OCP Publications, 5536 NE Hassalo, Portland, OR 97213: Lyrics from "Show Us Your Mercy, O Lord/Misericordia, Señor" by Bob Hurd. English lyrics © 1998 by Bob Hurd; Spanish lyrics © 1972 by Sobicain. Lyrics from "Lead Us to the Water" by Tom Kendzia and Gary Daigle. Lyrics © 1998 by Tom Kendzia and Gary Daigle. Lyrics from "Open My Eyes" by Jesse Manibusan. Lyrics © 1988 by Jesse Manibusan. Published by spiritandsong.com®. Lyrics from "Children of God" by Christopher Walker. Lyrics © 1991 by Christopher Walker. Lyrics from "I Will Praise You, Lord"/"Te Alabaré Señor" by Manuel Jose Alonso and Jose Pagan. Lyrics © 1979 by Manuel Jose Alonso and Jose Pagan. Lyrics from "Glory to God" by Daniel L. Schutte. Lyrics © 2007, 2009 by Daniel L. Schutte.

Photo/Credits
8 Our Sunday Visitor; 9 Our Sunday Visitor; 10 Blend Images/Thinkstock; 11 Our Sunday Visitor; 14 Our Sunday Visitor; 15 Our Sunday Visitor; 18 Our Sunday Visitor; 19 Our Sunday Visitor; 20 Royalty Free/Corbis; 21 (t) Our Sunday Visitor; 21 (b) iStock/Thinkstock; 24 Our Sunday Visitor; 25 Our Sunday Visitor; 28 Our Sunday Visitor; 29 Our Sunday Visitor; 30 Richard Hutchings; 31 Thinkstock/Comstock/Getty Images; 34 Our Sunday Visitor; 35 Our Sunday Visitor; 38 Our Sunday Visitor; 39 Our Sunday Visitor; 40 Our Sunday Visitor; 41 Our Sunday Visitor; 44 Our Sunday Visitor; 45 Our Sunday Visitor; 48 Our Sunday Visitor; 49 Our Sunday Visitor; 50 Our Sunday Visitor; 51 Pixland/Thinkstock; 54 Image Copyright Anneka, 2012 Used under license from Shutterstock.com; 55 Our Sunday Visitor; 58 Our Sunday Visitor; 59 Our Sunday Visitor; 60 Our Sunday Visitor; 61 Our Sunday Visitor; 64 Our Sunday Visitor; 65 Our Sunday Visitor; 88 (l) Our Sunday Visitor; 88 (c) Our Sunday Visitor; 88 (r) Our Sunday Visitor; 89 Our Sunday Visitor; 90 Our Sunday Visitor; 91 (l) Our Sunday Visitor; 91 (r) Our Sunday Visitor; 94 Our Sunday Visitor; 95 Bill & Peggy Wittman; 98 Our Sunday Visitor; 99 Our Sunday Visitor; 100 Our Sunday Visitor; 101 Our Sunday Visitor; 104 Our Sunday Visitor; 105 Bill & Peggy Wittman; 109 Amos Morgan/Photodisc/Getty Images; 110 Our Sunday Visitor; 111 Bill & Peggy Wittman; 114 Our Sunday Visitor; 115 Our Sunday Visitor; 118 (l) Our Sunday Visitor; 118 (c) Our Sunday Visitor; 118 (r) Our Sunday Visitor; 119 Our Sunday Visitor; 120 Our Sunday Visitor; 121 (t) Image Copyright Paul Orr, 2012 Used under license from Shutterstock.com; 121 (b) Our Sunday Visitor; 124 Our Sunday Visitor; 125 Our Sunday Visitor; 126 (tl) Jacqueline M. Koch/Corbis; 126 (tr) Keith Dannemiller/Corbis; 126 (bl) Xinhua/XINHUA/Corbis; 126 (br) Jordon R. Beesley/CNP/Corbis; 128 Our Sunday Visitor; 129 Our Sunday Visitor; 130 Zoonar/Thinkstock; 131 (l) Ed McDonald; 131 (r) iStockphoto.com/JohnArcher; 134 iStockphoto.com/small_frog; 135 Ed McDonald; 138 Chapter Opener Ed McDonald; 139 Ed McDonald; 140 iStockphoto.com/sdominick; 141 (t) Ed McDonald; 141 (b) Ed McDonald; 144 Our Sunday Visitor; 145 Ed McDonald; 148 Our Sunday Visitor; 149 Comstock/Punchstock; 150 Our Sunday Visitor; 151 Bill & Peggy Wittman; 154 (l) Our Sunday Visitor; 154 (r) Our Sunday Visitor; 155 Our Sunday Visitor; 158 Our Sunday Visitor; 159 Our Sunday Visitor; 160 Our Sunday Visitor; 161 Our Sunday Visitor; 164 Ed McDonald; 165 Our Sunday Visitor; 174 Our Sunday Visitor; 176 Our Sunday Visitor; 177 Our Sunday Visitor; 179 Our Sunday Visitor; 181 Our Sunday Visitor; 182 Our Sunday Visitor; 184 Our Sunday Visitor; 185 iStock/Thinkstock; 186 Our Sunday Visitor; 187 Our Sunday Visitor;

Call to Celebrate Reconciliation and Eucharist
ISBN: 978-1-59-276973-5
Item Number: CU5050

2 3 4 5 6 7 8 9 10   000287 15 14
RR Donnelley; Menasha, WI, USA; February 2014; Job #91703